Sponsorship
For a return on investment

Sponsorship
For a return on investment

Guy Masterman

ELSEVIER

AMSTERDAM BOSTON HEIDELBERG LONDON NEW YORK OXFORD
PARIS SAN DIEGO SAN FRANCISCO SINGAPORE SYDNEY TOKYO

Butterworth-Heinemann is an imprint of Elsevier
Linacre House, Jordan Hill, Oxford OX2 8DP, UK
30 Corporate Drive, Suite 400, Burlington, MA 01803, USA

Notice
No responsibility is assumed by the publisher for any injury and/or damage to
persons or property as a matter of products liability, negligence or otherwise, or
from any use or operation of any methods, products, instructions or ideas
contained in the material herein. Because of rapid advances in the medical
sciences, in particular, independent verification of diagnoses and drug dosages
should be made

British Library Cataloguing in Publication Data
A catalogue record for this book is available from the British Library

Library of Congress Cataloging-in-Publication Data
A catalogue record for this book is available from the Library of Congress

ISBN–13: 978 0 7506 8640 2

For information on all Butterworth-Heinemann publications
visit our web site at books.elsevier.com

Typeset by Charon Tec Ltd (A Macmillan Company), Chennai, India
www.charontec.com
Printed and bound in Great Britain

07 08 09 10 10 9 8 7 6 5 4 3 2 1

Working together to grow
libraries in developing countries

www.elsevier.com | www.bookaid.org | www.sabre.org

ELSEVIER   BOOK AID
              International   Sabre Foundation

This book is dedicated to:
Emma who is tireless in her editing and support,
Mum and Dad who support, tirelessly and
Alice, Katy and Edie who are just tireless (but nicely so).

Contents

List of figures

List of case studies

Acknowledgements

I would like to acknowledge the impact the late Lamar Hunt had on my career as a sports marketer, events promoter, academic and author. Lamar died in late 2006.

I had the pleasure and honour to work for Lamar at World Championship Tennis Inc (WCT), an organization he created in 1967. Through WCT he challenged amateur sport and devised the 'tour' that not only modernized and professionalized tennis but also created a model that many sports continue to follow even now. Tennis and many other major sports now run their own worldwide circuits and seasons that culminate with championship grand finales as a result. Lamar was a sports fan at heart and did remarkable things in many sports. He owned the Kansas City Chiefs, for example, and was a founder of the AFL and the Super Bowl in the USA. He helped introduce soccer to the USA and helped form the NASL, its successor MLS, and owned two club franchises. He was also a founding investor in basketball's Chicago Bulls and recently in an NHL club franchise.

Lamar's entrepreneurship in sport was second to none and yet he remained a humble and unassuming leader. In the mid-1980s I presented the details of WCT London's sponsorship programme to Lamar and the other WCT tournament management teams at the WCT Offices in the Hunt Building in Dallas, Texas. He then welcomed us to his family dinner table that night. My youthful north-eastern dialect must have been a difficult language barrier for them all to understand, but the following week back in London I received a tape of 'Geordie' opera music from him and his management team that even today reminds me that it is not just the big picture that counts in sport. Lamar and my time at WCT remain an inspiration to me.

My thanks go to Ingrid Abery at www.hotcapers.com, Clipper Ventures, Jonathan Rosenberg, Robert Kaspar, Trish Coll and Brian Masterman for allowing me to use their photographs.

Back cover photographs:
Panathenaic Stadium, Athens
Shea Stadium Scoreboard, New York – courtesy of Jonathan Rosenberg
Surridge Junior Football Tournament, County Durham
New York boat, Clipper Round the World Yacht Race 2005/2006 – courtesy of Ingrid Abery, www.hotcapers.com/Clipper Ventures

The Author

Guy Masterman is Head of Sport Sciences and Director of the UK Centre for Sports Events Research at Northumbria University. He was formerly at the Tisch Center for Hospitality, Tourism and Sports Management at New York University and at the UK Centre for Events Management, Leeds Metropolitan University, where he helped found and then lead the first Masters Degree in Events Management. He has worked in the sports and events industries for over 25 years, 15 of which were spent as an independent consultant. Early in his career he was an international racquetball player and was involved in the development of that sport in the UK and internationally.

His clients have included Coca-Cola, Pepsi, Nabisco, Capital Radio Group, Chelsea FC, Team Scotland, WCT Inc, The New York Mets and international governing bodies such as the ATP Tour, the International Yacht Racing Union and the International Stoke Mandeville Wheelchair Sports Federation. In 2005 he worked with the New York 2012 bid team on a new education legacy. He has worked extensively with charity groups, such as Muscular Dystrophy, Scope and Sparks, and with sports stars Seb Coe, Jody Scheckter, Steve Backley and Lennox Lewis. His event work extends across sport as well as the arts and music and includes EURO '96, World Games, Coca-Cola Music Festival, Pepsi Extravaganza, Nabisco Masters Doubles, and the promotion of concerts for Ray Charles, Santana, B. B. King, James Brown and Tony Bennett.

His research focuses on strategic sports event planning and legacies and sponsorship, and he regularly presents, reviews and edits in these areas. A second edition of his book *Strategic Sports Event Management: An International Approach* (Butterworth-Heinemann), first published in 2004, is due to be published in 2008 and he has also co-authored *Innovative Marketing Communications: Strategies for the Events Industry* Elsevier/Butterworth-Heinemann), with Emma Wood, published in 2006.

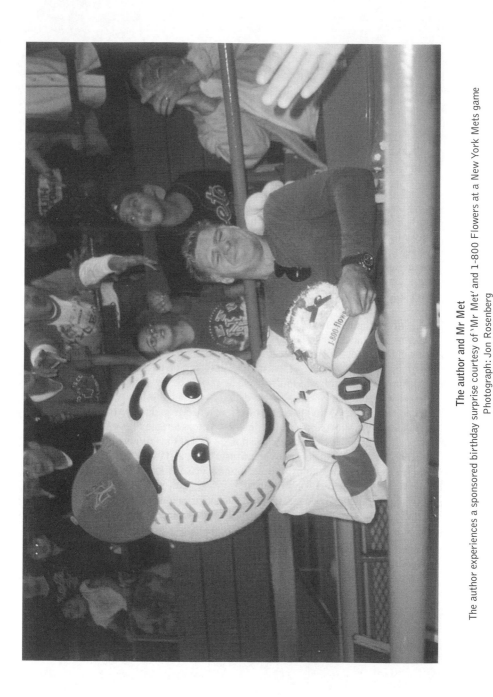

The author and Mr Met

The author experiences a sponsored birthday surprise courtesy of 'Mr Met' and 1-800 Flowers at a New York Mets game

Photograph: Jon Rosenberg

Introduction

It was a carpet, a flying carpet to be exact, that made Wilton Carpet Factory a fitting sponsor for a production of Aladdin at Salisbury Playhouse. Not only did a Wilton Carpet provide an active function for the pantomime, a number of activities away from the theatre also led to further exposure for the sponsor. Several weeks prior there were arts-, crafts- and theatre-linked activities staged in Salisbury Shopping Village and a carpet design competition was activated through local schools and media. The sponsorship fee was £3000 and included the sponsor's name and logo printed in theatre brochures and flyers but Wilton also worked hard to achieve local radio and newspaper coverage too (Arts and Business, 2006). They considered their return to be significantly more than what they might have achieved with £3000 worth of local advertising.

There is no doubt about it, sponsorship has risen rapidly and is an internationally accepted form of communication that can be used across a wide range of sectors. Whilst we have become more than familiar with corporate names and logos on football shirts, we are also becoming used to also seeing the likes of Wilton in the theatre, ScotRail at festivals (Edinburgh), O_2 at concerts (Wireless) and even the City of Newcastle local authority as sponsors of Northumbria Police speed cameras. We can also see sponsorship of events, institutions, buildings and individuals.

Whilst sponsorship has developed rapidly over the past 30 to 40 years it has also reached a critical point in its life cycle. Whilst sponsorship activity and expenditure continue to increase and the focus throughout this text is on the positive use of sponsorship, a critical view is also presented so that pointers to a number of issues can be made. Most significantly, sponsors are now looking hard at their sponsorships and increasingly demanding a demonstrable return on their investments.

A return on investment is not being widely achieved and significantly there are sponsors that have begun to turn away from sponsorship and look to other tools for the achievement of their communication objectives. However, this is not necessarily because these sponsors have not had a return on their investment. The issue is that there is too little evaluation undertaken, by sponsors or rights owners, and as a result many sponsorships, remain unmeasured. It is therefore unknown whether some sponsorships are successful or not. To compound this, for those that want to evaluate their sponsorships, there are too few reliable methods by which to do so.

A lack of evaluation and therefore feedback into future decision-making leads to another issue. There is, as yet, little understanding of the key factors that can make sponsorship the successful communications tool it probably is. Whilst we believe that sponsorship is and can be successful we are not providing unequivocal evidence for that.

Most sponsorships consist of a collection of communication activities, a mixed use of advertising, public relations, sales promotions and direct marketing tools and in that there is nothing mystical about what constitutes a sponsorship. However, what sets sponsorship apart from other forms of communication is that this mix can represent a unique relationship, the sponsorship relationship between the rights owners and the sponsors. If this relationship is based on a strong and exploitable 'fit', then every sponsorship is capable of delivering a bespoke set of communications that can lead to competitive advantage for sponsors and rights owners.

Early use of sponsorship did not achieve the true potential that was on offer. It has taken recent research to show that those sponsorship rights that are exploited are more likely to achieve success. Paying the sponsorship fee and expecting the rights to then achieve a sponsor's objectives is no longer good practice. This is how sponsors first went about their sponsorships and unfortunately this practice continues today. Building sponsorship into a set of integrated communications, at an expense that is beyond any fees, goods or services provided to the rights owner, is now an essential element of successful sponsorship.

Another general issue is that there is still too little research, writing or dissemination of knowledge for a better understanding of sponsorship.

These important issues are discussed in this text and presented alongside a process for sponsorship for a return on investment in what is intended to be a logical sequence. Whilst any text should have sufficient flexibility for its reader to dip in and out as they require, each chapter is presented here as a building block that hopefully assists in the cause for a better understanding of what sponsorship can do and how it can be successfully managed.

There are three sections. Section One focuses on providing an explanation of sponsorship and contains three chapters. Chapter 1 provides a historic context and looks at how sponsorship grew from being little more than an opportunity for advertising and corporate hospitality in the 1970s. In just 40 or so years sponsorship has developed to now provide an integrated way of achieving a number of marketing and corporate communication objectives, including driving sales, developing favourable brand associations and awareness, awareness of corporate image, and internal relations development. This chapter considers a number of key factors that played their part in the development of sponsorship, including the popularity of sport stars and other celebrities in endorsement activities, the impact of television and new forms of advertising and also how sponsorship was an opportunity for new ways of achieving advertising objectives, but less expensively.

Chapter 2 considers what sponsorship is and what it might achieve. It begins with a number of views and definitions of sponsorship. The differences between philanthropy and sponsorship and how sponsorship is a mutually beneficial arrangement are discussed whilst establishing that sponsorship consists of the provision of resources of funds, goods and/or services by the sponsor in return for a set of benefits provided by the rights owner. Several authors' categorizations and terminology are considered to establish that generally, there is agreement on what sponsorship can achieve. This is compared with industry practice.

Chapter 3 considers sponsorship as an integrated communications tool and the identification of specific objectives that are realistically achievable for sponsors.

This chapter also introduces the idea that if a rights holder wants to be successful in its recruitment of sponsors it needs to understand what its sponsors want to achieve. Sponsorship objectives are divided into four broad categories: direct sales, brand awareness, external and internal corporate awareness with an additional fifth category linking them all, competitive advantage being achievable when a rival company is shut out of the opportunity and then that opportunity is maximized via exploitation of the rights.

The process by which sponsorship decisions are made is discussed here highlighting that sponsorship needs to be assessed against other forms of communication for efficiency and effectiveness. An integrated marketing communications approach for sponsorship is explored.

This chapter also identifies a number of key elements in this process including targeting, distribution, managing resources, together with the introduction of the concept of sponsorship 'fit'. A case is made for sponsorship to be part of an integrated set of communications and because such an approach ensures that each communications selection needs to be justified, sponsorship therefore has to be more effective and efficient than other communications options if it is to be selected. It therefore has to be accountable.

Section Two focuses on rights and contains five chapters. Chapter 4 considers sponsorship accountability further by discussing how communication objectives can be best achieved. Whilst it has been and to some extent still is common practice for rights owners to approach potential sponsors with prescribed packages already determined, this is not an effective approach. The focus in this chapter is therefore on how sponsors need to measure against their objectives and how important it is that rights owners identify what a sponsor requires in order to tailor packages that meet communication objectives. The theme here is for both sides to seek the most appropriate rights. This tailored approach also requires rights owners to prepare by considering what rights it can eventually offer any one sponsor via an audit of its assets and the compilation of an inventory of potential rights that will provide a base from which to eventually tailor packages.

Chapter 5 considers endorsement and its links with sponsorship. Research shows that individual celebrity endorsers have more effect on target audiences than non-celebrities, although those with the highest of profiles are not necessarily the most effective choice of endorsers. It is the extent of the renown of the endorser within any target audience that is critical and so local endorsers may be effective within local communities too. Endorsement works by transferring positive values from the endorser to the endorsee and then on to the consumer and so the key factor of credibility is discussed here. A good fit is important too. If the endorsee and endorser, and the endorser and target audience, are a good match, then the endorsement can provide a return on investment. The links with sponsorship are made showing that endorsement can also be of mutual benefit, whereby both rights owner and sponsor can endorse, and be endorsed by the other.

A process for endorsement is identified highlighting the important elements of assessing familiarity, relevance, esteem, differentiation and decorum, aligning to specific objectives, and the necessity to review contractual limitations.

Chapter 6 considers the case for broadcast sponsorship. Is it really sponsorship when it fails to allow brands to play functional roles within programming? Product placement is also discussed and an analysis of how it can utilize a product, or a service, within the content of a film or a television programme for a credible form of sponsorship is undertaken.

Media partnerships are also identified as an essential element of most sponsorship programmes here. Media partners for example, may provide fees and/or exposure given in-kind and therefore provide an important promotional function for the rights owner and its sponsors as well as functions that add value to the content of the rights owner's property.

Chapter 7 considers the process for the recruitment of sponsors by rights owners and how to create sponsorship programmes with multiple sponsors. This consists of an audit and creation of an inventory of potential rights, research and selection, and then contacting specific sponsors, the identification of their communication requirements, followed by the provision of a sponsorship solution that meets those requirements, if they can. As part of that solution it is necessary to ensure that the sponsorship opportunities on offer provide a function(s) and can demonstrate a good sponsorship fit.

In managing sponsorship programmes that consist of more than one sponsor, a rights owner needs to be able to determine requirements and offer solutions to as many potential sponsors as possible in order to remain flexible and to not finalize a structure too early. The theme here is on how rights owners need to be able to analyse which sponsors in which type of structure will bring the most benefit.

Finally, this chapter considers the recruitment of sponsors as a continuous process. There are always sponsorships to either newly create, renew or replace.

Chapter 8 considers the recruitment of sponsors further and specifically the 'selling' stages of the process. It addresses some key questions: What expertise is required? What role do individuals play? What role does a sponsorship proposal play? At what price should a sponsorship be set and at what price one bought? How important is presentation?

Section Three focuses on the elements of successful sponsorship and contains four chapters. Chapter 9 considers sponsorship as a unique component in a strategic and integrated marketing communications approach. The aim for integrated marketing communications is to affect the behaviour of target audiences so strategies that can instigate action, and provide a measurable return, are therefore required. The task of managing this at various levels, via an organization-wide effort, is discussed.

Chapter 10 considers exploitation as one of the key success factors for successful sponsorship. As indicated above, the effectiveness of sponsorship is directly related to the degree to which sponsors are willing to exploit their rights and so sponsors therefore need to support their acquired rights with further communications activity in order to achieve sponsorship and ultimately communication objectives. Whilst exploitation communications have previously been seen as 'extra', they are now an essential component of successful sponsorship. How much exploitation is necessary is a key question. Proposed rules of thumb are critically discussed and an approach that views a sponsorship on an individual basis is offered as an alternative. Further questions of how and when to plan, and then how and when to implement exploitation, are also considered.

Chapter 11 considers another key factor for the development of sponsorship as a credible communications tool by focusing on the way forward for sponsorship evaluation. The implications of issues such as a lack of standardization and reliable and valid techniques are considered. Measures that are multi-faceted and consider the whole effect of sponsorship (sales, awareness, image and total communications) are required as are measures that evaluate the sponsorship relationship itself. However, whilst new measuring techniques are sought, an effective way forward is offered here. It consists of a framework, a combination of current measures that can focus on the whole range of integrated communications that are undertaken, that also provides measurement of what the competition is doing.

Chapter 12 discusses a range of issues. The increasing use of ambush marketing, the strength of the sponsorship relationship, the ethical management of sponsorship and the increasing trend towards multi-faceted sponsorship are all considered. These issues are used to highlight the need for awareness amongst rights owners and sponsors of the importance of strong sponsorship fit, exploitation and evaluation for the future development of sponsorship.

Reference

Arts and Business (2006). The Wilton Carpet Factory Ltd and Salisbury Playhouse. www.AandB.org.uk (accessed 4 January 2007).

Section One: Sponsorship Explained

The three chapters in this section provide a context for sponsorship by explaining its origins, defining its purpose and analysing its integrated use as a communications tool.

Chapter 1 explains how sponsorship has emerged. First used some 2000 years ago but developed more recently over the past 30 to 40 years for corporate communications, sponsorship is widely considered to be an effective tool but as this chapter discusses, there is now a need for sponsorship to provide measurable return on investment.

Chapter 2 provides a preliminary review of what sponsorship is and what it can achieve by considering various definitions and then how it is used across a range of sectors, whilst Chapter 3 considers sponsorship as an integrated communications tool and identifies realistic sponsorship objectives for sponsors.

1

The emergence of sponsorship

The objectives for this chapter are to:

- Examine how sponsorship has evolved
- Identify the key factors that have had impact on the evolvement of sponsorship
- Consider the extent and significance of sponsorship markets

The City of Liverpool and the Clipper Round the World Yacht Race
The 'Liverpool' sponsored boat in the 2005/2006 Clipper Round the World Yacht Race
Photograph: Ingrid Abery, www.hotcapers.com/Clipper Ventures

Introduction

Sponsorship has developed into a sophisticated communications tool from humble beginnings. What was once little more than an opportunity for advertising and corporate hospitality in the 1970s is now a way of achieving a number of marketing and corporate communication objectives. Sponsorship is now used to drive sales as well as develop favourable brand associations and awareness, develop awareness of corporate image and develop organizational internal relations.

The purpose of this chapter is to investigate how sponsorship has evolved by considering a number of key factors and developments over time. This begins with a consideration of very early use over 2000 years ago.

Ancient and philanthropic beginnings

Despite recent development over the past 30 to 40 years and the perception that sponsorship is a new communications tool, it does in fact date way back into history. In Ancient Greece for example, there were both sporting and arts festivals that were underwritten with the intent of improving the sponsors social standing (Sandler and Shani, 1993). One of the earliest examples of philanthropic benefaction in the form of buildings is at the Theatre of Dionysos at the Acropolis in Athens. The theatre could seat up to 17,000 arts lovers and was built by the Athenian statesman, Lykourgos in 326BC in order to gain favour and improve his position within society. Still standing today are two nearby Corinthian columns that are the remains of choragic monuments that were erected to celebrate a benefactor's team winning at the drama festivals held there. This site is the celebrated originating home of the Greek Tragedy genre (Dubin, 2004).

The sites of the Panhellenic Games in Ancient Greece, Isthmus (Isthmian Games, near Corinthe), Delphi (Pythian Games), Nemea (Nemean Games) and of course Olympia (Olympic Games) all became of widespread importance, not just for the development of sport and culture generally, but also for the political ambitions of both individuals and Greek States. Olympia in particular became an 'arena' for political rivalry between cities whereby athletes were made promises and offers if they could achieve as many victories as possible in what are early examples of support for individual sportsmen. It is important to note that there were not just awards for success after it had been achieved, there were also promises of awards prior to success. Awards differed from city to city, but may have included the right to dine for life at the Prytaneion, at Olympia, a privilege accorded only the most senior of public figures. There may also have been awards of exemption from taxes, citizenship, council seats for athletes in their own cities and money. There are records of large amounts of payments to Olympic victors that were as high as five talents, possibly 30,000 drachmas, as an Attic Talent may have been worth up to 6000 drachmas (Ekdotike Athenon, 2003).

The support and exploitation of the athletes and the games themselves at these times, for individual and civic political purposes, also involved the gifting of buildings, an example of which is the erection of the Philippeion, began initially by Philip II and then completed by his son and successor, Alexander the Great, as a memorial to their family. The Roman emperors that came later also recognized the importance of this kind of benefaction and sought to take part in and support

11

the games that were essentially restricted to those of Greek descent. By declaring their Greek descent and by making their appearances at Olympia for example, they attempted to integrate into Greek culture in order to intervene in political affairs by offering freedom and peace to a strife-stricken part of their empire (Ekdotike Athenon, 2003).

Sports events at the Panathenaic Stadium in Athens, also known as the Kallimarmaro Stadium, span both the Ancient Greek and Roman eras. First built again by Lykourgos in 329BC, the stadium was reconstructed in Roman Emperor Hadrian's time in AD138 for Gladiatorial Games and then again in AD144 by a wealthy benefactor, Herodes Atticus, for the Panathenaic Games. The stadium was restored by another benefactor, Georgios Averof, for four million drachmas, in time for the staging of the first modern Olympics in 1896. Over 2300 years since being first built, it was again used for athletics events at the 2004 Olympics (Dubin, 2004). The current stadium is an exact replica of the original and has a seating capacity for 60,000. It is a long-lasting example of how benefactors have supported sport, but with the communications objectives of winning political support.

Roman history shows us that the use of events for political purposes was widespread. Gladiatorial contests, for example, were underwritten by the wealthy nobility in order to gain popularity, social standing and office (Head, 1988). The extent to which this was the case is demonstrated by the fact that in 63BC the sponsorship of events had to be regulated. The political intent behind the staging of a 'Minus' (games), whilst seeking office, had clearly been critically reviewed by the Roman Senate. It became illegal for anyone to stage games in a 2-year runup to an election. At a later point, second level magistrates (praetors) were limited to two games with a maximum of 120 gladiators each during their terms of office (Connolly, 2003; Grant, 1975). It was not just the content of such activities that made these important communications however; it was also the extent of the reach. The capacities of the venues that were used were large even by today's standards. The stadium at Olympia, after it had been moved to the east of the Sanctuary, during the 5th century BC, could ultimately seat up to 45,000 spectators (Kaltsas, 2005), whilst Rome's Circus Maximus had space for audiences of up to 250,000 people some 2000 years ago (Connolly, 2003).

This type of benevolence re-emerged and grew from the middle ages onwards, with the church and then more recently aristocracy and royalty playing significant roles in patronizing the arts. In particular there are examples of artists, composers and theatre companies being supported. Pope Julius II is famed for his support of Michelangelo and particularly for the work done in Vatican City's Sistine Chapel and Leonardo da Vinci was supported by the Milanese, Lodovico Sforza. Perhaps the most famous patrons of this time were the Florentine Medici family who also supported Michelangelo as well as Donatello and Filippo Lippi (Bradbury, 2003; Head, 1988). Patronage of this kind was motivated by piety, prestige and pleasure. The compositions of Bach, Handel and Mozart for example, owe much to the patronage of Europe's royal houses throughout the 17th and 18th centuries for similar reasons (Burrows, 2005). The support of English theatre too, dates back to the 16th century when at least six companies were named after their noble patrons including the Elizabeth I Company and its work with William Shakespeare. James I continued this illustrious connection and in the early 1600s, whilst the Globe Theatre was the company's home base, the company also went on what were essentially sponsored tours (Head, 1988).

In similar ways individuals have also given to institutions throughout history for the benefit of society, but in so doing have received lasting recognition in return. The Bodleian Library at Oxford University and the Tate Gallery in London are two examples. More recently billionaire Texan Bill Bass and his wife Mercedes were reported to have donated $25 million to the Metropolitan Opera of New York, the largest single contribution this particular institution had ever received. Mr and Mrs Bass, stepped in when a previous pledge fell through. Despite the philanthropy in this case, as patrons their names were posted on the Met's Grand Tier and as a news item this story received coverage as far as the UK (Bone, 2006).

A return on investment

It is clear that throughout these times both individuals and organizations have philanthropically supported various activities for the good of society. In so doing, however, it is also clear that they have also sought a return on their investment. It is important therefore to trace these humble beginnings of sponsorship in order to identify how the seeking of a return on investment became important.

This takes us to the advent of advertising where we can identify that the early use of commercial promotion was a significant first step in the evolvement of contemporary and corporate sponsorship. As long ago as the 17th century advertising has been run in newspapers and in the 1760s one of the first uses of 'endorsement' was implemented. The Wedgewood brand of pottery and chinaware used royal endorsements to create an aura for the company and its products (Vemuri and Madhav, 2004).

Associating with sport for commercial gain was beginning to take shape through publishing in the 1860s. The gentlemen's outfitter John Wisden did more than simply advertise in a new cricket annual publication, it developed an early sponsorship by incorporating its name into the title (Head, 1988). Wisden's Cricketers' Almanac is still being published.

The use of endorsement was also beginning to gain momentum and grew significantly, from 1875, when trade cards came into use. These were small pieces of cards that were either handed along with the product to the customer at the point of sale or they were inserted into the product packaging. On the cards were product descriptions and pictures of celebrities chosen specifically for their fame and popularity from the film and sports industries (actresses such as Lily Langtree and Sarah Bernhardt, and baseball players like Cy Young and Ty Cobb for example). Even Mark Twain featured on three brands: Great Mark Cigars, Mark Twain Cigars and Twain Flour (Vemuri and Madhav, 2004). The cigarette industry in particular adopted this promotional tool to such an extent that these cards became known to many as 'cigarette cards'.

Until the 1930s the major endorsers of brands were athletes. One of the oldest brands of breakfast cereal in the USA, Wheaties, began using sports stars such as Babe Ruth, Joe DiMaggio and Jackie Robinson (the use of sports stars has continued to recent times with the use of Chris Evert, Michael Jordan, Michael Johnson and Tiger Woods to endorse the same brand). From 1945 and the emergence of the film industry, movie stars also became much sought after.

A very early use of other media came in 1924 with The 'Eveready' Hour on radio supported by a battery manufacturer (Skinner and Rukavina, 2003). Early television drama productions in the USA were also financially supported by detergent brands and as a consequence we now refer to these types of programmes as 'soaps'. Furthermore, over one hundred years ago, two contemporary sponsors first became involved in events. Coca-Cola and Kodak both had an involvement with the first modern Olympic Games, in Athens in 1896, albeit this involvement was limited to advertisements in the official programme (IOC, 2004). Then in 1912 at the Stockholm Games, the Granberg Industrial Art Company paid $3600 for the right to take and sell photographs (Puig, 2006). At the 1928 Olympic Games in Amsterdam however, Coca-Cola acquired product sampling rights, and has since developed its relationship at each and every Olympic Games in order to get to the level of sponsorship we recognize today (Pitts and Stotlar, 2002; Stotlar, 1993).

There are some perhaps surprisingly early commercial associations with events. One of the earliest recorded event sponsorships in modern sports is that of the England cricket team's 1861 tour of Australia by catering company Spiers and Pond (Gratton and Taylor, 2000) and the first Indianapolis 500 motor race in 1911 was sponsored by Firestone, an involvement the company still enjoys today (Firestone, 2004). However, it was the commercial links between manufacturers and their advertising on television that was one of the most important factors in the evolvement of sponsorship and in particular the companies from the tobacco, alcohol and automotive industries, that began to establish a further and significant link with cinema and sport in particular.

The role of television

With the advent of television and television commercials, in 1941 in the USA, came new opportunities for advertisers to reach wider and larger audiences. It was at this time that a combination of factors began to lay the foundations of the sponsorship industry we know today. The popularity of sport was an attractive television programming proposition and so as more sports events were broadcast, the greater the interest became in the use of sport as a tool for brand promotions.

Several promotional opportunities began to emerge. Firstly, advertisers became interested in placing their commercials in amongst sports programming, notably in commercial breaks before, during and after major sports events. It is significant that the first television commercial in July 1941 was taken by Bulova Watch Company. The advertisement cost $9 on WNBT and was shown in a break in the baseball game between the Brooklyn Dodgers and the Philadelphia Eagles. Secondly, advertisers began to extend their endorsement activities into television by featuring their endorsers and brands together. The use of endorsement on cards, until this point, had largely only been by association. There were generally no quotes that celebrated the product, nor pictures of the products being used by the endorsers. However, this changed with the emergence of television and, in particular from 1965 and the beginnings of colour television, the endorsement tool became increasingly well used. By 1975 it is reported that one in eight television commercials featured a celebrity endorsement. This research, conducted by Robert Clark and Ignatius Horstmann of Boston University, reviewed 1000 advertisements between 1920 and 1970, and identified that the brands endorsed were predominantly from the cigarette, beauty, beverage and audio equipment manufacturing industries (Vemuri and Madhav, 2004).

Endorsers were now being used to directly and verbally extol the qualities of brands as well as being pictured using them in their everyday lives in order to show their full endorsement of them. One of the earliest in the UK was the endorsement of a hair grooming product by the late Dennis Compton who is still referred to as the original 'Brylcreem Boy'. In the 1940s the cricketer was pictured on trams, buses and billboards as part of a 'Brylcreem keeps you right on top' campaign (Graff, 2006). In the 1980s there was the initial use of boxer Henry Cooper by Faberge for endorsement of their aftershave, Brut. The company then took on footballer Paul Gascoigne to carry on the mantle and the cult slogan, 'splash it all over'. More recently David Beckham has continued the association of sports stars with grooming products with his endorsement of Gillette's shaving systems.

A further opportunity also arose out of the increasing links between television and sport. Televised events created opportunities for sponsors to gain exposure without having to pay television advertising rates. Out of the sponsorship of teams and individual sports players, arose the use of rights that included pitch advertising and the placement of logos on playing gear, all with the potential for gratuitous broadcast exposure.

This also extended to a similar opportunity via event sponsorship. Initially event television rights and sponsorship rights were sold separately and so it was possible to gain television exposure without paying the broadcaster anything. Broadcasters, however, did recognize their loss and began to offer 'programme sponsorship' opportunities themselves and whilst event organizers recruited independently, the broadcasters did the same. Market research began to reveal that broadcast sponsors were being perceived to be the event sponsors by target audiences and so a change was required. Since the early 1990s, however, events have generally developed their relationships with broadcasters so that television rights are now sold in conjunction with event sponsorship title rights that often include integral television advertising packages. An example of how this has developed is the 2006 Royal Horticultural Society's Chelsea Flower Show where the event sponsor, Saga Insurance, received both verbal acknowledgements and graphic credits during its programming on BBC2 in the UK.

Broadcast sponsorship itself has flourished since 1989. It enables brands not only to have their name associated with a specific programme, but also to air short trailers around that programme. These trailers can use appropriate images about the brand although there are strict codes on the extent of the message that can be used. Further discussion of broadcast sponsorship is in Chapter 6.

A key impact in the 1970s came in the form of athlete free agency, implemented by law in the USA sports industry. Free agency allowed athletes to market themselves at best possible prices to a team. As a result, players in the major leagues of baseball, football and basketball were now also free to extend that marketability in order to increase their incomes via activities away from the field of play. Whilst players always had some limited capacity to do this, there was now the emergence of athlete representation and agencies and agents to negotiate deals on behalf of their clients. In order to maximize the revenue for clients and their representatives, the placement of teams and individual athletes of all kinds into new marketing opportunities began to increase.

There have been several key and iconic sports stars in the evolution of sponsorship and some, such as Michael Jordan and David Beckham, have taken this to new levels. There are also several key administrators to consider. Three such administrators were so entrepreneurial and influential that they created models by which sponsorship activity is still conducted today. Peter Uberroth is famed for his role in making the 1984 Los Angeles Olympics non-dependant on public sector funding. Arguably he turned the Olympics from a financial millstone into a desirable economic product and demonstrated that it could, if required, make a profit with commercial funding.

Another leading figure is David Stern, the Commissioner of the National Basketball Association (NBA), an administrator who is widely acknowledged as being the creator of the blueprint for the commercial maximization of USA major league sports. Under his guidance the NBA has opened eight offices outside North America and NBA Games are broadcasted in 175 countries. He created NBA properties which are now mirrored at the National Football League (NFL) and was the key figure in the 1976 wage settlement with NBA players that led to the 'free agency' across the USA sports mentioned above. He is also responsible for introducing collective bargaining that led to revenue sharing amongst NBA franchises and the salary cap, both of which have been adopted by other USA major league sports (International Jewish Sports Hall of Fame, 2006).

Finally, there is the first 'kingmaker', the late Mark McCormack. In 1960 McCormack signed his first client Arnold Palmer and by 1984 he had not only added golf's other 'big two', Gary Player and Jack Nicklaus, he also represented many more of the world's biggest sports stars, including Pele, Martina Navratilova and Jean Claude-Killy. More recently this roster has included Tiger Woods, Pete Sampras, Michael Schumaker, Derek Jeter, Charles Barclay and Roger Federer. McCormack's model was to turn his clients into marketable commercial properties for sponsorship and endorsement deals and higher appearance fees, and to manage their time more efficiently than they could do themselves (McCormack, 1984). The model soon expanded with the creation and management of events, the representation of other events and their recruitment of sponsors, and the representation of sponsors themselves and the development of their sponsorship programmes. Such was the impact of his athlete representation business, International Management Group (IMG), and later the associated sports television producers, Trans World International (TWI), that other agencies have not only followed, but prospered too. The importance of Mark McCormack is further highlighted by his extension into the Arts, Music and Fashion industries, whereby IMG has represented opera singers, artists and models (IMG, 2006).

From the 1980s companies began to make products around their endorsers. Standard Brands Inc created a candy bar called 'Reggie' after New York Yankees baseball star, Reggie Jackson. Faberge Inc named a range of cosmetics after actress Farrah Fawcett and in 1984 one single endorsement-based sponsorship became a milestone in the industry. Nike identified that a young Chicago Bulls basketball star, Michael Jordan, would provide them with a new image and a new brand range 'Air Jordan'. In addition to Nike, Jordan has been used to endorse over 70 products for companies including McDonald's and Gatorade. The use of Jordan as an endorser developed still further and into a role that saw him set a new trend for using celebrities as spokespersons for the brand.

The growth of the use of sponsorship as a communications tool began naively. Advertisers initially saw value in sponsorship rights that included potential media exposure and at a cost that was less than advertising rates. This, for some, may still appear to be the case, but there is a growing understanding that whilst the visible cost of a sponsorship (the fee) might appear to be small compared to advertising, the true cost of a sponsorship is certainly much higher because the exploitation needed for success will require further investment (Davies and Quattrocchi, 2002).

A further driver of the growth of sponsorship has been the increasing fragmentation of media and consumer cynicism towards advertising. Consequently, marketers have looked elsewhere for alternative communications and as a result the growth of sponsorship has exceeded the average growth of advertising (Davies and Quattrocchi, 2002).

Unfortunately, out of this came the use of 'equivalent advertising and media value' evaluation techniques whereby media coverage (numbers of seconds of sightings of logos or advertisements, heard or seen) are counted up and then priced according to advertising rate-card costs for that particular time on radio or television. Marketers were looking, and still do seek, a comparison with advertising in order to justify selection of sponsorship. These techniques are still commonly used today to evaluate sponsorship although the call for more accuracy and appropriate evaluation for sponsorship is now getting louder. Sponsors themselves have started to 'discount' equivalent media values as they are now increasingly aware that television and radio advertising are quite different communications from the sightings of logos or hoardings (Gillis, 2005). Such calculations are also flawed in that rate-card prices are seldom the final prices that are paid for television and radio advertising. There is further discussion of this in Chapter 11.

Whilst there is scepticism about the messages that are received via advertising, research has shown that sponsorship is popular. Customers acknowledge that events might not be staged if it were not for sponsorship, and that sponsors can provide services and added value to customers. As a result they look kindly upon associations with sponsors (Mintel, 2004).

Development as a communications tool

Up to the early 1980s, event sponsors were largely content to receive rights that consisted predominantly of signage, perhaps tickets and hospitality. There was little development of this simple association, yet sponsors expected to benefit, although often with no or few specifically set objectives. Indeed sponsorships were chosen either for the 'gratuitous' media exposure, the opportunity to corporately entertain, or unwisely, because of individuals' decisions to sponsor for personal rather than corporate needs. Up to this time there were many examples of sponsorships that were selected because there were personal benefits for company owners and executives (Abbratt and Grobler, 1989; Head, 1988; Stotlar, 1993).

There still remain examples of philanthropic giving and whilst many financial gifts are anonymously given for the good of society there are also plenty that are given in return for some sort of benefit. Many buildings continue to be built or supported by individuals for example. These acts can be extremely important and generous and should be recognized as such. However, if there is no anonymity and in particular if there is intentionally generated publicity or naming rights used, then such acts are also intended for some received benefits. There is nothing wrong in this and it is important to identify that here. For example, the Tisch family has generously given to New York University over a number of years and in return has naming rights to University departments, its teaching hospital and faculty buildings including its theatre.

The 1984 Olympics in Los Angeles was the start of a new era, as implied earlier. These games were entirely commercially funded by the private sector, made a profit of £215 million (Catherwood and Van Kirk, 1992; Gratton and Taylor, 2000) and in so doing allowed many events owners and sponsors to become aware of the potential use of sponsorship. The result was a development of new types of sponsorship rights and the beginnings of new thinking about the objectives for sponsorship. In addition to business-to-business activity via hospitality and increased brand and corporate awareness via signage, sponsors have seen the potential for brand and corporate image development. Via an integrated set of communications that might be anchored in a set of sponsorship rights, sponsors have begun to recognize the importance of spending more than just the sponsorship fee due to the role exploitation plays in the achievement of successful sponsorship.

This has been assisted by technological developments. The profusion of media channels, particularly television, has resulted in more events being broadcast to fill airtime thus creating more sponsorship opportunities. Since the 1990s the sponsorship fees have, as a result, also increased and with that has come a growing astuteness in how sponsorship is being used (Cooper, 2003).

The Internet, mobile communications, digital and high definition broadcasting, and broadband have all helped develop existing rights as well as new ways of benefiting from sponsorship. This has led to particular companies either becoming sponsors or increasing their use of the tool. Vodafone, the mobile telecommunications company, began trading in 1984 and has used sponsorship in cricket, rugby, Formula 1 and football on an international basis to good effect. Despite their decision to end its sponsorship with Manchester United early in 2006, the company's use of its rights to on-shirt brand advertising consistently achieved the highest of ratings. Over half the UK population (53 per cent) were seeing that brand at the time. O2, another mobile telecommunications company, and sponsor of Arsenal, were ranked in second place with 47 per cent recognition. Samsung, the audio-visual manufacturer, in only their first season on the Chelsea shirts, was successfully gaining 21 per cent recognition (Sports Marketing Surveys, 2006). Whilst football shirt branding is not a new way to develop awareness, the way these companies have developed further integrated rights that utilize their technology has maximized their awareness opportunities. The use of dedicated football services, such as interactive and mobile messaging products are new technologies that have been successfully incorporated for example.

Whilst the grocery, motor and sports manufacturers, and alcohol and beverage producers continue to sponsor, one of the earliest and greatest users of sponsorship, the tobacco industry has been excluded, since July 2005. At the time of the phasing out of tobacco sponsorship over a number of years for motor sports in particular, but also for snooker and cricket, there was a fear that the gap would never be filled. In 2003 the estimated spending by the tobacco industry on international motorsport alone was £222 million. However, technologically focused industries as well as the financial and media sectors have all produced a much wider and solid base of sponsors that now seek a wider range of sponsorship objectives.

A more unusual set of sponsors has been innovatively recruited by the Clipper Round the World Yacht Race (see Case Study 1.1). Cities have utilized an integrated

Case Study 1.1 Clipper Round the World Yacht Race

The Clipper Round the World Yacht Race is an innovative example of how an event sponsorship programme has been used for the objective of developing tourism. All 10 boats of the 2005/2006 race were sponsored by the main stopover cities on the race route.

The race, created and managed by Sir Robin Knox-Johnston's Clipper Ventures plc, lasts for approximately 10 months and is designed to take fee-paying amateur crews.

The cities and the sponsors involved are:

- Liverpool 08 (European Capital of Culture 2008)
- Glasgow (Scotland with Style)
- Qingdao (Olympic Sailing City 2008)
- Freemantle (Western Australia.com)
- Durban (South Africa's Playground)
- Channel Islands (Jersey)
- New York
- Singapore (Uniquely Singapore)
- Victoria BC, Canada
- Cardiff, Wales

The sponsoring cities received sponsorship rights that enabled them to brand the boat hulls and sails. In addition there were opportunities for individuals to apply and pay for their berths and roles on board a boat and there were various hospitality opportunities when the race was 'in-town'.

The brand awareness is dependent on television and press photographic coverage and so Clipper Ventures appointed TWI to produce and distribute television programming both locally and internationally – BSkyB were the broadcaster in Europe with numerous other stations contracted to deliver in South Africa and throughout South-East Asia and India. HotCapers were appointed to provide the much needed on-the water shots for the publicity photographic campaign.

The sponsorship recruitment took an unusual but perceptive approach in order to offer sponsors a uniform tourism development objective that was both non-competitive and complementary. The programme is also an example of how a number of cities have been introduced to sponsorship as a communications tool and an indication of the evolution that sponsorship is continuing to undergo.

Sources: Clipper Ventures (2006), Liverpool 08 (2006), Sports Marketing Surveys (2006)

programme of sponsorship rights with the Race in order to achieve tourism objectives. Ten boats have been sponsored by stopover cities on the race route and each has taken advantage of traditionally used boat branding and corporate hospitality. The importance of international media coverage is quite clearly a critical part of the achievement of tourism objectives. However, in addition there are a number of other rights that have been specifically developed. The innovation has led to a rather unique set of organizations coming into sponsorship.

The continued growth in sponsorship is reflected by not only the increase in the numbers and types of sponsors, but also in the integration of a wider set of types of corporate players in general. With the increasing use of sponsorship as a communications tool since the 1980s there has been an ever-increasing growth in the number of marketing and public relations agencies and sponsorship agencies that offer sponsorship recruitment, management and consultancy services. These services have developed to include consultancy to sponsors for the selection of sponsorship, recruitment services to rights owners and in some cases the guarantee of sponsorship revenue for the right to sell those rights at their own negotiated prices, and also evaluation services for both rights owners and sponsors. Amongst these agencies there are also those that specialize in sport, music, arts and community sponsorship.

In 1985 the Institute of Sports Sponsorship was formed to promote best practice and from 1992 it administered the government incentive scheme for grass roots sport, Sportsmatch. Not long after, the European Sponsorship Consultants Association was formed in 1990 to provide an independent voice on sponsorship with the European Union Commission and to promote sponsorship. These two important bodies merged in 2003 to form the European Sponsorship Association (ESA) to encounter the surge in media interest, the growth of the Internet and the increased spending on sponsorship in the public sector.

The emergence of more research in sponsorship is also a sign of its importance and recognition as a communications tool. There are increasing numbers of sponsorship-specific journal articles, research papers and trade publications. In education too there has been considerable demand from students for sports marketing and sponsorship led higher and further education, particularly in the USA since the 1990s, and now more so in Europe. Consequently sponsorship is becoming increasingly professionalized. In the 1980s most executives at sponsoring companies had learnt their trade whilst on the job with some beginning to come from the advertising and public relations communications sectors. Now there is another generation of expertise, and companies are able to recruit experienced executives that have a number of years of direct sponsorship work behind them. Over three-quarters of the sponsorship executive respondents in the European Sponsors' Survey (Redmandarin, 2004) indicated that their teams were made up of sponsorship, event management and marketing experienced staff.

Sponsorship markets

As a marketing communications vehicle used for commercial gain, sponsorship, as we know it today, began around the 1970s. Event sponsorship spending in 1970 totalled only £4 million (Meenaghan and Shipley, 1999). Despite its youth, there has been considerable and rapid growth in sponsorship on a worldwide basis and particularly in the two largest growing regions of Europe and the USA. Mintel (2002, 2004) estimated that the UK sponsorship market alone was valued at £798 million in 2002, and whilst it contracted in 2003 to £783 million it was expected to remain constant in 2004.

Sports sponsorship has always dominated the overall sponsorship market but is also dipping from £429 million in 2002 to a predicted £398 million in 2004 (Mintel, 2004). The arts too have experienced a recent decline from £150 million in 2000 down to below pre-1998 levels at £111 million in 2002. Alongside the fact that there are smaller marketing budgets, this is also a sign that there are increasing opportunities in other forms of sponsorship. Whilst football sponsorship in the UK continues to thrive (twice as many deals as for the second ranking sport, rugby) the take-up of opportunities in broadcasting and community-based sponsorships is increasing (Mintel, 2004). Sponsorship in the broadcast sector has risen by 25 per cent to £205 million in 2004 with television revenues at about two-thirds of that. Community sponsorship also continues to thrive with growth from £58 million in 2002 to an estimated £69 million in 2004 (Mintel, 2004).

The European Sponsor's Survey (Redmandarin, 2004) provides an interesting comparison. Whilst it does not contain actual spending data, 34 per cent of the respondent sponsorship executives said that their sponsorship budgets would increase and 32 per cent said that they would remain the same in 2004 as they were in 2003. Only 34 per cent said they would increase spending in sport (17 per cent in the arts) whilst 44 and 48 per cent said that they would increase spending on entertainment and community/cause related sponsorships, respectively.

The UK sponsorship market consists of four main sectors, Sport (51 per cent share), Broadcast (26 per cent), Arts (14 per cent) and Community (9 per cent) (Mintel, 2004). The long-term prediction is for a shift towards a greater share for sport. In 2009, whilst the market overall is expected to rise to a value of £848 million (at 2004 prices), Mintel envisages an increase in market share for Sport to 54 per cent, decreases for Broadcast to 24 per cent and the Arts to 13 per cent, with Community sponsorship remaining the same. This does not take into account the impending London 2012 Olympic Games but is based on an assumption that sponsors will be able to evaluate better, spend more successfully in exploiting their rights and thus achieve greater return on investment (Figures 1.1 and 1.2).

On a worldwide basis, sponsorship expenditure reached a height of US $43.1 billion in 2005 representing a 65 per cent increase in spending since 2000 (Sponsorclick, 2006). It is important to also note that these figures represent the amount of spending on sponsorship fees only and do not include the greater amounts that are spent on exploiting sponsorship rights. This data is clearly difficult to calculate as many sponsors are unlikely to reveal such information into the public domain.

In 1998 it was estimated that USA companies spent US $800 million on acquiring celebrities for advertisements and promotions. In 2004, Nike alone spent US $338.6 million on its endorsements. A substantial proportion of this was associated with the company's use of the golfer, Tiger Woods. Since they began their association in 1996, the company claims that its golf ball revenue grew by 25 per cent in 6 years to US $250 million (Vemuri and Madhav, 2004).

Davies and Quattrocchi (2002) maintain that the market is divided into three sectors and might thus be modelled in a pyramid. At the top there are the large deals that are over US $1 million or more, of which there are relatively few and

Sport	No. of Companies	Key companies	Partner and size of sponsorship deal (£million)	Years
Football	101	Barclays Bank	57 FA Premier League	3
		Carlsberg	40 FA Partner	4
			15 Liverpool FC	3
		Vodafone	36 Manchester United FC	4
		Nationwide BS	30 FA Partner	4
		McDonald's	30 FA Partner	4
		Pepsi	20 FA Partner	4
Rugby Union	64	Royal Bank of Scotland	23 Six Nations Championship	3
		Heineken	20 European Cup	3
		Zurich Insurance	15 Premiership	3
		British Telecom	12 Scottish Rugby Union	3
		O2	5 England National team	4
Golf	42	Barclays	12 Scottish Open	5
Cricket	34	Vodafone	12 England Cricket team	4
		Norwich Union	6 One Day League	3
Rugby League	20			
Athletics	19	Norwich Union	20 Various major events	4
Tennis	17	Ariel	15 Lawn Tennis Association	3
Equestrian Sports	16			
Bowls	12			
Motor Racing (excluding international)	11			

Figure 1.1 UK Sports Sponsorship Market (2003)
The leading sports in order, and the leading individual sponsors during 2003 (adapted from Mintel, 2004)

as such represent 20 per cent of worldwide sponsorship spend. Next there is the sector with the most activity, where the deals are US $5000 to US $1 million. This sector is 75 per cent of the total market. The remaining sector (5 per cent) is represented by hundreds or thousands of companies that have deals of US $5000 or less. There are of course relatively few companies that can afford to be in the upper part of this pyramid especially when exploitation costs are in addition to fees and increase relatively as fees get higher.

Since the mid-1990s, a new phenomenon has emerged. There has been a greater turnover of sponsors than was the case earlier, largely as a result of global economic downturn. This greater 'churn' also sees sponsors in shorter lasting

Art form	Sponsorship revenue (£million)	Key companies and art organization
Museums & Galleries	25	JP Morgan (Hayward Gallery) Barclays (National Gallery and Tate) British Telecom (Tate) EDS (The Lowry Project)
Drama & Theatre	10	Barclays (Royal National Theatre) Eversheds (New Theatre, Cardiff) SAP (Donmar Theatre)
Music	9.4	T-Mobile (Rolling Stones Euro Licks Tour) HSBC (Royal Philharmonic Orchestra) Sage (Gateshead Centre)
Opera	8.5	Artsworld (English Opera) BSkyB (English Opera) Coutts Bank (Glyndebourne) YTL (Three Tenors Concert, Bath)
Film	7.5	National Australia Bank (Barbican)
Visual Arts	6.4	
Festivals	6.3	
Arts centres	3.2	
Community arts	3.2	
Services	2.5	
Heritage	2.2	
Dance	1.9	AEG (English Ballet) Angelina Ballerina (English Ballet) Halifax (Northern Ballet Theatre)
Literature	1.3	
Photography	0.4	
Crafts	0.1	
Other	8.7	

Figure 1.2 UK Arts Sponsorship Market (2002)
UK Arts sponsorship by art form during 2002 (adapted from Mintel, 2004)

deals as a result of longer-term deals being less appropriate for shorter-term marketing strategies. For example, rapid developments in technology require shorter lead times for decision-making, and there is an increasing demand from sponsors for return on investment. Sponsors are far more discerning now. Consequently, Mintel (2002, 2004) warns that whilst there is an increase in opportunities as rights owners segment and create more fragmented sponsorships, there remains a need for continued and an increased use of sponsorship as a fully integrated communications tool and the leveraging of rights in order to maximize success. Worryingly for sport, and as an example of how sponsorship spending has developed, there is a polarization effect, with the premium properties exhibiting the lowest levels of churn. The highest churn is therefore having an effect on the bulk of the market.

Summary

From little more than an opportunity for advertising and corporate hospitality in the 1970s, sponsorship has grown rapidly into a significant and increasingly sophisticated communications tool. Over four decades, the tool of sponsorship has developed into an integrated way of achieving a number of marketing and corporate communication objectives. Sponsorship is now used to drive sales as well as develop favourable brand associations and awareness, develop awareness of corporate image and develop organizational internal relations.

A number of key factors have played their part in this rapid evolvement. The popularity of sports stars and other celebrities was acknowledged early in the last century as being a way of reaching target audiences and the endorsement they gave on and in pack, and in particular when used by tobacco products, proved to be a successful form of promotion. With the advent of television, and new forms of advertising, these types of endorsement began to reach wider and larger audiences. This was compounded further with the interest in sport events by television programmers. As television advertising became more widely used it also became more expensive and marketers looked for value elsewhere.

Sponsorship was an opportunity that offered new ways of achieving advertising objectives, but less expensively. It began as a fairly misunderstood practice with few rights owners knowing what prices to charge and few sponsors knowing how to evaluate that spend and their perceived benefits. Now, around 40 years later, we have a communications tool that is widely used, continues to grow but is at a critical stage in its evolution. Now it has to justify its role as a communications tool. It has to show that it can provide a return on investment.

Tasks and discussion points

- By referring to examples of your own, produce a detailed timeline from the 1970s that demonstrates how critical the impact of television has been on the evolution of sponsorship.
- Select one sponsorship where technology has played a key role in the development of the sponsorship rights concerned.
- Propose how the Clipper Round the World Yacht Race, in Case Study 1.1, might continue to use its sponsorship recruitment approach to attract new sponsors for a different but similarly themed programme.

References

Abbratt, R. and Grobler, P. (1989). The evaluation of sports sponsorship. *International Journal of Advertising*, Vol. 8, pp. 351–362.

Bone, J. (2006). Billionaire bails out opera to tune of $25million. *The Times*, 6 January.

Bradbury, K. (2003). *Essential Michelangelo*. Bath: Parragon.

Burrows, J. (Ed.) (2005). *Classical music*. London: Dorling Kindersley.

Catherwood, D. and Van Kirk, R. (1992). *The complete guide to special event management: Business insights, financial strategies from Ernst & Young, advisors to the Olympics, the Emmy awards and the PGA tour*. New York: John Wiley & Sons.

Clipper Ventures (2006). www.clipper-ventures.co.uk/2006 (accessed 23 May 2006).

Connolly, P. (2003). *Colosseum: Rome's arena of death*. London: BBC Books.

Cooper, A. (2003). The changing sponsorship scene. Admap, November. www.warc.com (accessed 5 April 2006).

Davies, N. and Quattrocchi, X. (2002). Integrated marketing agencies and sponsorship. Admap, February. www.brand.warc.com (accessed 14 March 2006).

Dubin, M. (2004). *Greece*. London: DK.

Ekdotike Athenon, S. A. (2003). *The Olympic Games in Ancient Greece*, Athens.

Firestone (2004). Racing news: Firestone legacy continues to 2004. www.bridgestonetire.com/news/us (accessed 9 May 2006).

Gillis, R. (2005). The media value problem. *Sportbusiness*, February.

Graff, V. (2006). So what's in a name? *Business Life–British Airways*, October.

Grant, M. (1975). *The Twelve Ceasers*. New York: Barnes and Noble Books.

Gratton, C. and Taylor, P. (2000). *Economics of sport and recreation*. London: Spon.

Head, V. (1988). *Successful sponsorship*, 2nd Edition. Cambridge: Director Books.

IMG (2006). www.imgworld.com/history (accessed 23 May 2006).

International Jewish Sports Hall of Fame (2006). www.jewishsports.net/biopages (accessed 23 May 2006).

IOC (2004). *2002 Marketing Fact File*. Lausanne: IOC.

Kaltsas, N. (2005). *Olympia*, 5th Edition. Athens: Archaeological Receipts Fund Directorate of Publications.

Liverpool 08 (2006). www.liverpool08.com (accessed 23 May 2006).

McCormack, M. (1984). *What they don't teach you at Harvard Business School: Notes from a street smart executive*. New York: Bantam.

Meenaghan, T. and Shipley, D. (1999). Media effect in commercial sponsorship. *European Journal of Marketing*, Vol. 33, No. 3, pp. 328–348.

Mintel (2002). *Sponsorship Report*. UK: Mintel.

Mintel (2004). *Sponsorship Report*. UK: Mintel.

Pitts, B. and Stotlar, D. (2002). *Fundamentals of sport marketing*, 2nd Edition. Morgantown, WV: Fitness Information Technology.

Puig, J. (2006). Olympic marketing: Historical overview. University lectures on the Olympics. www.olympicstudies.uab.es/lectures (accessed 5 April 2006).

Redmandarin (2004). *The 2004 Redmandarin European Sponsors' Survey*. Full Report. In Association with The Sponsorship Research Company. London: Redmandarin Sponsorship Consulting.

Sandler, D. and Shani, D. (1993). Sponsorship and the Olympic Games: The consumer perspective. *Sport Marketing Quarterly*, Vol. 2, No. 3, pp. 38–43.

Skinner, B. and Rukavina, V. (2003). *Event sponsorship*. New Jersey: Wiley.

Sponsorclick (2006). www.sponsorclick.com (accessed 22 May 2006).

Sports Marketing Surveys (2006). *The inside track*. April Newsletter.

Stotlar, D. (1993). Sponsorship and the Olympic Winter Games. *Sport Marketing Quarterly*, Vol. 2, No. 1, pp. 35–43.

Vemuri, K. and Madhav, T. (2004). *Celebrity endorsement through the ages*. Hyderabad, India: ICFAI Business School Case Development Centre. The European Case Clearing House.

2

Sponsorship defined

The objectives for this chapter are to:

- Examine the definitions of sponsorship
- Review objectives for sponsorship
- Evaluate how sponsorship is utilized as a communications tool
- Consider the use of sponsorship across different industry sectors and markets

Sturdy Savings Bank and the Stone Harbor 10K Run
Sponsorship signage is used to identify the route for this locally sponsored race
in Stone Harbor, NJ, USA

Introduction

This chapter focuses on an examination of what sponsorship is by considering a variety of definitions differentiating sponsorship from other related practices, such as philanthropy, and then identifying how it fits with other communications tools. A number of key aspects are analysed in order to arrive at a practical and workable definition and a focus for this text.

The objectives of sponsorship are reviewed through a consideration of previous academic research and industry practice. This analysis provides the underpinning for the objectives for sponsorship that are proposed in Chapter 3.

What is sponsorship?

In trying to determine what can be achieved by utilizing sponsorship it is important to first consider what sponsorship entails. In Introduction, there was consideration of how sponsorship evolved from humble beginnings and how in a relatively short space of time, it grew into a well-used tool. But exactly what is sponsorship? There are a number of views on this in the literature.

Firstly, and as has already been discussed, sponsorship evolved out of philanthropic gifting. Indeed there are those that propose that there are two forms of sponsorship; 'philanthropic sponsorship' and 'commercial sponsorship'. Calderon-Martinez et al. (2005) define philanthropic sponsorship as a tool for improving corporate image and social recognition in the context of the community. On the other hand they identify commercial sponsorship as something that is used to achieve business objectives such as increased awareness or sales. Meenaghan (1991) considers corporate sponsorship to be an investment for commercial ends and direct benefits whereas he views philanthropic sponsorship as a business donation with indirect benefits that are found in society not in the donating organization. Philanthropy is a service for general welfare and doing good to and for others, sometimes via the benevolent gifting of money (Oxford, 2006). Arguably though, even an indirect benefit in this case is still a benefit for the organization. For example, the organization is seen to make the donation (unless anonymous and therefore altruistically) and is therefore seeking recognition and goodwill, however little that might be, by not remaining anonymous. Secondly, the perceived goodwill the organization engenders in society is a benefit that can be used in order to gain commercially (Hoffman, 1998; Mullen, 1997; Polonsky and Speed, 2001). Cornwell (1995) agrees and describes sponsorship as an investment in causes or events in order to achieve overall corporate objectives and/or marketing objectives whilst Shank (2005) also maintains that corporate objectives, marketing goals or promotional strategies can be addressed via a sponsorship investment. A donation for the good of others that is anonymously gifted by an organization is philanthropic with no commercial gain intended. Likewise a donation by an individual, anonymous or not, that is not made for any commercial gain is also a case of philanthropy as opposed to sponsorship. The conclusion to be drawn is that sponsorship is a commercial activity (Cornwell, 1995; Meenaghan, 1991; Pope, 1998a; Sandler and Shani, 1993; Shank, 2005; Sleight, 1989).

Another conclusion that may be drawn is that an anonymous donation is one-dimensional, in that it is a gift going one way with nothing given in return.

That being the case, sponsorship should be considered as two-dimensional in that it involves mutual benefit to both sponsor and sponsored. This too is widely accepted. Jiffer and Roos (1999) maintain that sponsorship should benefit all those that are involved and Olkkonen (2001) proposes that it is a mutually beneficial business relationship. Similarly, Skinner and Rukavina (2003) also describe sponsorship as an activity that puts buyers and sellers together, so that both receive benefits and Sleight (1989) describes sponsorship as a business relationship between a provider (sponsor) and a receiver (sponsored or sponsee) whereby the former gains rights and an association that may be used for commercial advantage, the latter receiving funds, resources and/or services.

If sponsorship is two-dimensional then who or what are the parties that are involved? On the one hand the sponsor has been established here as anything or anyone that can gain commercially. An individual, organization or an institution could therefore be a sponsor. On the other hand the sponsored could be an event, an individual, a group of individuals, a body, an organization, authority or an institution, even a building or sets of physical infrastructure.

The next key question to be addressed is, if sponsorship is for the mutual benefit of both parties, what are the benefits that are received? A traditional misconception for some time was that sponsorship only ever involved receipt of money by the sponsored. This is far from the reality in an industry that in fact is dependent on sponsors providing a whole range of resources. For example it could involve money in the form of sponsorship fees, but it could also be equipment or services and indeed people as resources (Pope, 1998a; Sleight, 1989). It might also be any combination of these. For example with no money exchanging hands the agreement may be described as a contra deal, a trade-out or more popularly as sponsorship-in-kind. This latter term derives from the way in which an agreement may be made on what value of goods or services are received by the sponsored in return for what value of rights are received by the sponsor. The idea is that sponsorship-in-kind is on a dollar for dollar or pound for pound basis. Thus an event can be supplied with resources such as IT hardware and software, transportation, accommodation, equipment, clothing, utilities as well as financial, insurance, legal, medical and marketing services that may also involve the provision of staffing. Similar provision might be made to an arts body, a school, a local authority or an individual. In return for this provision a sponsor will receive a set of sponsorship rights. The increasing use of sponsorship-in-kind supports the notion, that without sponsorship in this form, many events would not be able to run (Mintel, 2002). A sponsorship agreement may also be a combination of money in the form of fees and sponsorship-in-kind.

Whilst the sponsored receive resources, Sleight (1989) and Mullin et al. (2000) refer to the receipt or acquisition of 'rights' by the sponsor. These are the sets of benefits a sponsor receives by which it affiliates or directly associates with the sponsored. The sponsored or sponsee is in fact the owner of the rights/benefits it passes on to the sponsor and as such is referred to as a 'rights owner'. The rights owner is in effect entitling a sponsor to an affiliation or association that it can then use for corporate, marketing or media objectives (Pope, 1998a). Sponsorship rights can take the form of verbal or visual acknowledgement or promotion via advertising, public relations, sales promotions, personal sales or direct marketing activity.

In determining what these rights are used for and how they are used, another conclusion can be drawn. Sponsorship is a communications tool (Jiffer and Roos,

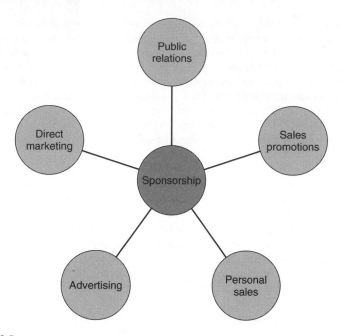

Figure 2.1 Sponsorship as a Communication Mix

1999). Sponsorship can be used to disseminate either corporate or marketing messages, and as indicated above, this can be via the use of advertising, public relations, sales promotions and personal sales and/or direct marketing tools. As such, sponsorship is a combination of communications tools. Any sponsorship, for example, can utilize any level or combination of these tools, and in such cases the term sponsorship is effectively a collective name for this programmed and integrated activity.

The relationship sponsorship has with other communications tools is a complex one. As a collective term for a range of communications it is in itself a communications mix in that it can consist of advertising, public relations, direct marketing, personal sales and/or sales promotions activity (see Figure 2.1). On the other hand it is also a tool for corporate as well as for marketing communications (MarComs) and as such might be seen by some as either a corporate public relations tool or a promotions tool. Hence the early issues of deciding on where sponsorship co-ordination lay, with a public relations or a marketing department (see Figures 2.2 and 2.3).

The discussion above has led to the formation of the definition of sponsorship below and it is this definition that will provide the necessary underpinning structure for this text:

> Sponsorship is a mutually beneficial arrangement that consists of the provision of resources of funds, goods and/or services by an individual or body (the sponsor) to an individual or body (rights owner) in return for a set of rights that can be used in communications activity, for the achievement of objectives for commercial gain.

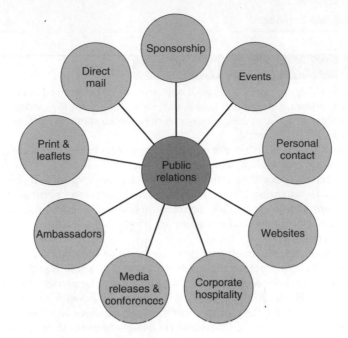

Figure 2.2 Sponsorship as a Public Relations Tool

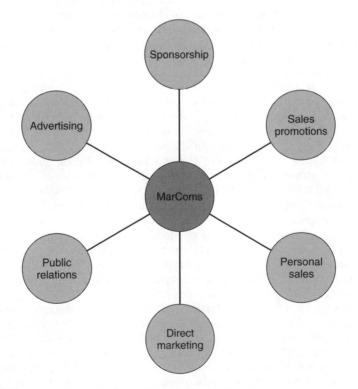

Figure 2.3 Sponsorship as a MarComs/Marketing Promotions Tool

A review of sponsorship objectives

There would appear to be a range of objectives that are believed to be attainable through sponsorship. The aim here is to review what is put forward in the literature in order to arrive at the definitive set of potential sponsorship objectives that are discussed in Chapter 3.

Generally there is little depth to the coverage of sponsorship objectives in marketing and even marketing communications texts. There are also few dedicated sponsorship texts available, although sponsorship and sponsorship objectives do receive more attention in the sports marketing literature, particularly that of USA origin. However, the links between theory and practice are increasing as research in sponsorship and consideration of what sponsorship can be used for continues to grow.

Most commentators imply that there are two levels of objectives for sponsorship, these being corporate and product related (Clow and Baack, 2004; Milne and McDonald, 1999; Mullin et al., 2000; Pickton and Broderick, 2001; Pitts and Stotlar, 2002; Shank, 2005; Skinner and Rukavina, 2003; Smith and Taylor, 2004). Irwin et al. (2002) use the terms 'corporation-related objectives' and 'product- or brand-related objectives'. Another school of thought proposes three levels of objectives, corporate, marketing and media (Pope, 1998a: Sandler and Shani, 1993). A fourth area, that of personal objectives, has also been identified (Abbratt and Grobler, 1989; Stotlar, 1993). This is where management's interests might be perceived as reason enough to undertake sponsorship. For example, personal interest in the sponsorship entity, the sport, arts or music concerned. Whilst such personal objectives are acknowledged as having been used, they are not contemporarily accepted as good enough reason to enter into sponsorship. The argument against is that an individual's personal reasons cannot be corporately justified (Pope, 1998a; Sleight, 1989). The origins of corporate sponsorship do derive from such decisions and the use of personal objectives in undertaking sponsorship is not unheard of even today. As recently as early 2006 Sir Anthony Bamford, Chairman of JCB, indicated that his company's sponsorship of a team attempting to break the world diesel land speed record had much to do with a personal desire to being involved with a potential world record (Dunn and Taylor, 2006). Generally though, sponsorship now has more corporate focus with a desire for return on investment (Meenaghan and Shipley, 1999; Pitts and Stotlar, 2002).

Several authors relate to marketing communications theory in order to identify and categorize the key areas of influence of communications, or more commonly communication effects. As previously established, sponsorship is a key communications tool and so it is pertinent to consider this theory and the role that sponsorship might play in the customer decision-making process.

One of the oldest yet still prevalent categorization of communications effects was developed by Strong (1925) and was related to direct sales. The four-stage model is collectively known as AIDA and refers to awareness, interest, desire and action. Two further and similar categorizations are Colley's (1961) DAGMAR stages (unawareness, awareness, comprehension, conviction and action), and Lavidge and Steiner's (1961) hierarchy of effects model (awareness, knowledge, liking, preference, conviction and purchase). Each of these models refers to the mental processes undertaken by the target audience, and whilst the ultimate desire may be for target audiences to make a purchase the first stages are concerned with achieving awareness.

The range of communication objectives that are available may be summarized into four general categories. The following is an adaptation of those provided by Rossiter and Percy (1987) and Boone and Kurtz (2002) in Masterman and Wood (2006):

- To provide information and through that create brand awareness.
- To enhance attitudes through changing perceptions of the organization, product or brand.
- To influence intentions by building product category wants and facilitating purchase.
- To increase or stabilize demand.

These broader communication objectives need to be set within the individual constraints of the corporate or marketing objectives of the organization and once set will be the targets against which the success of a communications plan will be measured. Sponsorship is one of several communications tools that can be used to achieve such objectives. More specifically there are a number of key areas that emerge from the literature. These are discussed as follows.

Competitive advantage

Most commentators agree on the potential for sponsorship to facilitate competitive advantage. The opportunity arises with the acquisition of exclusive rights for a particular area of business and only one sponsor is recruited into a sponsorship programme from an industry or sector of that industry. One soft drink producer (Coca-Cola not Pepsi), one financial services company (HSBC Bank not the Royal Bank of Scotland) or one car manufacturer (Mercedes not BMW) for example. If only one sponsor is recruited then exclusivity has been achieved as a result of blocking, even pre-empting the competition from taking the opportunity (Clow and Baack, 2004; Irwin et al., 2002; Mullin et al., 2000; Pope, 1998a; Sandler and Shani, 1993). This might be a case of taking the opportunity before a competitor does so. If the sponsorship opportunity is in demand, then even if this is the only objective a sponsor achieves it will at least have prevented the opposition from taking up the opportunity (Shank, 2005).

Direct and indirect objectives

There is some distinction made between direct and indirect objectives. On the one hand direct objectives may be for the achievement of short-term impact on consumption behaviour and the increasing of sales. Indirect objectives on the other hand, would ultimately be over a longer term, and would at some future point lead to increased sales (Shank, 2005). In this latter case the sponsor has to generate awareness and create a desired image for their product before consumers will purchase. The aims here would be to do this by developing brand/product awareness and image in new target markets, or developing more awareness and improving image in the same target markets. This might be achieved and measured by increased sales revenue directly over the short term or indirectly over the long term (Milne and McDonald, 1999).

A further distinction between direct and indirect objectives may also be in their measurement. As indicated above, a sponsorship might lead to a sale over the longer term. The operative words here are 'might' and 'lead'. It is difficult to determine that a sale of a product has definitely occurred because of a sponsorship. Indeed if there were better measurement techniques available and a sponsorship could be shown to have directly caused a sale then that kind of assured return on investment would ensure that the use of sponsorship would escalate dramatically. The fact is that a greater awareness and an improved image for a sponsor's product can be measured but that is not a measure of whether there have been sales. Indeed even whilst market share and sales revenue can be measured and shown to have increased over a period of sponsorship, it is very difficult to then determine unequivocally that the sponsorship has been the cause of that improvement. Whilst this kind of assumption is made in many cases, there are too many other market and external factors at play for it to be acknowledged as being directly attributable to the sponsorship. At best it is an indirect cause.

If a sponsorship can be shown to have undoubtedly been the cause of increased sales revenue and market share then clearly the sponsorship can be determined as being directly attributable for the increases. These are direct sales, and objectives such as these can be achieved by securing rights to sell on-site (Irwin et al., 2002) for example. In recent years industry practice has shown that direct sales opportunities are in fact more available than previously thought, and as this practice develops the theory will no doubt catch up. Some credit card companies for example, have achieved direct sales by entering into event sponsorships where they are the exclusive method by which tickets can be purchased via a credit card. Mastercard did this for the 2006 FIFA World Cup and Visa for the 2004 Olympic Games.

Awareness

It is widely agreed that the setting of sponsorship objectives for increasing awareness can be for corporate or marketing (product) reasons. Increasing visibility and therefore awareness of a product in target markets, possibly via brand positioning tactics, is possible via sponsorship (Clow and Baack, 2004; Irwin et al., 2002; Sandler and Shani, 1993; Shank, 2005). Some commentators refer to this as showcasing the product and its attributes (Clow and Baack, 2004; Skinner and Rukavina, 2003). This might be with existing or new target markets, as targeting can be made more effective and specific so that associations can be established with particular market segments (Mullin et al., 2000; Sandler and Shani, 1993). Thus a new product may be launched by a relatively unknown company via a sponsorship and gain its desired awareness levels in its target markets (Smith and Taylor, 2004).

Increasing a firm's corporate visibility and awareness with its target publics/audiences is also an achievable objective via sponsorship (Clow and Baack, 2004; Sandler and Shani, 1993). Mullin et al. (2000) maintain that associating the company name with an event, for example can develop and reinforce public awareness of that company.

Sandler and Shani (1993) include media objectives alongside corporate and marketing sponsorship objective categories. Arguably though, this is not a separate category as the media are a conduit for the achievement of corporate and marketing objectives rather than a means to an end in themselves. For example, generating publicity is not an objective but a tactic for achieving increased awareness. Similarly, the enhancement of a campaign, achieving target specificity and avoiding communications clutter are marketing aims for more effective development of awareness.

Image building

The aim for developing awareness, whether for a corporation as a whole or an individual product, is to increase the size of the target audiences/markets reached. This is merely an increase in the numbers of people who know of the product/company. The image of that corporation or product is held by that target audience is a different issue.

A company seeks to attain a particular image with its stakeholders and if the right property is selected then the relationship can be used to enhance the company's or product's image (Clow and Baack, 2004; Sandler and Shani, 1993; Shank, 2005). Quester and Thompson (2001) for example, maintain that arts sponsorship can be an effective vehicle for image change and Mullin et al. (2000) and Irwin et al. (2002) agree that image association and image transfer opportunities via sponsorship can mean that public perception can be influenced and even altered. For the latter to be achieved it is likely that a long-term commitment is necessary, and therefore a successful and durable sponsorship that builds a strong and positive perception of a company or its product is required.

An involvement with the community is suggested as a separate sponsorship objective by some (Irwin et al., 2002; Mullin et al., 2000). In fact Milne and McDonald (1999) list it as a way for a sponsor to demonstrate community responsibility. That being the case, this is another way of developing the positive corporate image of the company via 'good-citizenship'.

The measurement of image perception via sponsorship has been rare, with few studies of personality attributes for sponsorship purposes conducted. A belief that sponsorship can deliver changed image perceptions is based more in 'informed' judgements than objective measurement (Meenaghan and Shipley, 1999). However, following research, Meenaghan and Shipley (1999) maintain that the achievement of image-related sponsorship objectives is dependent on the right choice of sponsorship. An advertising message is a controlled communication involving designed and bought media space but in sponsorship the image of the event is a critical element in its success. The concept is that a sponsored activity, such as an event or an individual, already has a personality, set of values and attributes, and collectively this inspires a perceived image. In effect a sponsor is buying in to the ready-made image of the rights owner's activity, indeed the rights owners themselves, and by doing so is hoping to gain a 'rub-off' effect (Meenaghan and Shipley, 1999). The same might also be said of the rights owner who can also gain from an association with the product, brand or organization.

This highlights the mutual nature of sponsorship. Both the sponsor and rights owner become involved in a symbiotic relationship where there is transference of inherent values between the parties. The aim of the communications strategy is that target audiences learn to associate the sponsor and rights owner with one another. Clearly the task for both is to ensure that this achieves a positive effect.

In some contrast, and of value, is the concept put forward by Erdogen and Kitchen (1998) who refer to 'balance theory' whereby a sponsor seeks to gain a higher perceived image as a result of associating with an activity that has a highly positive image. The theory states that when a belief may be unbalanced and unstable about two objects, the mind unconsciously attempts to link the lowly valued object with the highly valued object. The sponsor's aim here being to create, in the minds of target audiences, a link between themselves or their brand and an event, organization or individual that the target audiences already value highly. One party providing an endorsement for the other.

Developing and maintaining relations

The improving or maintaining of relations with customers, suppliers and employees is listed by some as an objective (Clow and Baack, 2004; Irwin et al., 2002; Sandler and Shani, 1993; Shank, 2005; Smith and Taylor, 2004). Shank (2005) maintains that sponsorship can be used to build key relationships, via the use of tools such as corporate hospitality, but there is in fact little research in this area. One of the few to study the area is Bennett (2003) who undertook an exploratory study that revealed that most organizations use corporate hospitality to build relationships in order to retain and develop business with existing clients rather than develop new business with new clients.

Maintaining relations with customers and suppliers might be viewed as a means by which greater awareness and improved image are gained. Milne and McDonald (1999) even list corporate hospitality as a sponsorship objective for example, and whilst sponsorship has long included this kind of entertainment as highest on the list of sponsors' most desired sponsorship rights (IEG/Sponsorship Research, 2004) it is a tool to garner stronger relationships rather than an objective in itself.

The building of internal relations is also a key corporate objective. Employee pride in the company and motivation for more effective and efficient performance may be achieved via sponsorship (Meenaghan, 1991; Milne and McDonald, 1999). Irwin et al. (2002) maintain that inspiring employees to follow and support, perhaps participate in, a sponsorship, can lead to increased pride in and loyalty to the company and then increased motivation.

Other objectives

A number of other objectives are proposed in the literature. These include building goodwill with decision-makers (Mullin et al., 2000), post-merger identity building and enhancing financial sector confidence (International Marketing Reports, 2002). Each of these though can be seen to be concerned with corporate and/or product awareness and/or image building. Whereas circumventing advertising bans (Smith and Taylor, 2004) is very specific, it is still concerned with increasing product awareness and enhancing image. Unloading excess inventory

(Clow and Baack, 2004), also a very specific objective, is concerned with generating direct sales.

The use of sponsorship

It was noted in Chapter 1 that sponsorship is not a new communications tool. As a marketing activity used for commercial gain, however, it is a more recent development. In a matter of 40 years or so the increase in spending has been significant and with such, sponsorship looks to remain extremely buoyant. However, as will be argued in the remainder of this text, there is an increasing need for sponsorship to be accountable. The future of sponsorship as a communications tool depends on objectives being set and measured to demonstrably show a return on the sponsor's investment.

Having reviewed the literature and examined the types of objectives believed to be achievable through the use of sponsorship, it is now important to compare this theory with industry practice. An overview of how sponsorship is currently being used is now discussed.

A good place to start is with the IOC. They list the following as the reasons why its 'TOP' sponsors associate with the Olympic Movement (IOC, 2004a):

- building of brand equity and awareness,
- brand repositioning,
- driving revenue,
- enhancing internal relations,
- showcasing products and services,
- retaining competitive advantage by keeping other sponsors out,
- demonstrating altruism.

All bar one of these objectives are reflected in the literature. The building of brand equity and repositioning are concerned with the enhancement of product image, driving revenue with the achievement of direct and indirect sales, and the showcasing of products and services with the achievement of increased product awareness. It is also quite clear that the IOC maintains that by joining the TOP sponsorship programme, a sponsor can seek competitive advantage as a result of denying a competitor the opportunity.

The IOC list makes no explicit references to either corporate awareness or corporate image enhancement, although it might be assumed that the latter is implicit with the inclusion of an objective that is related to 'demonstrating altruism'. In analysis this is more a case of the development and maintenance of relationships. By giving/donating to society a sponsor is seeking to develop customer loyalty and the achievement of bargaining power with suppliers in order to build brand equity. Finally, the IOC also clearly sees the importance of delivering sponsorships that not only work externally but also for the development of internal relationships.

Whilst it is not necessary for practitioners to ordinarily define sponsorship in writing there are a number of key examples in industry where this does occur. Hampshire County Council has a set of guiding principles it uses in its recruitment of sponsors. It defines sponsorship for its use as 'a business deal between itself and other parties whereby the latter meet part or all of the costs of a project in exchange for commercial benefit' (Hants, 2006). BDS Sponsorship, a UK sponsorship agency, also describes sponsorship as a 'business relationship between a provider of funds, resources or services and an individual, event or organization which offers rights and association in return that may be used for commercial advantage' (BDS, 2006). In New South Wales in Australia, Ashfield Council is somewhat more specific. It defines sponsorship as 'a means of contribution of money or kind by an individual or organization, in support of a public sector activity' and further maintains that it does not include the selling of advertising space, joint ventures, consultancies and gifts or donations where the benefit received from the council does not extend beyond modest acknowledgement (Ashfield Council, 2006).

Each of the key areas of discussion that emerged from the literature is now taken in turn as follows.

Gaining competitive advantage via sponsorship

It is reasonable to assume that Coca-Cola maintains its long relationship with the IOC and the Olympics in order to keep its competitors from gaining from the opportunity. Similarly, whilst they may not make it explicit and it is amongst the use of other objectives, their partnership with FIFA and sponsorship of the World Cup also denies rival soft drinks a sponsorship opportunity and potential competitive advantage. This is a complicated area to analyse however. For example, Pepsi, Coca-Cola's key direct competitor, was an official sponsor of the England team that featured in the 2006 FIFA World Cup in Germany and as a result was able to legitimately use sponsorship communications offensively in the soft drinks market in order to gain competitive advantage.

This demonstrates that simply taking out a sponsorship does not automatically achieve competitive advantage. What it does do is enable a sponsor to take advantage of the opportunity to gain competitive advantage. The work to achieve competitive advantage only successfully begins with the effort and resources that are then put in to the exploitation of the opportunity. Competitive advantage in itself is not measurable but depending on the desired outcomes of any one sponsor, it may use increased awareness, increased positive perception of the brand, increased sales or even improved staff recruitment performance as measures.

In 2003 at the Cricket World Cup in South Africa, Pepsi demonstrated how it defended its position as an event sponsor in order to maintain competitive advantage, at least on-site at the event itself. An agreement was made whereby the event would not allow any non-Pepsi soft drinks into its venues. One outcome was a lawsuit from an ejected spectator who had bought a ticket and had tried to enter one of the grounds with a can of some other drink (Du Toit, 2003).

Two early industry examples demonstrate that sponsorship does offer an opportunity for competitive advantage. These both come from the Nabisco Masters Doubles in the 1980s.

In 1986 Minolta were an official supplier to this world tennis doubles championship at the Royal Albert Hall in London. Their agreement was for 1 year and on expiry they were asked if they wanted to renew. Their marketing manager indicated that their prime objective was to renew in order to stop Xerox from replacing them. Their sponsorship was subsequently renewed with a 3-year agreement with increased rights and at double the annual fee paid the year before.

Nabisco International were the title sponsors for this event but WCT Inc, the rights owners, were intent on selling additional presenting rights. Mercedes were amongst several targeted companies. The result would have been a title that would have read 'The Nabisco Masters Doubles presented by Mercedes'. WCT presented the idea to Nabisco before approaching any potential presenting sponsors and ended up agreeing to sell these rights to Nabisco itself. The fee was paid out of Nabisco UK's budget in an effort to prevent another sponsor coming in at that level and potentially dilute Nabisco's presence and competitive advantage. The example here demonstrates that the opportunity for competitive advantage needs to be protected from indirect as well as direct rivals.

A final example from the 1980s provides another early but different lesson learned by many sponsors. Sponsorship was used as a means to gain a number of objectives when a new daily newspaper, 'Today' launched in the UK in 1986. The paper became the title sponsor of The Football League to gain both brand awareness and competitive advantage. Football of course is a staple reporting area for most newspapers and what materialized was their widespread boycotting of the use of the official title of the newly sponsored league. It is not surprising though that rival media would not want to acknowledge a competitor and the result was that the 'Today Football League' sponsorship lasted only 1 year and the newspaper itself subsequently soon went out of business.

Research has also shown that competitive advantage is a specific sponsorship objective in the industry. Respondents in a 2004 survey of sponsorship decision-makers at European sponsoring organizations identified competitive advantage as their seventh most important objective for sponsorship (Redmandarin, 2004).

Achieving direct and indirect objectives via sponsorship

The same survey identified that increasing brand loyalty (5th), increasing sales (11th), driving retailer traffic (12th) and selling to co-sponsors (19th) as sponsorship objectives (Redmandarin, 2004). Indeed 60 per cent of respondents indicated that increased brand loyalty was 'very important' (rated as eight, nine or ten on a scale of ten). These objectives are perceived as indirect because sponsorship is not clearly the sole cause for increased sales. Whilst brand-focused sponsorship objectives are rated the most important, the survey acknowledges that current sponsorship evaluation methods are unable to link the propensity to purchase directly with shifts in awareness or brand perception.

Conversely, direct objectives, whereby sales could be linked to sponsorship success were not conspicuous in the survey. 'Gaining on-site sales rights', for example, was ranked 15th with only 17 per cent of recipients rating it as very important. However, direct sales objectives are not necessarily just related to on-site activity and therefore the survey does fall short in identifying the degree to which the respondents valued direct as opposed to indirect objectives. For example, it is not clear if respondents measure 'brand loyalty' (rated fifth by 60 per cent of the respondents indicating that it was very important) in increased sales or not.

In 1984 Puma, the sports manufacturer, sold 15,000 tennis rackets. In the following year, having agreed a sponsorship with Boris Becker, their sales rose to 150,000

(Pope, 1998b). Becker won his first Wimbledon that year and gained considerable exposure for his sponsor as a result. As this is an example of increased awareness, possibly resulting in increased sales, the sponsorship can be said to have indirectly contributed to increased sales.

It is clear that elsewhere in the industry, direct objectives, where sales are indisputably as a result of a sponsorship, are being increasingly used. In some cases this can be limited to sales on-site at an event as in the case of Boddingtons, an official sponsor of the 2002 Commonwealth Games. However, perhaps greater results may be had via the exploitation of sales before and during an event by a sponsor. Whilst Mastercard and Visa have negotiated exclusivity in order to achieve direct sales as reported above, other card companies have had to be more innovative due to a lack of exclusivity. For example, American Express, as sponsors of the 2006 Tribeca Film Festival in New York City afforded themselves the opportunity to increase sales through the sponsorship. It was possible to use both Mastercard and Visa cards to make bookings for this Festival, however American Express members (card holders) could make bookings in advance for all kinds of tickets and special events. There was also the important opportunity for anyone to apply for American Express membership, gain a card and then make ticket bookings. The time it takes to process and deliver a membership was a barrier to overcome and so clearly the key for Amex was to ensure that they promoted (exploited) this opportunity early enough, so that as many customers could take advantage as possible (see Case Study 2.1).

Increasing awareness via sponsorship

Increasing awareness, whether for a brand or the company as a whole, is a significant objective for sponsorship. There is some indication that it is predominantly brand focused rather than corporate objectives that are sought however (Redmandarin, 2004). Creating awareness/visibility for the brand, for example, is the second-ranked objective in the European Sponsors' Survey (Redmandarin, 2004) with 69 per cent of recipients rating it as very important. On the other hand the only objectives that were related to gaining awareness for the company were, showcasing social or community responsibility which was ranked 13th (22 per cent).

American Express can be seen in Case Study 2.1 to be demonstrating their targeting of new customers in Manhattan, New York and further a-field via various advertising and promotions activities in order to increase awareness of their credit card brands. They use other sponsorships to target this audience as well. The company is a sponsor of the US Tennis Open, played at Flushing Meadow in Queens, New York and prior to the event there is a significant use of advertising to exploit their association. In 2004 for example their focus was on key tennis players (Agassi, Roddick and the Williams sisters) and used a theme whereby they are all pictured endorsing the use of American Express cards. Placement for the advertising included complete saturation of all space on subway trains using the route to and from the stadium.

Corporate awareness, whilst not as prevalent as brand awareness, is nevertheless still an important sponsorship objective. Whilst the IOC, as indicated earlier, does not explicitly identify the development of corporate awareness as one of the objectives TOP sponsors have the opportunity of pursuing, there are several

Case Study 2.1 Sponsorship objectives: Tribeca Film Festival presented by American Express

The Tribeca Film Festival began in New York in 2002 and American Express was its founding principal sponsor. Celebrating its 5th year, the Festival, founded by Robert De Niro, Jane Rosenthal and Craig Hatkoff, featured 274 films including 96 world premieres.

In 2004 the Festival attracted 350,000 visitors and only 2 years later in 2006 there were over one million event goers. The event sponsorship programme included American Express as 'presenting' sponsor and another 18 'signature' sponsors, including Budweiser, Nokia and General Motors.

American Express' sponsorship objectives can be categorized as follows:

Direct sales

The American Express card was the official credit card for the event and tickets for the event could be purchased at cinemas, by telephone and on-line by using an American Express card. Other credit cards could be used, but using an American Express card gained exclusive opportunities of purchasing tickets earl-ier than anyone else. Those without an American Express card could also apply for one on-line at the time of booking in order to take advantage of the opportunity. As a result American Express enjoyed sales that it otherwise would not have gained via customer loyalty and card activation development.

Brand awareness

Brand awareness activities included advertising in print news media, billboards, fly posters, television and radio. Via the American Express website there was Festival information, wireless alert promotions and photograph opportunities.

A 'film poster' theme was used in 2004 across all advertising and promotions including 'The man with the Golden card' mechanic that was used specifically with the company's gold card brand.

A new idea for 2006 was a 'What's your fondest memory' film competition where any one could send in a 15-second film via the American Express website (linked to the Festival website). The judges included Director Martin Scorsese and the theme linked into the wider American Express 'My life, My card' marketing communications programme thereby integrating the sponsorship into their overall marketing strategy.

Image enhancement and awareness

The focus for the launch of the 2006 event on 24th April was an association and reflection back to the '9/11' attacks on Manhattan, New York. The World Trade Center did stand in the Tribeca district.

A press release and launching speech by Robert De Niro picked up on this theme and the dedication of the event to the whole of New York. In so doing American Express were thanked for their founding and continued support and as a result were able to consider the opportunity to enhance their image.

Relationship development

For the 2006 Festival, American Express employees were offered 20 per cent discount on ticket purchases in order to develop internal relations.

American Express also enjoyed various opportunities for the entertainment of clients in order to develop further corporate awareness and image enhancement.

Competitive advantage

The above were all opportunities for American Express to achieve competitive advantage in the credit card market. In taking the sponsorship opportunity in 2002 they were able to prevent other credit cards from enjoying such opportunities. By exploiting the sponsorship over the 5 years with new ideas and rights it was able to strategically maintain that position.

Source: The Village Voice (2004), Downtown Express (2004), American Express (2004, 2006), Tribeca Film Festival (2004, 2006)

significant TOP sponsors that clearly aim for such. In Athens, for example, both Cosmote and Samsung utilized their sponsorships for corporate awareness which included exploiting their rights by taking out advertising on public transportation.

Building image via sponsorship

Enhancing brand image was ranked first by the respondents in the European Sponsors' Survey (Redmandarin, 2004); 75 per cent of the respondents rated this as very important. In addition they ranked the improvement of brand credibility third (67 per cent) and shifting brand or corporate perceptions fourth (62 per cent). Thus brand image enhancement and increased awareness are the top two ranked objectives respectively, but what is not necessarily clear from this survey or in the industry generally are the following critical factors when it comes to setting objectives:

- Increased awareness via sponsorship need not necessarily provide positive results.
- To build a corporate or brand image via sponsorship there needs to be increased awareness.

The point here is that setting objectives for brand or corporate image enhancement and increased brand or corporate awareness, whilst clearly separate in the theory reviewed earlier, are in fact linked. For example, awareness for a brand is desired as positive, there is no justification in increasing awareness if it is going to be otherwise and for it to be positive a clear message for that brand is required. The message needs to build the image of that brand. Even when building a new position for a brand with an existing audience via sponsorship, the objective is for increased awareness of that image.

American Express, via a combination of its sponsorships in New York for example, was looking to increase awareness but for a particular brand image. Ultimately the sponsor was attempting to create awareness, interest, desire and action, and it was doing that via different types and levels of communications activities. Increased awareness was achieved whilst focusing on a brand image that was of interest to target audiences because it was endorsed by successful international heroes, local events and facilities that also happened to be local.

In order to examine this more closely we can consider the use of sponsor logos. For some time logos on sports shirts, theatre programmes, ceremonial lecterns, motor racing cars, arena advertising boards and concert merchandise have been synonymous with sponsorship. Many sponsorship proposals have identified logo opportunities as beneficial rights for potential sponsors. There is no doubt of their value but that value is only achieved when a logo is used as an integral communications component of the sponsorship as a whole. In 10 pages in Sunday Times on 6th January 2006 there were 15 different logos pictured in sports photographic action shots. These consisted of only corporate or brand symbols and/or single names and included logos for Castle, '3', Vodafone, Fedcom, Puma, Mitsubishi, HL Mercedes, Carlotti, Coca-Cola, Sony Ericsson, adidas and Churchill Insurance. Not all readers looking at these logos would have been aware of which brands these names and symbols represented at the time and this is a demonstration of the lack of power of a logo in isolation. Unfortunately many sponsors in time have planted their logo on a shirt or as a flash on an advertisement and relied on that to achieve a successful sponsorship. The widespread sighting and visibility of such logos resulting in measures of increased awareness does not lead to any indication of the degree of knowledge the audience has about the company or product behind the logo. However, as part of an integrated communications effort, a sponsorship can support the use of logos so that they can work alongside other brand-building activities.

Developing and maintaining relations via sponsorship

Enhancing relations was ranked tenth by the respondents in the European Sponsors' Survey with 37 per cent of respondents indicating that it was very important (Redmandarin, 2004). The survey report does indicate that this is viewed as a brand-focused objective and as such is considered as a means by which brand awareness and/or image are developed.

The continued use of the hospitality rights associated with sponsorship is evidence that the development of relationships is at least perceived to be possible via sponsorship (IEG/Sponsorship Research, 2004). Bennett's (2003) study referred to above, for example, shows that client organizations that utilize corporate hospitality do so in order to develop relationships with existing rather than potential clients. This demonstrates that corporate hospitality is more successful in helping to retain and increase business with current clients and is therefore viewed as a reward for previous business. This is predominantly a business-to-business activity where the cost of the entertainment is a relatively small amount to pay compared with the potential increased revenue. However, there is increasing use of hospitality as prizes for mass consumer competitions where sponsors can tempt target audiences to enter and in so doing increase involvement with the brand. In addition to the entertainment of customers, it is common for sponsors to entertain their key suppliers. The theory is the same in that an enhanced relationship can still affect the bottom line but via decreased costs.

Sponsorship is also increasingly used for the development of internal relations with staff and in more ways than just via hospitality. As can be seen in Case Study 2.1 the Tribeca Film Festival offered 20 per cent discount to the staff of its sponsor American Express. Innovatively McDonald's have made an incentive out of qualifying to get to go and work at the Olympics. They take staff from their restaurants around the world to work at the outlets they install at the games. Similarly, BUPA and Flora arrange guaranteed runner spots for their employees at The Great North Run and The London Marathon respectively.

Delta was an official Grand National sponsor for milk and ice cream products at the 2002 Olympics in Athens and it used its sponsorship to develop both internal and external relations (IOC, 2004b). Internally it distributed Olympic pins to each employee, gave out souvenirs at its staff parties and in particular to the children of employees, and organized an excursion to Olympia, the ancient and original Olympic Games site for all its employees. More than a year before the games it offered its retail partners the opportunity to win Olympic merchandise by reaching sales targets and keeping their freezers and advertising materials in good condition. It also offered its consumers the chance to win 1 of 50 Olympic hospitality packages and 1000 tickets for the games via ice cream purchases. Finally, in order to develop corporate awareness amongst a wider stakeholder group, it staged a 'Clean Beach' project at 25 beaches in Greece with the objective of raising environmental awareness for a cleaner country. These examples demonstrate Delta's use of sponsorship for the development of a wide range of relationships.

Summary

In order to establish a framework for this text a number of views and definitions of sponsorship have been considered. Whilst sponsorship evolved out of philanthropic beginnings, there is no justification in categorizing it into two types of sponsorship: commercial and philanthropic sponsorship. An anonymous donation gifted either by an individual or an organization is an altruistic gesture because if there is anonymity there is no gain for the donor. On the other hand, an organization or an individual that makes a donation, however little, and not anonymously, is seeking recognition and goodwill in return. If the goodwill that is engendered in society can then be of commercial benefit then this can be identified as sponsorship.

As there are two parties or more involved, sponsorship is a mutually beneficial arrangement. The arrangement itself consists of the provision of resources of funds, goods and/or services by the sponsor in return for a set of benefits provided by the rights owner. Whilst the latter benefits from the use of the resources, the sponsor uses the rights for communications activity in order to achieve corporate and/or product-related communications objectives.

Whilst different authors use differing categorizations and terminology, there is generally agreement on what sponsorship can achieve. This theoretical discussion also generally reflects what is happening in industry. Firstly, sponsorship can be used for corporate- or product-related communications objectives and as there are a number of sponsorship objectives that overlap there is sense in categorizing them into those that concern direct sales and those that can lead indirectly to sales. It is also arguably correct to identify that all sponsorship objectives are related to the achievement of competitive advantage. In addition to these, sponsorship objectives are also concerned with the achievement of increased awareness, enhanced image and awareness of that image, and the development of key relationships.

This chapter has provided the preliminary review and discussion of what sponsorship is, and what sponsorship can achieve. Chapter 3 considers sponsorship as an integrated communications tool and identifies the objectives that are realistically achievable for sponsors.

Tasks and discussion points

■ Select a sports event sponsorship programme and identify the objectives sought by each sponsor. Support your analysis with examples of how each objective is being achieved or not as the case may be.
■ Consider American Express in Case Study 2.1 and identify how the organization might further develop product image and awareness of that image through sponsorship.
■ How might American Express further develop direct sales through sponsorship?
■ Select an organization that has previously not been involved with sponsorship. Devise a programme of sponsorship activity for the development of staff relations for this organization via an association with a music event.

References

Abbratt, R. and Grobler, P. (1989). The evaluation of sports sponsorship. *International Journal of Advertising,* Vol. 8, pp. 351–362.

American Express (2004, 2006). www.americanexpress.com (accessed 9 May 2004 and 25 April 2006).

Ashfield Council (2006). Sponsorship and the receipt of money, gifts and in-kind assistance. www.ashfield.nsw.gov.au/policy_pdfs/sponsorship_policy (accessed 3 April 2006).

BDS (2006). The definition of sponsorship. www.sponsorship.co.uk/in_sponsorship/in_ sponsorship (accessed 3 April 2006).

Bennett, R. (2003). Corporate hospitality: Executive indulgence or vital corporate communications weapon? *Corporate Communications: An International Journal,* Vol. 8, No. 4, pp. 229–240.

Boone, L. and Kurtz, D. (2002). *Contemporary marketing 2002.* London: Thomson Learning.

Calderon-Martinez, A., Mas-Ruiz, F. and Nicolau-Gonzalbez, J. (2005). Commercial and philanthropic sponsorship: Direct and interaction effects on company performance. *International Journal of Market Research,* Vol. 47, No. 1. www.warc.com/fulltext/JMRS/ 79731 (accessed 5 April 2006), pp. 75–99.

Clow, K. and Baack, D. (2004). *Integrated advertising, promotion, and marketing communications,* 2nd Edition. Upper Saddle River, NJ: Pearson/Prentice Hall.

Colley, R. (1961). *Defining advertising goals for measured advertising results.* New York: Association of National Advertisers.

Cornwell, T. (1995). Sponsorship-linked marketing development. *Sport Marketing Quarterly,* Vol. 4, No. 4, pp. 13–23.

Downtown Express (2004). *Special section: Tribeca Film Festival*, Vol. 16, No. 49, 30 April–6 May 2004.

Du Toit, M. (2003). Press and publications: Ambush marketing. www.bowman.co.za/ LawArticles (accessed 18 April 2006).

Dunn, J. and Taylor, J. (2006). Judgement day for the big banana. *The Sunday Times*, 20 August.

Erdogen, B. and Kitchen, P. (1998). Managerial mindsets and the symbiotic relationship between sponsorship and advertising. Marketing intelligence and planning. *MCB University Press*, Vol. 16, No. 6, pp. 369–374.

Hants (2006). *Sponsorship policy*. Hampshire County Council. www.hants.gov.uk/TC/cg/ sponsorship (accessed 3 April 2006).

Hoffman, A. (1998). Two sides of the coin, corporate giving is business. *Fund Raising Management*, Vol. 29, No. 1, pp. 27–30.

IEG/Sponsorship Research (2004). 4th Annual sponsorship decision-makers survey. *IEG Sponsorship Report*. Sample Issue. Chicago: IEG.

International Marketing Reports (2002). www.im-reports.com/sample3 (accessed 15 April 2002).

IOC (2004a). *2002 marketing fact file*. Lausanne: IOC.

IOC (2004b). *Athens 2004 marketing*. Lausanne: IOC.

Irwin, R., Suton, W. and McCarthy, L. (2002). *Sport promotion and sales management*. Champaign, IL: Human Kinetics.

Jiffer, M. and Roos, M. (1999). *Sponsorship – a way of communicating*. Stockholm: Ekerlids Forlag.

Lavidge, R. and Steiner, G. (1961). A model for predictive measurements of advertising effectiveness. *Journal of Marketing*, October.

Masterman, G. and Wood, E. H. (2006). *Innovative marketing communications: Strategies for the events industry*. Oxford: Elsevier/Butterworth-Heinemann.

Meenaghan, J. (1991). The role of sponsorship in the marketing communications mix. *International Journal of Advertising*, Vol. 10, pp. 35–47.

Meenaghan, T. and Shipley, D. (1999). Media effect in commercial sponsorship. *European Journal of Marketing*, Vol. 33, No. 3, pp. 328–348.

Milne, G. and McDonald, M. (1999). *Sport marketing: Managing the exchange process*. London: Jones and Bartlett Publishers.

Mintel (2002). *Sponsorship Report*. UK: Mintel.

Mullen, J. (1997). Performance based philanthropy: How giving smart can further corporate goals. *Public Relations Quarterly*, Summer, pp. 42–48.

Mullin, B., Hardy, S. and Sutton, W. (2000). *Sport marketing*, 2nd Edition. Champaign, IL: Human Kinetics.

Olkkonen, R. (2001). Case Study: The network approach to international sport sponsorship arrangement. *Journal of Business and Industrial Marketing*, Vol. 16, No. 4, pp. 309–329.

Oxford (2006). *Oxford English Dictionary*, 11th Edition. Oxford: Oxford University Press.

Pickton, D. and Broderick, A. (2001). *Integrated marketing communications*. Harlow: Pearson Education.

Pitts, B. and Stotlar, D. (2002). *Fundamentals of sport marketing*, 2nd Edition. Morgantown, WV: Fitness Information Technology.

Polonsky, M. and Speed, R. (2001). Linking sponsorship and cause related marketing: Complimentarities and conflicts. *European Journal of Marketing*, Vol. 35, No. 11/12, pp. 1361–1389. www.emeraldinsight.com/Insight/ViewContentServlet?Filename-Published/ Em (accessed 3 March 2006).

Pope, N. (1998a). Overview of current sponsorship thought. *Cyber-Journal of Sport Marketing*. www.ausport.gov.au/fulltext/1998/cjsm/v2n1/pope21 (accessed 29 April 2004).

Pope, N. (1998b). Consumption values, sponsorship awareness, brand and product use. *Journal of Product and Brand Management*, Vol. 7, No. 2, pp. 124–136.

Quester, P. and Thompson, B. (2001). Advertising and promotion leverage on arts sponsorship effectiveness. *Journal of Advertising Research*, January/February, pp. 33–47.

Redmandarin (2004). *The 2004 Redmandarin European Sponsors' Survey.* Full Report. In Association with The Sponsorship Research Company. London: Redmandarin Sponsorship Consulting.

Rossiter, J. and Percy, L. (1987). *Advertising and promotion management.* London: McGraw-Hill.

Sandler, D. and Shani, D. (1993). Sponsorship and the Olympic Games: The consumer perspective. *Sport Marketing Quarterly*, Vol. 2, No. 3, pp. 38–43.

Shank, M. (2005). *Sports marketing: A strategic perspective*, 3rd Edition. Upper Saddle River, NJ: Pearson Prentice Hall.

Skinner, B. and Rukavina, V. (2003). *Event sponsorship.* Hoboken, NJ: John Wiley & Sons.

Sleight, S. (1989). *Sponsorship: What it is and how to use it.* Maidenhead, Berkshire: McGraw-Hill.

Smith, P. and Taylor, J. (2004). *Marketing communications*, 4th Edition. London: Kogan Page.

Stotlar, D. (1993). Sponsorship and the Olympic Winter Games. *Sport Marketing Quarterly*, Vol. 2, No. 1, pp. 35–43.

Strong, E. (1925). *The psychology of selling.* New York: McGraw-Hill.

The Village Voice (2004). Vol. XLIX, No.17, 28 April–4 May 2004.

Tribeca Film Festival (2004, 2006). www.tribecafilmfestival.org (accessed 9 May 2004 and 25 April 2006).

3

Sponsorship: An integrated communications tool

The objectives for this chapter are to:

- Examine the development and importance of sponsorship as a fully integrated marketing communications channel
- Identify the process for the selection of sponsorship as an integrated marketing communications choice
- Understand the corporate sponsorship decision-making process
- Identify corporate sponsorship objectives
- Analyse sponsorship accountability and it's capacity for return on investment

Coca-Cola Championship

A Coca-Cola billboard, located in Huddersfield, UK, promotes the brand's sponsorship of the Championship in 2004

Introduction

This chapter focuses on the process by which sponsors select sponsorship in order to achieve their marketing communications objectives. The discussion focuses on the importance of sponsorship as an integrated corporate communications tool and in so doing considers a successful approach for both sponsors and rights owners. In the latter case a clear understanding of the objectives sought by sponsors, the process by which sponsors make selections and their requirement for sponsorship to be accountable is needed in order to target, sell and grow sponsorship.

Chapter 2 examined a number of views on how sponsorship is used and reviewed the range of objectives that are perceived to be achievable in the field, both academically and industrially. In this chapter a definite set of objectives are identified and discussed following an analysis of the sponsorship planning process. This is the process by which a sponsor can successfully determine whether sponsorship is the most effective and efficient way of achieving communications objectives, make the decisions to sponsor and what to sponsor, and then implement that sponsorship.

Sponsorship planning process

The discussion in Chapter 1 identified the velocity with which high spending has been achieved in the industry and one conclusion drawn was that there was a need for a continued and increased use of sponsorship as a fully integrated communications tool. The emphasis on a return on sponsorship investment has therefore never been so significant. This process of accountability, the requirement for sponsorship to be a justified choice of communication, begins with the decision of whether to sponsor at all. Thus the question, 'will sponsorship perform better than all the other marketing communications that are available' is an early consideration. The focus here then is on the process that is required in order to ensure that sponsorship is well chosen and does provide this return.

Pitts and Stotlar (2002) propose a four-stage process for the execution of a sponsorship by a sponsor. The first stage precedes the decision to sponsor and addresses the need for sponsorship to be integrated into wider communications activity. The second involves a set of steps for review and selection in order to identify the most appropriate sponsorship vehicle. The third and fourth stages are concerned with implementation and exploitation, and then evaluation. These last three stages provide a general route through the decision-making process but only once the decision to sponsor has been made. Whilst the first stage is pre-sponsorship decision it does not fully acknowledge the need for an assessment of whether sponsorship can provide the most effective and efficient communications solution and the process by which that decision might be made – in particular by evaluating it against the use of other communications tools.

Whilst sponsorship has developed rapidly, it has still not reached the level of use of other significant communications tools, advertising for example. Sponsorship activity makes up 17.7 per cent of a sponsors overall market and communications budget according to the European Sponsors' Survey (Redmandarin, 2004) and the report further indicates that that is inflated by large spending by small numbers of sponsors. It suggests that it is as low as 10 per cent on average. Other sources suggest that for industry as a whole, firms spend less than 5 per cent on average of their marketing budget on sponsorship (Gratton and Taylor, 2000) whilst they spend approximately 35 per cent on media advertising, 23 per cent on direct marketing and 14 per cent on sales promotions (Redmandarin, 2004). Gratton and Taylor's (2000) view is that sponsorship is a part of the profit-maximizing behaviour that is generally only undertaken when the risk and uncertainty of a return on advertising investment indicates other strategies should be used. Of course, this is an economic perspective and one that does not consider the wider range of sponsorship objectives. However, it does at least identify one of the criteria by which sponsorship decisions should be first considered. The way in which tobacco manufacturers have gradually been legally restricted over time in their choice of communications and particularly in their use of television advertising, provides a clear example of this. The manufacturers' alternative strategies were to focus on motor racing and snooker sponsorship communications in order to achieve their image-building marketing objectives. A strategy that enabled them to still gain significant television exposure.

The attraction and rapid growth of sponsorship has been due to its apparent ability to offer effective and efficient alternatives to advertising. However, the lack of evaluation of sponsorship in the industry and the lack of objective methods by which to measure success has clearly held back the further penetration of sponsorship into the communications mix. An average of 5 per cent communications budget spend by firms on sponsorship (see above) does suggest that there is still a lack of trust in sponsorship and what it can achieve and indeed if it achieves. The rapid increase in the use of sponsorship from the 1970s in part was down to this ambiguity. It appeared that sponsorship offered more cost effective returns than advertising but did so without any evidence. This is still disputed and is by no means comprehensively accepted. For some customers sponsorship is only perceived as another form of advertising (Thwaites, 1995). The European Sponsors' Survey (Redmandarin, 2004) revealed that of its 99 respondent sponsorship decision-makers, only 24 per cent indicated that their organizations fully understood the use of sponsorship. Over half indicated that they did not understand it at all.

There is one aspect, albeit also only perceived rather than proven, that gives sponsorship a competitive edge over advertising. Its effectiveness may be derived from the perception that it has third party-credibility due to its use of a combination of public relations tools and vehicles. A sponsor is usually buying into a ready-made image and is thereby borrowing and integrating with an image that, if it is a worthy fit, effectively endorses the sponsor.

The decision to use sponsorship communications and then which sponsorship vehicles to select, are clearly critical and as with all decisions a level of specific information is required in order to make them reliable. The categories of information required are as follows.

Target customer potential

The sponsor needs to determine whether the sponsorship opportunity has the capacity to target markets and/or publics that the sponsor desires to reach. Reaching desirable target segments is a pre-requisite for sponsorship choices but in order to determine the extent to which they are an attractive proposition, the sponsor requires details of target segment profiles and the size of target that can be reached. This selection procedure is essentially a demographic- and psychographic-based exercise and it is incumbent on both the sponsor and rights owner to ensure that this is undertaken.

Target exposure potential

The extent of the target reach can be evaluated by considering all of the potential points of exposure. Depending on the type and scale of the sponsorship vehicle, this can involve the size and numbers of live audiences, recipients of communications, and viewers, listeners and readers via media broadcasting and reporting. In addition it is also dependent on the size and amount of targets reached via the sponsors own exploitation and leveraging. This can often come down to the question of how newsworthy the sponsorship vehicle is going to be. However, considering a wider set of available sponsorship objectives, other questions will include whether the sponsorship will reach the right targets in sufficient numbers and also whether this will be hitting them with the right message. This highlights the need for thorough and early exploitation planning in addition to an assessment of the rights on offer by the sponsor. For an accurate assessment of the potential reach of a sponsorship, a sponsor will need to determine the total amount and the quality of the potential target reach and do that prior to any decision to go ahead with that sponsorship.

Distribution channel benefit

Some sponsors require sponsorships that provide value for their intermediary distributors in order that their target reach can be achieved. Those sponsors with wholesale operations for example will look for ways in which they can provide sales promotions that 'push', with incentives, those that are doing the selling in their distribution chains. The incentives are something the distributor can either benefit from directly or pass on to their customers in turn. The idea is that they are 'pushed' in order to produce more sales (Boone and Kurtz, 2002; Pickton and Broderick, 2001).

An event sponsorship can provide the necessary mechanics for 'push' promotions. Event tickets, VIP invitations or hospitality can be used as rewards for reaching sales targets and can therefore act as incentives for distributors. The sponsor can also allocate tickets to distributors for them to then pass on to their customers via competitions and loyalty schemes, for similar results. In both cases the distributor is being provided with incentives to perform better and the sponsorship vehicle is the catalyst. T-Mobile, the mobile telecommunications company, devised both push and pull strategies for the UK in order to exploit its rights as an 'official partner' for UEFA EURO 2004. The end user 'pull' promotions involved free downloads, texting, free call minutes and exclusive event content packages whilst the incentives for its key retail partner, Carphone Warehouse, consisted of event ticketing (Masterman and Wood, 2006).

Advantage over competitors

The benefits of addressing all of the above-mentioned factors means that a sponsorship has the capacity to offer a sponsor competitive advantage in its market sector. In successfully reaching targets and providing incentives for distribution channels, sponsors can gain competitive advantage via their communications efforts. This is an additional consideration when assessing a sponsorship opportunity. There is an important consideration here though. In identifying the extent of any advantage gained there needs to not only be an evaluation of what competitors are being denied, but also an assessment of the platform that is being created for the competition to exploit. The fact that a competitor has taken out a sponsorship might well be viewed by some organizations as an opportunity to target marketing communications more clearly, for example directly at an event that they do not sponsor and at a sponsor that is a direct competitor. The question has to be raised, 'how much is the sponsor creating an opportunity for others as opposed to shutting them out?' This can be a platform that sets a competitor up with opportunities for ambush marketing. This is not to say that a sponsor should decline a sponsorship opportunity just because it offers a competitor such communications choices. The sportswear manufacturer, adidas does not resist its opportunities as a sponsor of the FIFA World Cup despite Nike's persistent offensive marketing strategies. Rather the strategy should always be to undertake the sponsorship if it is right, but to ensure that there is potential for sufficient protection from ambush tactics whilst making that decision. This kind of protection is achieved with an offensive exploitation of the sponsorship rights by the sponsor. Further discussion of ambush marketing is in Chapter 12.

Resource investment

An obvious consideration for the sponsor is the amount of resources the sponsorship will require. Clearly the costs of the sponsorship are an important consideration but this does not only concern an identification of whether finance is available at the right time to pay sponsorship fees. There are in fact three key financial considerations for any sponsorship:

1. *Fees*: How much are the fees, for what range of rights and when are they payable to the rights owners?
2. *Facilitation*: How much will it cost to facilitate the sponsorship with product and services?
3. *Exploitation*: How much will it cost to exploit the sponsorship rights?

All three considerations need to be implemented and then full costs determined prior to a decision to sponsor. Knowing what costs are involved in anything we buy is something that may well be considered common sense to most individuals. The fact is that sponsors are known to enter into agreements without full knowledge of product/service costs and also into agreements without full knowledge of how much it is going to cost to exploit their newly acquired rights.

This occurs at all levels of sponsorship. Several partners of the 2002 Commonwealth Games agreed their sponsorship rights prior to their creation of any exploitation strategies or costs were calculated. The organizers of the event, Manchester 2002, identified that this was also an issue for them and that there might be a loss of potential event promotions so they provided master classes for key executives from each of their sponsors in order to help them develop exploitation programmes.

A less high-profile case involved the sponsorship of Newcastle Falcons, the UK rugby premiership club by Northumbria University. The sponsor was offered sponsorship rights at a price that it could not refuse. The rights included the placement of logos on team shorts, advertising around the stadium and opportunities for corporate hospitality. The university had already been purchasing corporate hospitality match packages and for only a small increase on that spend it was offered these and other rights. Northumbria did not exploit those rights in any way but took them anyway because it was relatively little extra to pay. The only question the University might have considered was whether further investment in order to exploit those rights might have provided an even greater return. For a return on investment, and even to determine if there has been a return on investment, the investment in fees, facilitation and exploitation should be identified and agreed prior to agreeing to sponsor.

Characteristics and fit

Any sponsorship opportunity has either an established or an emerging brand image and a critical question for any interested sponsor is whether this image and its characteristics will provide a positive or negative effect on the sponsoring brand. This is referred to as 'sponsorship fit'.

Schema congruity theory can be used to further explain this concept. A schema is generally a preconception that has been developed by an individual and through their experiences. Consumers can therefore maintain preconceptions about individual brands (Milne and McDonald, 1999). When a sponsor associates with a sponsorship vehicle, consumers assess the congruency between the two and if the result is that they are seen to share perceptual characteristics there is an increased likelihood of congruence, a sense that there is a connection. This can result in a closer acceptance of the association between the sponsor and the sponsorship vehicle (Jobber, 2003; Martin, 1996). The greater the congruence, the greater the chance of a stronger acceptance (Martin, 1996). The aim for any sponsorship should therefore be based on a suitable 'fit'.

Milne and McDonald (1999) sought to test this hypothesis, that the 'matching' of a sponsor with the 'characteristics' of the sponsorship vehicle is one factor that is critical for success. Their research indicated that not only would a good match enhance the image of a sponsor's brand, the reverse would happen if there were a poor match, the brand would be damaged. As the sponsor's message becomes inextricably bound up with the attributes of the sponsorship vehicle any incongruity would be perceived as confusing by target audiences (Meenaghan and Shipley, 1999). Milne and McDonald (1999) concluded that whilst the use of demographic-based criteria, such as finding a sponsor and sponsorship vehicle that were targeting the right markets (identifying mutual target markets), might be successful in the goal of increasing target market awareness, the achievement of image-enhancement objectives is better served by matching a sponsor and vehicle that have complementing image characteristics, in other words that they 'fit' together better.

Some steps for the achievement of a better fit would include the following (Martin, 1996):

1. Identify the sponsor's product/corporate image characteristics, not by internal processes but via external research such as customer surveys and focus groups. The aim is to identify the current perception of the image held by customers and potential customers.
2. Identify and select which type of sponsorship has the closest match: arts, music, sport, community, cause-related. Again this is reliably gained via market research.
3. Identify sponsorship vehicle options that more finely match and then select the vehicle that is evaluated via market research as the most positive.

The credibility of the rights owner is also an important issue when it comes to sponsorship fit. The ability of a rights owner to organize and deliver the rights as agreed is a key area of concern for a sponsor and something the latter should be diligent in exploring and ensuring prior to any decision to sponsor. In many cases the profile of the rights owner is inextricably linked to the sponsorship vehicle itself and so evaluation of them is simultaneous. For example, it is difficult to divorce the International Olympic Committee (IOC) from the Olympics, the Royal Shakespeare Company (RSC) from their production of Hamlet, and perhaps even more difficult to separate the Rolling Stones from their Bigger Bang Tour and David Beckham from his football boots sponsorship rights. A sponsorship of the RSC by Allied Domecq was undertaken in order to enhance corporate awareness for example. It was based on a fit between the sponsor's international alcohol and restaurant brands, and the international fame and repute of the theatre production company (Charity Village, 2004). The strong reputation of the RSC is arguably maintained as much by its image off-stage as well as its performance on-stage and Allied Domecq bought in to that whole fit.

The task of identifying the credibility and ability of rights owners is naturally much easier when there is a history to examine. The identification of a good fit between a sponsor and an organizing body is more difficult when the sponsorship vehicle and/or the rights owners are new. A series of unknown variables disrupts the decision-making process and the way through to an informed decision is often to closely examine the individuals who will be delivering the rights concerned. The growth of the number of sponsorship agencies in the 1980s was underpinned by those individual managers that gained their credibility working for one agency and then moving out to form their own, often taking their clients with them. This continues to be the case although the growth rate has slowed down considerably.

The media impact of event sponsorships is often evaluated through audience reach, size and demographics data just as with conventional advertising. What is rare is the measurement of image perception. Few studies of personality attributes for sponsorship purposes have been conducted with more trust being placed in the use of subjective 'informed' judgements (Meenaghan and Shipley, 1999). The value of a sponsorship fit that can result in the achievement of image-related objectives is clearly important and so a more objective approach and considerably more use of an identification of good fit between the two parties is not only desired but critical for a return on investment. An advertising message is a controlled communication involving designed and bought media space. A sponsorship on the other hand is reliant on the matching of its image with that of the sponsorship vehicle and this match is thus a critical element in its success. The sponsor, therefore, has a duty to consider an objective route for its decision-making and the selection of a sponsorship.

It is important to consider the nature of the images and perceptions that can be sought by sponsors. From a macro perspective Meenaghan and Shipley (1999) conducted research that revealed that sport in general is seen as healthy, young, energetic, fast, vibrant and masculine, that the mass arts are also seen as young, accessible, friendly, current, innovative but commercial whilst high-brow arts are seen as elitist, sophisticated, discriminating, serious and pretentious. There are perhaps no surprises in these outcomes but what is of interest are the research methods that were used for this evaluation. Consumer focus groups were required in order to acquire sufficient knowledge and it is at this level of research that sponsors and rights owners need to operate in order to provide effective evaluation that can aid decision-making and determine whether or not there can be a return on investment.

Potential risks

The potential risk of any sponsorship is also a calculated decision. The decision to select a sponsorship should not just concern fit at the time of selection. A forecast of what the image and characteristics of the sponsorship vehicle will be throughout the lifetime of the sponsorship is also critical. Clearly this is a subjective forecast but one that needs to be made reliably in order to reduce the risks. In order to ascertain the risks, the following should be considered.

Negative association

Negative association is where the sponsorship vehicle might become a poor fit in terms of image and characteristics. This might involve poor performance and association with 'losing', not just a 'losing' individual but also failing groups, events or corporations. This might be a sportsperson losing a match, a rock concert losing money, a film festival losing respect or a charity losing support. This is not to say that losing per se is necessarily going to cause negative association. It depends on the objectives of the sponsorship and the nature of the fit.

Volvo invested £30 million for a 4-year deal to sponsor the Volvo Ocean Race (round the World Yacht Race) and when one leg of the race encountered difficulties in early 2006 it was forced to enact various forms of communications to counteract any negative associations. Volvo positions itself as a manufacturer of reliable and safe cars but unfortunately four of the boats in the race had failed to complete the leg due to technical problems. The UK's Guardian newspaper adopted a critical stance of the association and forced the company's commercial director to issue a statement saying that by the end of the race 'the talk would be all about how tough and strong' the boats really were (Weaver, 2006).

Negative association can also concern other factors, particularly away from the actual 'field or stage of play'. However, even anti-social behaviour that results in bad publicity is not necessarily going to mean that there will be negative association. Again it depends on the objectives sought and the fit involved. In the termination of its sponsorship of professional footballer Stan Collymore after poor publicity, Reebok UK was sending a message to the public firmly demonstrating its disassociation with its ex-client. However, following poor publicity during a court case in the USA, Philadelphia 76er's basketball player Allen Iverson was not dropped by his sponsors Reebok US. Whilst they publicly maintained that they did not condone anti-social behaviour in their continued association with the player they were demonstrating that they were keen to maintain a certain 'edge' with their audiences (CNN, 2006). Termination itself, for whatever reason may result in negative publicity (Jobber, 2003).

Sponsorship clutter and over-commodification

Sponsorship clutter is the excessive number of other messages that interfere with the message of the sponsor and lead to the perception of over-commercialization. Events can display too many advertising hoardings for example, as can sponsorship vehicles such as motor racing cars. The way in which advertising can also impact on the ambience of an event venue is also an important consideration. Tennis provides a number of examples. Wimbledon limits its commercial messages on-court, much more than the French Open does in Paris, with few commercial names allowed and only for supplied products such as the clock (Rolex), umpires chair (Dunlop Slazenger) and drinks (Robinsons). The Paris event has a large number of advertisement hoardings at various levels in its arenas although it does at least ensure that, whatever the brand, they are all uniformly produced in a green and black colour way. The Royal Albert Hall has proven to be an impressive amphitheatre for tennis since WCT ran its events there in the 1980s. Their policy was not to carry any advertising on the fascias of the corporate boxes. However, a current event there, the Masters Tennis end-of-season finale to the Delta Tour of Champions, has no such policies and adorns all three tiers of the venue with different advertisers, in all colours and thus runs the risk of over-commodification.

Over-commodification also occurs via other media. Websites and public relations activity can become over-laden from the customers' perspective. The danger is that this might involve too many messages that prevent or interfere with recognition or recall.

Ambush marketing

The risk of being ambushed as a sponsor is getting higher. There are sponsors that have decided to drop their sponsorships and adopt other marketing tactics that are directed at their previously sponsored vehicles because it is a less expensive and more effective option. Nike frequently scores higher in polls for event sponsorship recognition and recall than adidas even though they are not a sponsor (Performance Research, 2003). As a sponsor, adidas takes a risk when it indirectly invites its competitors to use new communications platforms.

Decision to sponsor

All management decisions follow a process and the decision to sponsor and then which sponsorship to undertake are two key steps in an integrated marketing decision-making process. An integrated marketing communications plan derives from the master marketing plan and its purpose is to achieve harmony in relaying messages to customers and other publics (Clow and Baack, 2004; Pickton and Broderick, 2001; Smith and Taylor, 2004). Planning should incorporate all of the key promotional efforts so that the total communications plan is in synchronization. In order to achieve this, each communications component (advertising, public relations, direct marketing, sales promotions, sponsorship) must be selected so that it is an effective and efficient tool that also complements each of the other components. The optimum communications plan consists of tools that are selected for their effectiveness and efficiency in meeting overall marketing aims and specific marketing communications objectives. With so many tools available a process is required that determines which tools will be selected.

In order to determine if, firstly, sponsorship should be a tool and then secondly which sponsorship provides the best solution, a sponsor can follow the sponsorship planning process outlined in Figure 3.1. This process consists of three key stages (Masterman and Wood, 2006):

1. Organizational marketing decisions: the alignment of marketing planning with organizational objectives. Firstly identify organizational objectives and then prepare a marketing plan to meet them (Boxes 1 and 2 in Figure 3.1). Key information for this planning will come via a situational analysis and an audit of current marketing activity. Marketing objectives and strategies should then be devised with a clearly identified marketing position. An integrated communications mix is then required and as part of the selection process for this, sponsorship options need to be considered.
2. Sponsorship selection decisions: in order to determine if sponsorship options are an effective and efficient selection, all potential sponsorships have to be evaluated. This involves targeting potential sponsorships, the consideration of those sponsorship proposals that may have been received and the identification of new or existing sponsorships opportunities. To achieve this, sponsorship rights, ambush potential and protection requirements, costs (fees, facilitation and exploitation) and strategic options have all to be identified (Box 3). The steps proposed earlier for identifying the closest sponsorship fit are also undertaken at this stage. The strengths of these options are then evaluated against other communications options. The key question is whether sponsorship will increase the effectiveness of the other integrated marketing communications (Box 4). If it does, then all negotiations and agreements for sponsorship are then completed (Box 5). If it is not, then the marketing object-ives will be met with a communications programme that does not include any sponsorship.
3. Sponsorship planning and implementation: the planning and execution of the sponsorship (Boxes 6 and 7) incorporates continuous evaluation in order to ensure alignment with marketing objectives, to help develop the sponsorship relationship and provide feed back to aid any realignment that may be required (Box 8). End-on/post-sponsorship evaluation is also implemented after the sponsorship or one cycle/unit has concluded. For example, after the first event in a sponsorship that consists of three events. Feedback can be provided in order to aid future sponsorship selection decision-making and the development of the current sponsorship relationship for renewal and/or enhancement.

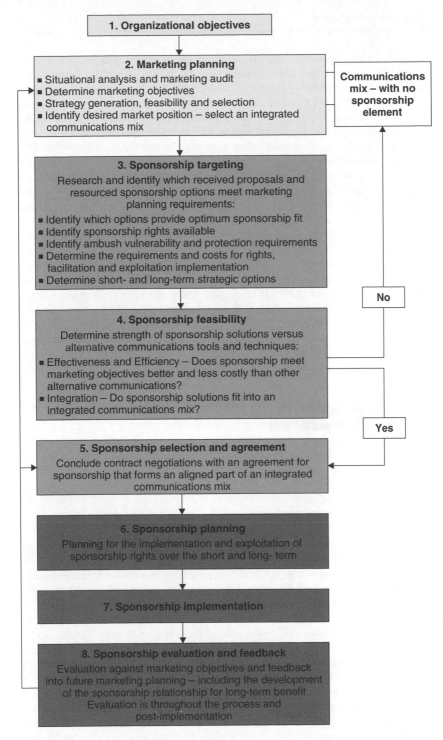

Figure 3.1 Sponsorship Planning Process
Process for the planning of sponsorship incorporate integrated marketing communications (adapted from Masterman and Wood, 2006)

This process provides effective planning for sponsorships that are to be integrated into a sponsor's wider communications programmes. The sponsorship must have the capacity to sit alongside other communications vehicles in order to achieve the sponsor's overall marketing objectives and therefore a decision to sponsor at all must be part of a wider communications decision process. The process begins with questions that determine if sponsorship is a communication tool that could be used to good effect alongside or instead of other tools. This planning process therefore allows a sponsor to decide to sponsor independently of any other marketing communications considerations. This process does not always guarantee that sponsorship will be undertaken. However, it does ensure that sponsorship is always a consideration when determining a communications mix. There is, therefore, an emphasis on the ability to determine if sponsorship can achieve a better return on investment than other options and in so doing the tool of sponsorship is always, at least, considered.

There is some evidence to suggest that sponsors are integrating their sponsorships and that is being achieved via the use of public relations and/or advertising agencies (Redmandarin, 2004). If this is an increasing trend then rights owners need to be aware of how their offerings will match and fit into a potential sponsor's marketing plans. If a sponsor that exploits their rights to the full is desired, then a critical element of the rights owner's sponsor recruitment process is determining how well their proposed sponsorship will work within a larger and varied communications programme. This is discussed again in Chapter 10.

Sponsorship objectives

In Chapter 2 there was a review of pertinent literature and discussion of what sponsorship is believed to have the capacity to achieve. It is proposed here that the following categories of objectives are achievable (Masterman and Wood, 2006).

Direct sales development

Direct sales are a more recent sponsorship objective. A sponsorship can drive sales for a sponsor and if the sales only occur because of the sponsorship then this is considered to be direct sales development. More recently this has been recognized as one of the few sponsorship objectives that can be objectively and accurately measured. The increase in the demand for sponsorship return on investment has therefore meant that this has become an increasingly utilized sponsorship facet. In particular, events offer practical opportunities for selling and because evaluation is a simple process of accounting for sales at the event, this objective is being implemented by an increasing number of sponsors. The key is that without the event sponsorship and the opportunity afforded to the sponsor, the sales would not have occurred. The sales are therefore directly attributable to the sponsorship.

All kinds of consumer products can lend themselves very well to event environments for this purpose. For example, those that offer simultaneous consumption such as food and drink will attract these manufacturers as official suppliers. The 2005 Wimbledon Tennis Championships had as many as seven official drinks sponsors. With sufficient audience numbers, direct sales at events can be significant and so brands like Lanson as the official champagne, Coca-Cola as the official carbonated soft drink, Buxton as the official mineral water, Nescafe as the official beverage, Jacob's Creek as the official Australian wine, Powerade as the official sports isotonic drink and Robinsons as the official non-carbonated soft drink have all been attracted to the event. The bargaining power of the rights holder in this case is demonstrated in its ability to attract so many drinks suppliers and segment the drinks sector exclusivity it offers down into such small categories. It can be seen too that should they wish to exercise their bargaining power further they might develop their drinks sponsorship programme with even more drinks sponsors. The fact that they negotiated with Jacob's Creek and agreed rights to be 'official supplier of Australian wine' affords them the opportunity to bring in other wines. Another example of direct sales involves Tennents, the oldest and number one selling lager in Scotland. They began sponsoring 'T in the Park' in 1994 and in 2004 the music festival attracted over 52,000 on each of 2 days thereby enabling them to sell beer to those music fans on an exclusive basis.

There are similar advantages for manufacturers of consumables that will not necessarily be instantly consumed. For example, merchandizers clearly have an opportunity to sell at events and may become sponsors too. Media sponsors have also recognized the opportunity with newspapers, for example, negotiating event sponsorship rights that include selling their offerings on the day(s) of the event. If they were to give their newspapers away though, the objective would be considered to be brand awareness development.

The sale does not necessarily have to be at the event in order for direct sales to be achieved. In the last decade credit card companies have seen the advantage of taking out event sponsorships in sport, music and arts by becoming exclusive partners. The types of rights that are now being negotiated by these companies entitle their cards to be the only card that can be used for ticket purchases for that event. Visa's and Alpha Bank's collaboration around their respective sponsorship rights for the 2004 Olympics included the launch of a new Olympic Games Gold Card. More than 110,000 subscriptions were achieved by June 2004 against an objective of 30,000 (Athens 2004 Marketing Report, 2004). Without the sponsorship these sales would not have been possible.

From an events perspective there is no loss in offering this exclusivity as not only can it ensure that it does not pay card commissions, it can still offer its customers other ways to buy tickets. To purchase tickets by credit card for the FIFA World Cup, Germany 2006, fans had to have a MasterCard. However, they could also elect to pay by bankers draft or by debit card. If the purchase was being made via the event website there was also the opportunity to open a new MasterCard credit card account thereby enabling two forms of direct sales revenue for the sponsor.

As part of the decision-making process a potential sponsor that aims to achieve direct sales should also evaluate whether there is a greater opportunity for sales that will be lost in taking out the sponsorship. This opportunity–cost evaluation will help determine if a sponsorship will give the optimum return on investment.

Brand awareness and image development

In contrast with direct sales development, brand awareness development objectives are less tangible. It is more difficult to confirm that sales have resulted from an increase in awareness and that they are therefore directly attributable to a sponsorship. A sponsorship can be implemented and the sponsor's market share can be seen to increase, but because there are many other variables, the increase can, at best, only be indirectly linked to the sponsorship. This applies to decreases as well of course. Other variables that may have impact include the intervention of the carry-over effects of the sponsor's own past or other marketing communications, any changing economic conditions, any competitors newly entering the market or leaving it and any competitor marketing communications activity (Bennett, 1999). A more reliable evaluation approach would use market research techniques for a clearer picture. The use of consumer survey instruments or focus groups for example can capture an insight into the depth of perception of the awareness and this might help determine whether it was sponsorship driven and what links there may be with sales behaviour.

In order to achieve market penetration, sponsorship can be used to increase recognition of a brand, within existing target markets, in order to help develop greater sales to existing and/or new customers. Getting the existing customers to eventually buy in greater volume also increases consumer loyalty, an objective that ranks high amongst corporate decision-makers when assessing the value of a sponsorship's properties. The IEG/Sponsorship Research (2004) annual survey of decision-makers reveals that 79 per cent of respondents made awareness and 71 per cent made increased brand loyalty the two most important reasons for taking a sponsorship on. Coca-Cola, via its sponsorship of the 2003 Houston's Livestock Show and Rodeo, achieved incremental store presence and volume sales by offering incentives to distributors and consumers in 'push and pull' style sales promotions. Its tactics included attaching coupons to 400,000 event-themed '18-can packs' of Coca-Cola for discounts on various items of co-sponsors merchandise. Sales were noted to have grown by 67 per cent on the previous year. However, these are not sales that can be directly attributed to the sponsorship but they are assumed to have been driven by the sponsorship and the brand awareness that developed.

The Puma case referred to previously in this text provides another example. In 1984 the company was just entering the tennis racket market and in so doing sold 5000 tennis rackets. Their sponsorship of an ascendant Boris Becker, who won his first Wimbledon a year later however helped to develop awareness of the brand and consequently helped sales to rise to 150,000 rackets that year (Pope, 1998). These examples demonstrate why sponsorship was and still is attractive.

Sponsorship is also used to develop brand awareness in new target markets and as a strategic tool for market development. A sponsor may be able to extend its brand equity into similar but new markets, or stretch it into dissimilar new markets with a well-selected sponsorship. Nike used various sponsorships to penetrate the USA soccer market. In a sophisticated linking of activities the sportswear manufacturer used its sponsorship of Fox television soccer programming, its own website, advertising and local team sponsorships to try and develop new business. In addition it used its sponsorship of Manchester United and utilized rights that included communications via the club's website, exclusive match coverage on the USA-based Yes television network, use of the club's players in USA television advertising campaigns (including their USA national team goalkeeper) and club tours of the USA (2003 and 2004) all in an effort to launch new products into new territories.

Sponsorship is also a tool for helping increase the knowledge of target consumers and thereby developing market position. Sponsorships offer ideal opportunities for brands to function for example whereby a sponsor's products and services can perform valuable, or more convoluted roles and functions at an event or for an individual. As the sponsor's brand is seen to be assisting the event to function, for example, the functionality helps to develop congruence and showcases the brand operating as it is intended but now with the added endorsement of the sponsored vehicle. This is why it might cost a lot of money for Police sunglasses to provide (and be seen to provide) shading from the sun for David Beckham. If this usage also involves seeing the products/services in a new light then this will also help to increase consumer knowledge. Image and reputation as well as awareness are therefore resources from which competitive advantage may be derived and sponsorship is an effective tool by which image might be altered in order to develop knowledge (Amis et al., 1999). Sponsorship can therefore be used to secure, sustain and redevelop market position.

Similarly, this functionality can also help to reinforce or revitalize brands in existing markets and in so doing achieve competitive advantage and then ultimately affect sales performance.

Many of the lists of objectives that are offered in the literature, and as reviewed in Chapter 2, identify the development of awareness and image as separate items. In fact they are interlinked. In seeking an improved image a sponsor needs to achieve awareness of that image. Whilst an organization can make decisions to change an image, the sponsorship is selected in order to communicate that image to target audiences in order to then try and achieve increased awareness of that.

External corporate awareness and image development

The same applies to the development of corporate image. Sponsorship can be used by organizations in order to position or reposition by developing awareness of a corporate image. In 1993, Allied Domecq's objective was to reinvent its corporate image. It strategically used the earlier mentioned $8 million sponsorship of the RSC to achieve awareness of that repositioning. The organization conducted research and identified that it was perceived as a conglomerate made up of individual trading companies and that few consumers understood what Allied Domecq, the company, was and what it stood for. It determined that it was losing competitive advantage as a result. Its portfolio of alcohol brands, Canadian Club, Beefeater Gin and Courvoisier Cognac, together with its outlets of Dunkin Donuts and Baskin Robbins, lacked an identifiable personality and as a result the organization was falling behind its competitors. It used sponsorship to help solve that issue. Its RSC principal sponsor status rights allowed Allied Domecq to reach target markets via venue branding, joint media relations projects, corporate hospitality and tickets, and print acknowledgements.

Awareness through sponsorship exposure can also help to position a new corporate merger/takeover. An event sponsorship for example offers opportunities for launching new organizations because they can be newsworthy and have wide target reach thus giving relatively quick and integrated solutions to a problem of how to inform but not spend too much time in transition.

Sponsorship can also provide an organization with access to wider public awareness of its mission and values. This kind of exposure can be critical in times of hardship and in response to adverse public perception. Equally it can be used to enhance public perception. For example Merrill Lynch, as part of its sponsorship of the education programmes at the Weill Music Institute at Carnegie Hall in New York, exploited its rights with magazine advertising that was targeted at children and focused on the benefits of learning music (*The New York Times Magazine*, 2004). The benefit to the sponsor included rights to communications for awareness of its website, but made no references to any products or services thereby providing a less commercial and therefore more appropriate approach for a better sponsorship fit.

Another corporate objective is the development of financial relations with investors, lenders and pertinent financial markets. For example, sponsorship can be used to defend market status and performance by demonstrating future intention for growth. Nabisco International demonstrated this in the 1980s when it was seen as a vulnerable conglomerate that was ripe for takeover and subsequent portfolio break-up. By using its corporate name rather than any of its individual brand names such as Jacob's Cream Crackers or Huntley and Palmers, it became sponsor of the worldwide Association of Tennis Professionals (ATP) Tour and end of season championship events in order to demonstrate a position of financial stability and strength.

Sponsorship of government projects and events can enhance key relationships that can lead to new business or bear influence on future performance. The fit with government, whatever the level, may be seen as a key to perceived endorsement and credibility. Partnerships between the public and commercial sectors are also well practised. The sponsorship of local authority-owned roundabouts (orbital highway junctions) in the UK is not new but is now more widespread. By definition, however, this is advertising on available sites not sponsorship. The income received by Bridgend County Borough Council for this activity is used to enhance local amenities such as planting and hanging baskets (Bridgend County Borough Council, 2006). Worthing Borough Council sells hanging basket sponsorship and has 20 high street retailers involved in its scheme (Worthing Borough Council, 2006). Perhaps more innovatively, Northumbria Police Authority was sponsored in 2006 by six local authorities from the City of Newcastle, Gateshead and City of Sunderland areas by providing them with speed cameras and funding for extra staff to manage results. The objectives were to stop more road accidents and the strategy to detect and fine more speed offenders. Their measurable benchmark was set at 20,000, the average number of offenders prior to 2006 (Northumbria Police, 2006).

Corporate hospitality has always played a big part in sponsorship rights. In the IEG/Sponsorship Research (2004) annual survey of corporate sponsorship decision-makers it was ranked the highest desired rights element with 77 per cent of respondents indicating that it was a part of their programmes. The entertainment of key customers as a reward for past dealings and the further development of business-to-business relationships can be well facilitated by corporate hospitality alone, but can be further developed by placing the hospitality into a wider sponsorship programme where customers can see the sponsor's brands providing a function.

Sponsorships can be used to communicate corporate messages to target publics as well as support the product marketing effort directed at target markets. Local communities for example are key target publics for all organizations, and sponsorship is a vehicle by which the company might be perceived as one that is concerned with community welfare. Involvement with the community is important for such activities if they are to be viewed credibly and sponsorship can offer suitable solutions for such. The Bank of Ireland was the main sponsor of the 2003

Special Olympics 'Host Town' programme in Ireland. The initiative was developed in order to build local community support for the games all around Ireland and was used by the sponsor for similar reasons. In the 3 years prior to the games the focus was on recruiting towns into the programme. A large number of towns (177) were active with signage and associated events by the time the games opened in June 2003. The Bank of Ireland played a significant part in this recruitment with 85 per cent of the towns having a bank representative on local committees. To further support this integrated marketing effort the sponsor advertised on national television with themes that promoted the programme and featured bank employees. In one small town of only 1400 people, Kilkenny of Callan, the bank manager instigated the committee so that the community could apply and participate as a host town. In so doing the town played host and housed a games delegate from the Ivory Coast (Business 2000, 2004). The whole exercise was designed to create goodwill on a local basis where involvement could be directly implemented, but also achieve this in nationally significant numbers. As a result, the Bank of Ireland might have considered itself to have achieved significant integration directly with its target audiences at a local level.

In an attempt to develop awareness, Leeds Metropolitan University and Huddersfield University have sponsored rugby league teams, Leeds Rhinos and Huddersfield Giants, respectively. Both universities have claimed that their links with this particular sport have helped them raise awareness along the M62 corridor and amongst male key target audiences in a region that is considered to be the heartland of rugby league (Sanders, 2006).

Internal relations development

Employees are a key target public and sponsorships offer all kinds of vehicles by which to develop internal communications. Sponsorship of an event can create goodwill via an involvement with the employees' community, become a theme for employee team-building activities and provide opportunities for involving employees' families. Allied Domecq's sponsorship of the RSC included 1-year free memberships for all its UK employees and the creation of an internal newsletter dedicated to the sponsorship with performance information. It expanded the latter with benefits to all its 70,000 employees worldwide (Charity Village, 2004). Flora, the margarine brand, has implemented similar internal activities that are focused on its sponsorship of the London Marathon that include guaranteed entry to the race, other staff acting as race stewards and parties for runners, and their families and pre-event internal communications focused on personal fitness and health.

Competitive advantage

Competitive advantage can be gained by achieving any or all of the above objectives, but in taking a sponsorship on an exclusive basis a sponsor also manages to gain an advantage by not allowing its competitors to take advantage of the opportunity. This is providing the sponsorship on an exclusive basis whereby only one sponsor is recruited from any one industry sector.

Sector exclusivity is now considered to be the norm, but there are still cases where a sponsorship programme can involve several sponsors from one particular industry sector. In the early 1990s the Capital Radio Group owned Pepsi Extravanganza, a 2-week lifestyle interactive exhibition in London, had no less than three car manufacturers as sponsors: Ford, Vauxhall and Nissan. It managed this by agreeing a different set of sponsorship rights that each sponsor was happy with. The bargaining power of the event was strong enough to inspire all three to play a functioning role in the event. For those rights owners with less bargaining power, the provision of sector exclusivity is considered a necessity rather than an additional benefit.

The IOC is clear that one of its sponsorship attributes is the objective of achieving competitive advantage and that a sponsorship is a defence strategy. There are two elements to this objective. On the one hand in taking an exclusive sponsorship the sponsor does in fact deprive a rival from doing the same. It is perhaps clear why Coca-Cola has been associated with the IOC and the modern Olympic Games since 1896. In taking out a sponsorship, however, the sponsor is immediately opening up other platforms for competition from its rivals. Ambush marketing is predominant in sports and sponsors need to be aggressive in their defence of the position they have taken in order to make their competitive advantage count. In developing competitive advantage through sponsorship, sponsors need to recognize that they are setting themselves up for retaliatory competitor activity and therefore have to be capable of defending that position. The feasibility and extent to which this defence needs to be taken should be ascertained before the sponsorship is undertaken and particularly when assessing future sponsorship costs. The willingness and capacity for a sponsor to exploit its sponsorship is vital.

Another important element for competitive advantage is building a sponsorship that is difficult to imitate (Pickton and Broderick, 2001). If a competitor can easily imitate the opportunity either via ambush tactics or other sponsorship opportunities and then does so, there is no competitive advantage. The key is for a sponsor to 'tie-in' the sponsorship with its other facets. This is achieved by ensuring that the sponsorship appears synonymous with the image of the sponsor and that there is a strong fit. The difficulty for any sponsor in taking on the London Tennis Championships at Queens Club for example, would be to follow Stella Artois and an event that is known as 'the Stella'. The aim is to ensure that the sponsorship is non-tradable (Pickton and Broderick, 2001). In other words developing a sponsorship vehicle that is worth more when it is with the sponsor than it would be with another. Being the first sponsor can help, but longevity is clearly critical and a sponsorship that has longevity is likely to have been redeveloped and realigned to objectives several times in order to maintain that competitive advantage.

In creating a sponsorship that is difficult to imitate a sponsor is also exploiting the sponsorship fit and at the same time developing that fit on to new levels. The sponsorship itself therefore becomes a tool for enhancing the fit in order to secure competitive advantage.

Accountability

Following the discussion above, it can now be established that in an integrated marketing communications approach, sponsorship needs to be accountable. It needs to stand up to the same scrutiny that any other communication option might be subject to. The discussion now turns to how this is done.

Two elements for sponsorship evaluation have so far been identified; efficiency and effectiveness. A key question is, therefore, can sponsorship provide marketing solutions that are more efficient and effective than other marketing communications options? In addition, there is one further consideration for many firms and that is that the sponsorship probably has to work within a specified budget.

This is unfortunately a dichotomy. Determining the budget before marketing communications decisions are made is counter-productive. The process involved in selecting a sponsorship explained earlier, clearly entails an identification of the right tool for the right job and then determines costs to then determine and finalize a budget. Smith and Taylor (2004) recommend starting with a zero budget in order to build a communications plan that specifies what is needed financially to achieve the objectives.

It is reasonable however to understand that economic limitations are necessary. It is therefore proposed that the correct approach, an approach that ensures that sponsorship can be accountable, is one that determines what it would cost to achieve the marketing objectives (in fees, facilitation and exploitation), then identifies whether that is more economical than other options and finally if that is not affordable (it is not economical) then other communications options are considered instead. In industry the overall marketing communications budget received is often less than what is required and so there will have to be prioritization (Smith and Taylor, 2004).

Return on investment

A sponsorship that is accountable and has been determined via this process should therefore be able to achieve a return on the investment. The sponsorship planning process is designed to firstly align with objectives and then realign iteratively if required. It is accepted that measurement of success is determined by whether or not objectives are achieved and that a return on investment is easier to identify with the use of measurable objectives (Dolphin, 2003; Jiffer and Roos, 1999). Therefore the successful achievement of objectives is equal to the return on investment that was originally prescribed. Furthermore, if the objectives are measurable then the extent of that return is also calculable. The problem is that not all objectives are easily set with clear measurability. The prescription is to link the generic categories of objectives identified earlier in this chapter to organizational targets (Clow and Baack, 2004; Drucker, 1974) that are SMART (specific, measurable, achievable, relevant and time specific) (Case Study 3.1). The following types of organizational targets can be implemented:

- *Market share*: Demonstrating sales, brand loyalty and competitive advantage.
- *Profitability*: Demonstrating the efficiency and effectiveness of sales.
- *Performance targets*: Demonstrating efficient and effective internal productivity.
- *Productivity targets*: Demonstrating the gaining of new customers and sales.

- *Social responsibility targets*: Demonstrating brand equity and loyalty and corporate awareness.
- *Innovation targets*: Demonstrating the capacity for new and different ways to communicate for competitive advantage, brand and corporate awareness.

Case Study 3.1 Sports sponsorship objectives: Audi – Audi Quattro and alpine skiing

Audi AG, the German-based car manufacturer, allocates 15 per cent of its total marketing budget into sponsorship- and event-related activities, 90 per cent of which is focused on sports-related sponsorship. The company has been involved with the sponsorship of the Swedish alpine skiing team since 1990.

Decision-making criteria

The decision to sponsor was made centrally at Audi AG headquarters in Germany with the following key criteria:

- A good fit. Selection of a sponsorship vehicle that demonstrated the same values as Audi cars – depending on the car model to be associated.
- Develop media exposure. In particular via Swedish television and lifestyle print media/magazines – depending on the model.
- Develop retail relationships.
- Generate goodwill with key target audiences.
- Gain and maintain competitive advantage.

Sponsorship selection

- Alpine skiing in general was identified as having the same values as the Audi Quattro 4-wheel drive car series. 'Safe on winter roads' and the 'ability to tackle rough terrain' were seen to fit.
- Mutual target audience demographics were identified – younger age groups with greater incomes.
- There was no history of a previous car manufacturer sponsoring skiing – this was deemed an important aspect for gaining competitive advantage.
- Measurable television and other media exposure objectives were set and were to be evaluated using methods the company has used since 1988. This involved an equivalent advertising costs (EAC) method whereby television exposure in the form of logos, advertising hoardings and verbal acknowledgements are counted. The total exposure times are compared with how much it would cost to buy that amount of regular advertising time and space. A good result is seen to be had when the value attached to the exposure is greater than the EAC. The company admits that this method requires upgrading but it is reluctant to lose the opportunity to track results from year to year. Audi also uses interviews, focus groups and surveys to identify customer attitudes towards its cars.

Decision-making process

The process Audi implemented was as follows:

1. Identification of the car models to be associated with the sponsorship.
2. Needs of the target audiences identified.
3. Identification of the image and values to be communicated to these audiences.
4. Identification of sports options that (a) matched this image and values to ensure a good fit, and (b) could attract the desired target audiences.
5. Risk analysis – policy of non-sponsorship of individuals, evaluation of potential poor performance and lack of media coverage conducted.
6. Selection and final decision to sponsor taken – a long-term strategy was also identified to be beneficial.

Audi generally follows a pattern of starting with its overall marketing objectives (product and target audiences are identified first) and works through to determining which sports options will suit before making its risk-assessed selection. What is not clear is whether Audi considered its sports sponsorship options in comparison with other forms of communication in order to decide if it was the most effective and efficient strategy to follow in an integrated approach to its marketing communications.

Source: Mannberg and Muotka (2004)

Summary

Whilst a sponsorship relationship should be mutually beneficial and is therefore often regarded as a partnership, it is still a business relationship and as a result there will always be two agendas. The objectives of a sponsor are different from those of the rights holder, but if the latter wants to be successful in its recruitment of sponsors it needs to understand what its sponsors want to achieve. Sponsorship objectives can be divided into four broad categories: direct sales objectives, brand awareness, external and internal corporate awareness. By achieving any or all of these a sponsor can also gain competitive advantage by shutting rival companies out of the opportunity and then maximizing that opportunity via exploitation of the rights.

The process by which sponsorship decisions are made is critical for the achievement of these objectives, but it is a process that begins with the decision of whether to sponsor or not. The decision to implement any communications tool has to be taken only once all options have been assessed for efficiency and effectiveness. In an integrated marketing communications approach therefore, a sponsorship has to prove more successful in reaching marketing objectives than other advertising, public relations, sales promotions and direct marketing options.

A number of key areas of information are therefore required throughout the planning process in order to support decision-making. These include identification and size of the target audiences the sponsorship will reach, whether there is an appropriate 'fit', how distribution channels can be provided with incentives, where competitive advantage can be gained, and the extent and type of resources that will be required. The sponsorship planning process is therefore comprised of three key stages: organizational marketing planning where marketing plans are initiated and aligned with corporate objectives, research, targeting and evaluation of sponsorship opportunities against other channels and contact points in an effort to ensure that communications are integrated and sponsorship is a justified selection and planning, execution and evaluation of the sponsorship.

Sponsorship has to stand up and be counted. In more effective marketing communications, where there is an integrated approach, it has to justify itself to be selected, it has to be more effective and efficient than other communications options. It has to be accountable. That accountability now drives sponsorship whereby any evaluation of it needs to show that there has been a return on investment. Whatever the objective or combination of objectives, the focus is on a return on investment through mutual benefit. The next section covers how these objectives can best be achieved?

Tasks and discussion points

■ Consider the case of Audi in Case Study 3.1. Critically analyse the car manufacturers decision-making and identify how their sponsorship of alpine skiing might be further developed.

■ Select a sponsorship and identify the objectives for each sponsor. Critically analyse the extent to which each of these objectives are met.

■ Select a sponsorship that you consider has provided a return on investment for the sponsor. Critically examine how and why this was the case.

■ Select a sponsorship that you consider has not provided a return on investment for the sponsor. Critically examine how and why this was the case and recommend ways in which this might have been rectified.

References

Amis, J., Slack, T. and Berrett, T. (1999). Sport sponsorship as distinctive competence. *European Journal of Marketing*, Vol. 33, No. 3, pp. 250–272.

Athens 2004 Marketing Report (2004). Lausanne: International Olympic Committee.

Bennett, R. (1999). Sports sponsorship, spectator recall and false consensus. *European Journal of Marketing*, Vol. 33, No. 3, pp. 291–313.

Boone, L. and Kurtz, D. (2002). *Contemporary marketing 2002*. London: Thomson Learning.

Bridgend County Borough Council (2006). www.bridgend.gov.uk (accessed 24 January 2006).

Business 2000 (2004). Case study: Bank of Ireland. Sponsorship of the Special Olympics: A partnership approach. www.business2000.ie/cases (accessed 26 April 2004).

Charity Village (2004). www.charityvillage.com/cv/research (accessed 11 May 2004).

Clow, K. and Baack, D. (2004). *Integrated advertising, promotion, and marketing communications*, 2nd Edition. Upper Saddle River, NJ: Pearson Prentice Hall.

CNN (2006). www.money.cnn.com/2003/07/21/news/companies/kobe (accessed 26 January 2006).

Dolphin, R. (2003). Sponsorship: perspectives on its strategic role. *Corporate Communications: An International Journal*, Vol. 8, No. 3, pp. 173–186.

Drucker, P. (1974). *Management: Tools, responsibilities, practices*. New York: Harper and Row.

Gratton, C. and Taylor, P. (2000). *Economics of sport and recreation*. London: E & FN Spon.

IEG/Sponsorship Research (2004). 4th Annual sponsorship decision-makers survey. *IEG Sponsorship Report*. Sample Issue. Chicago: IEG.

Jiffer, M. and Roos, M. (1999). *Sponsorship – way of communicating*. Stockholm: Ekerlids Forlag.

Jobber, D. (2003). *Principles and practice of marketing*, 4th Edition. London: McGraw-Hill.

Mannberg, M. and Muotka, D. (2004). *Sport sponsorship: A case study of Audi*. Lulea University of Technology.

Martin, J. (1996). Is the athlete's sport important when picking an athlete to endorse a non-sport product? *Journal of Consumer Marketing*, Vol. 13, No. 6, pp. 28–43.

Masterman, G. and Wood, E. H. (2006). *Innovative marketing communications: Strategies for the events industry*. Oxford: Elsevier.

Meenaghan, T. and Shipley, D. (1999). Media effect in commercial sponsorship. *European Journal of Marketing*, Vol. 33, No. 3, pp. 328–348.

Milne, G. and McDonald, M. (1999). *Sport marketing: Managing the exchange process*. London: Jones and Bartlett Publishers.

Northumbria Police (2006). www.northumbria-police-authority.org/latestnews/news32 (accessed 24 January 2006).

Performance Research (2003). British football fans can't recall Euro 2000 sponsors. www.performanceresearch.com/euro-2000-sponsorship (accessed 10 September 2003).

Pickton, D. and Broderick, A. (2001). *Integrated marketing communications*. Harlow: Pearson Education.

Pitts, B. and Stotlar, D. (2002). *Fundamentals of sport marketing*, 2nd Edition. Morgantown, WV: Fitness Information Technology.

Pope, N. (1998). Consumption values, sponsorship awareness, brand and product use. *Journal of Product and Brand Management*, Vol. 7, No. 2, pp. 124–136.

Redmandarin (2004). *The 2004 Redmandarin European Sponsors' Survey*. Full Report. In Association with The Sponsorship Research Company. London: Redmandarin Sponsorship Consulting.

Sanders, C. (2006). Teamwork gets results on and off the pitch. *The Times Higher*, 1 September.

Smith, P. and Taylor, J. (2004). *Marketing communications: An integrated approach*. 4th Edition. London: Kogan Page.

The New York Times Magazine (2004). The earlier they start. Merrill Lynch advertisement, 28 March.

Thwaites, D. (1995). Welcome to the Pirana Club. November 12, pp. 46–50.

Weaver, P. (2006). Ocean race gives sponsors their wildest ride. *The Guardian*, 26 January.

Worthing Borough Council (2006). www.worthing.gov.uk/leisure/ParksampOpenSpaces/ Sponsorship (accessed 24 January 2006).

Section Two: Rights

The chapters in this section focus on sponsorship rights, what they are, the role the media play alongside in their support of sponsorship and how they are devised in order to create sponsorship programmes.

Chapter 4 considers the recruitment of sponsors with tailored and bespoke rights in an approach that seeks to identify and satisfy sponsors needs. Types of rights are discussed here and Chapter 5 continues this discussion by considering the use of endorsement.

Chapter 6 explores the often interdependent nature of the relationship sponsorship has with various media and in particular the securing of media exposure in order to support the rights that are offered to sponsors. Chapter 7 turns to the recruitment process to be undergone by rights owners, the choices available and the decisions required in order to acquire sponsors and place them into sponsorship programmes. Finally, Chapter 8 considers a specific approach for the successful selling of sponsorships including the use of sponsorship proposals.

4

Sponsorship rights

The objectives for this chapter are to:

- Identify and analyse approaches for the development of sponsorship rights
- Understand and analyse the levels of status that may be provided to sponsors as part of their sponsorship rights
- Evaluate and understand basic sponsorship programme structure
- Explore the role of asset audits in the development of sponsorship inventory
- Understand the process by which sponsorship rights can be developed
- Identify types of sponsorship rights
- Understand the importance of functional rights and the role of the media

Kodak, IOC TOP partner

Kodak promotes the long association it has had with the IOC and the Olympic Games since 1896 via a poster outside the Panathenaic Stadium, Athens in 2006

Introduction

This chapter considers the benefits, in assets and associations, that rights owners can pass on to their sponsors. These rights are tangible and intangible entitlements that by agreement are bundled together into sponsorship packages for prescribed lengths of time. The chapter begins with a discussion of the approach that rights owners can adopt in the sponsor recruitment process. Current and evolved practice is included and the need to achieve relationships that will achieve a return on investment is considered in order to develop an approach for best industry practice. This approach steers away from fixed packaging and moves towards bespoke tailoring to better meet sponsors' objectives.

The discussion here considers the various categories of sponsorship rights and attempts to make sense of the wide range of terminology that is used in the industry. The focus then turns to packaging by firstly considering how rights owners can structure their sponsorship programmes. In order to determine what rights a sponsor eventually receives, a rights owner has to consider whether it will have one or several sponsors, and if it is several then whether they will fit into a tiered or flat programme structure.

Rights owners have to multi-task in their recruitment process. Whilst they consider how many sponsors they want and how their programme will be shaped, they also have to consider all the types of rights that they have to offer so that they are prepared for future negotiations. In order to be fully prepared they need to audit their assets and produce a sponsorship inventory; a list of all possible assets that might be shaped into rights for any particular sponsor. In particular the importance of sponsorship function is highlighted. At the same time a further task is to agree any media partnerships, bookings and schedules so that the rights that are associated with media exposure and coverage are secured prior to negotiations with sponsors.

There are two basic types of sponsorship a rights owner can offer a sponsor, fixed or bespoke. These are discussed below.

Fixed packaging

A fixed approach offers a sponsor a set of rights that are pre-determined prior to any consultation with that sponsor, a fixed package. Essentially this was how the sponsorship industry developed in its early years. Rights holders bundled their rights together into packages that could sit together in one programme. These packages were predominantly placed into tiered programmes whereby each package at each tier would be almost exactly the same and more often than not sold at the same fee. This was an 'off-the-shelf' approach and one that was totally non-customer focused. Whilst it served well to evolve sponsorship as a communications tool it also helped to develop the issues that surround sponsorship today. By offering a pre-determined set of rights, a rights owner demonstrates no interest in its potential sponsors' needs. As a result of this lack of understanding of the need for 'sponsorship fit', and because generally there is a lack of effective evaluation and methods by which to evaluate, many rights owners are guilty of not making their sponsorship accountable and therefore find it difficult to demonstrate a return on investment to their sponsors.

Sponsors were continually asked to consider packages via 'cold-sell' approaches. In effect a sponsor was being asked to take out a sponsorship without any consultation about their needs, they were being asked to fit their requirement around what was on offer. Whilst this approach is now considered obsolete by many theorists, the practice of selling fixed packages is still surprisingly widespread and is even common amongst some major rights owners. Visit any one of a number of websites to discover this practice. The National Lacrosse League (NLL) in the USA for example, regularly uses its website to describe various sponsorship opportunities. In one case it described 'Game of the Week – Presenting Sponsor' package details that included specific advertising details at eight arenas around the country, opening and closing television 'billboards' and 30-second commercials throughout the season. The advertising signage was specifically itemized and it referred to 64 'promotional opportunities during the intermission'. At the end of the description it mentioned that additional benefits included tickets, hospitality and 'meet and greets'. It also stated that the fees involved were $100,000 to $250,000 and that they would be customized to each individual sponsor. The issue with this approach is that it is specifically itemized and has a price range that has already been determined. The package was actually pre-determined and any interested sponsor would find it difficult to perceive that it might receive a tailored approach from the NLL (2004).

There is no harm in presenting possible rights that might be later bundled together or in doing that via a website, after all this is a relatively cheap option and interested parties may just visit on the off-chance. However, such an approach should not use itemized numbers of rights nor should it indicate prices if it is to credibly demonstrate flexibility for tailoring to meet a sponsor's needs.

The fact that this is still industry practice raises the question, where does the fault lie? Clearly rights owners are intent on overestimating their bargaining power by assuming that they will attract sponsors by offering them packages they have previously defined. There is also blame to cast on the sponsors that take out these sponsorships. Proponents of the practice would point out at this juncture, that if the sponsorships are getting sold then why worry about it. In fact there is a worry because an ill-founded sponsorship that is unlikely to meet sponsors objectives has a greater chance of failing and then not being renewed. There is a greater chance of this happening if there is no consultation undertaken and the sponsor's objectives are not identified.

Bespoke packaging

If a fixed package approach is at one end of the spectrum then a bespoke approach is at the other. A bespoke approach will develop sponsorships so that they are mutually beneficial by meeting both rights owners and sponsors objectives. At this level the tailoring of a set of rights into a package that meets a targeted potential sponsor's objectives might be considered as fulfilling a brief. A sponsor might even be asked to supply a brief as part of the initial consultation. For example, a rights owner contacts a potential sponsor and discusses what their needs would be from a sponsorship then goes away and returns later with a solution in the form of a package of rights. In such a case the rights owner has attempted to provide the sponsor with a sponsorship that has been tailored to meet requirements and as such might be praised for their bespoke approach to the task.

However, whilst the sponsor might admire the rights owners for their efforts, they might even then view this from a negative perspective. The sponsor wants a marketing solution and if it is itself following an integrated marketing communications approach it will want to explore all other forms of solution to its requirements before accepting the solution on offer via a sponsorship route. Other forms of media and communications might provide solutions too. From this perspective, the rights owner is still only able to offer a limited set of rights. These rights, bundled up into a package that meets the requirements, may still not be as lucrative a solution as other options; the sponsorship solution may not offer the best return on investment. Indeed, this sponsorship may be also outdone by other sponsorships. This is not a dilemma for potential sponsors as they can effectively, either in-house or by outsourced agency, seek and find their best marketing solution. It is, however, a dilemma for rights owners and raises the question, what is the best approach to adopt?

The answer is that it is still via a bespoke and tailored route. A well-tailored sponsorship solution may not get accepted because there are other options that work better, but if there is a process that is implemented prior to this that involves researching and targeting the right potential sponsors before they are approached, in order to discuss their requirements, then the rights owner is greatly reducing its risk of failure. If the approach is any less than this then the risk of failure is at its greatest. The future of sponsorship may very well depend on this premise, because if sponsors cannot evaluate to determine if they have met their requirements, then they will select other forms of communications solutions. So sponsorship is very much going to be held accountable and as such it needs to demonstrate a return on investment. The process for a successful targeted and tailored approach is more closely identified and discussed in Chapter 7.

Categories of sponsorship rights

When sponsorship rights are bundled together they include some kind of acknowledgement of the status the sponsor acquires through the relationship. This will normally involve a title of some description. Throughout the last 40 years and the development of sponsorship, these titles have incorporated a diverse range of vocabulary and terminology. Sponsors have been acknowledged as simply 'sponsor' and over time this has also developed some negative perception. As a result other terminologies have developed with 'official suppliers', 'presented by', 'in association with', all in wide use throughout all kinds of sponsorships. In recent years, and perhaps as a result of closer relationship building, there are now 'partners' and 'partnerships'. The International Olympic Committee (IOC) refers to its current key sponsors as partners in its TOP programme. The 2006 FIFA World Cup (Germany) refers to its sponsors as 'official partners'. Manchester United refers to AIG, its shirt sponsors, as its 'principal sponsor' and The English Football Association (The F.A.) has F.A. partners and previously referred to them as 'pillars'. Other acknowledgements across the industry include 'hosts', 'friends', 'supporters' and 'corporate champions', and the variance only demonstrates that rights owners can acknowledge their sponsors as they and their sponsors mutually see fit.

With such a variety of acknowledgements it is difficult to categorize sponsorship status and apply analysis in order to identify the nature of such associations.

However, in general there are five categories of sponsorship rights that can be sold on to a sponsor (see Figure 4.1).

It is possible to have more than one category of rights. For example, a title sponsor is likely to have sector rights and exclusivity and may have supplier rights. Depending on the programme of sponsorship, a sponsor with naming rights to a building may very well be considered to be the most important and in that sense may be referred to as a title sponsor, even 'the' sponsor if they are the only one. A presenting sponsor may also have naming, sector and supplier rights. A sponsor with sector rights may have supplier rights however, not all sponsors receive supplier rights although the argument for doing so is increasingly getting stronger.

Title rights
These rights include the sponsor in the title of the sponsorship vehicle so that all references pertaining to the title of the event include the sponsor's corporate, product or brand names as agreed. These rights usually extend to the graphics that are produced, for example event logos. The rights owner then has to manage the use and proper acknowledgement of this title by others, including media, so that these rights are maximized. Communications partners can also be successful title sponsors but to maximize the opportunities with all media and get other broadcasters and publishers to acknowledge the title in full requires careful management.

Presenting rights
These rights allow an acknowledgement of the sponsor alongside the title rather than being incorporated into it. Presenting rights may or may not extend to the graphic acknowledgements. Typically a sponsor's corporate, product or brand name will feature prior to or immediately after the event title. Again the rights owner has to manage the use of the title and accompaniments carefully as it is easier for media in particular to omit a presenting sponsor acknowledgement. Title and presenting rights can be used together but are rarely done so.

Naming rights
These rights are associated with physical structures such as arenas, stadia, halls and galleries. They are usually long-term agreements whereby a sponsor's corporate, product or brand name will be associated with a renaming of the building concerned.

Sector rights
Sponsors with category or sector rights have exclusive representation from their trading sector of the market. In other words a rights owner contracts not to sell rights to more than one sponsor from any one industry sector. Once seen as a negotiable right and benefit, sector exclusivity is now more contemporarily seen as a pre-requisite. A sponsorship programme should allow for all sponsors to enjoy sector exclusivity so that they can fit comfortably and work together. Communications partners can also be successfully incorporated into a sponsorship programme and also enjoy sector exclusivity.

Supplier rights
Supplier rights can, and wherever possible should be, enjoyed by all sponsors. In some way the event should incorporate all its sponsors, their products or brands, as functions of the event. The agreement to supply services, people and product can be in the form of sponsorship-in-kind or be in addition to sponsorship fees.

Figure 4.1 Categories of Sponsorship Rights (adapted from Masterman, 2004)

The potential for providing a function in the sponsorship via supplier rights is an opportunity to highlight and demonstrate product/brand assets to target audiences and is therefore an important right, consequently this receives due attention at other points in this chapter.

Such is the power of some sponsorship messages that the title need not be acknowledged for there to be successful communication. The London Tennis Championships have over the length of its current title sponsors involvement become known more commonly by the sponsors own brand. The event is frequently referred to by tennis aficionados as the 'Stella', the brand of course being Stella Artois beer. Perhaps more significantly the event can be recognized instantly by many simply through the use of the brand colour (red) all around the event.

Acknowledgements for presenting sponsors can take different forms. In 1998 the F.A. sold presenting rights of its prize asset, the F.A. Cup, to French insurance organization, AXA. Under pressure from supporters not to sell title rights and the name of this famous old football knockout competition, the F.A. decided that only presenting rights would be acceptable. The deal lasted 4 years and throughout that time there were two different acknowledgements in use. On the one hand the website in 2001 referred to the event as 'The AXA sponsored F.A. Cup'. However, the photograph on the same site showed Liverpool, the winners that year, behind a media sign board that had graphics which said, 'the F.A. Cup sponsored by AXA'. The sponsorship ended in 2002 having suffered fan criticism and a negative perception of the F.A. and sponsorship in general. Interestingly, the F.A. has recently sold a similar presenting package to E.ON the German utilities firm and parent company of Powergen in the UK. The 4-year deal is reputed to be worth around £8 million per year and is being used to build awareness of the brand beyond power and gas provision over that time. The F.A. acknowledge E.ON as a 'headline' sponsor and the sponsorship rights extend across a number of assets such as the F.A. Women's Cup, the F.A. Youth Cup as well as the F.A. Cup (Gibson, 2006a). The event is acknowledged as the 'F.A. Cup sponsored by E.ON'.

Naming rights are not that new although the term 'naming rights' has become a buzz-word in the sponsorship industry in the last 5 years or so. Possibly the first naming rights agreement was completed in 1973 when the Rich Corporation paid $1.5million for a 25-year relationship at the Rich Stadium, the home of the Buffalo Bills NFL team (McCarthy and Irwin, 1997). In the UK, naming rights were sold by Scarborough Football Club as long ago as 1988 to McCain, the frozen food producer, based over the road from their stadium. The sponsorship of the McCain Stadium is still in place today. The growth in this category of sponsorship rights though has been in the USA where today more than 50 per cent of all the stadia used in the NBA, NHL, NFL and MLB have naming rights sponsors. The Harris County Sports and Convention Corporation, in conjunction with Houston Livestock Show and Rodeo, and NFL team, the Houston Texans, sold naming rights for its new stadium in 2000 for $300 million to Reliant Energy. The new stadium opened in 2002 and the rights were agreed in a 32-year contract (HCHSA, 2000). Research shows that for new stadia there is relatively little resistance from fans against naming rights (McCarthy and Irwin, 1997). This might help to explain why naming rights have not seen as much usage in Europe and the UK in particular. There was little resistance to the naming of the new Reebok Stadium in Bolton, the McAlpine and now Galpharm Stadium in Huddersfield, nor the prospect of Arsenal's Emirates (Airline) Stadium in London. However, the prospect of a new name for Old Trafford sprang a whole series of objections from Manchester United supporters early in 2006. Generally these are long-term deals and the key is to discard the original name. If the media are to be convinced at all and become a consistent user of a sponsors name via this approach, then it is essential to make a complete and concise change.

Sector rights can take different forms and originated with the use of 'official supplier' acknowledgements. In the early use of sponsorship in the 1980s manufacturers in particular were attracted into sport as 'official suppliers' to events and individual sports stars. The products and brands were used or were seen to be used as well. With development and maximization of sponsorship rights, however, an increasingly diverse range of firms are now taking sector rights, and as a result are not necessarily exercising any supplier rights to a point where they provide a function in that sponsorship, thereby maximizing the fit between them and the sponsorship vehicle. Examples of sports sector rights used in conjunction with supplier rights in order to provide a function include the following:

- *Asda*: Supplier of clothing to the 2002 Commonwealth Games using their 'George' brand of clothing on the event tracksuit uniforms – one of which was incorporated into the script of Coronation Street the UK television soap programme prior to the event in 2002.
- *Gatorade*: The official energy drink to the NFL and all of its 32 teams with exclusive presence at all NFL training camps, practises and on sidelines at games.
- *Proctor and Gamble*: Providing Super Bowl XXXVIII with 27 luxury restrooms whilst promoting its 'Charmin' toilet tissue.

Use of sector rights together with supplier rights that also provide function is less common away from sport and in many cases more difficult to devise. Hence the recruitment of sponsors to event-led solus sponsorship programmes, for example New York's Metropolitan Opera and its 'Free Parks Concerts' was sponsored by the Bank of America and its 'Opening Night Gala' was sponsored by Deutsche Bank. The English National Ballet (ENB) recruited Linklaters, a London law practice, for its 'Christmas Season'. The rights given over to the sponsors in these cases were predominantly corporate hospitality based and the fit was less obvious due to a lack of sponsor function in the respective events.

If arts organizations can recruit longer-term sponsorship agreements then they are often relatively straightforward official supplier type arrangements. For example Freed of London, makers of ballet shoes, supply their products to the ENB via a welcome cost reducing sponsorship-in-kind agreement. Continental Airlines are the 'official airline' to the home of the Metropolitan Opera, the Lincoln Center in New York, and provide air transportation so that the Center can bring in artists at less cost. However, it is more difficult to see the function that Movado watches provides as an 'official sponsor' of the Center. Whilst there are personal rights and associations made with the Center's artistic director of Jazz, Wynton Marsalis (by providing him with his timepiece) the tagline 'the art of time' and link with the organization is tenuous. A more innovative approach was Claridge's, an up-market London hotel, and a fit, even if somewhat convoluted, between a competition prize consisting of a night at the hotel and an ENB event called an 'Evening of Pure Indulgence'.

Programme structures

These sponsorship rights and the levels of status that accompany them can be useful for differentiation when it comes to developing sponsorship programmes. When developing a number of sponsorships into a series or programme, the key is to design each one so that it can complement and sit comfortably alongside others. To do this successfully a rights owner needs to consider the whole picture and balance the sets of rights, so that there is sector exclusivity and that there is no unnecessary duplication that will lead to over-commodification. As previously discussed in this text, sector exclusivity was once seen as a benefit and right in itself but is now expected by most sponsors.

The temptation for rights owners may be to attempt to recruit as many sponsors as possible, but those that do this do it at the risk of cluttering the commercial messages of their sponsors and thereby run the risk of causing dissatisfaction. The Mastercard Alamo Bowl, an American football event in south Texas in the USA, describes how its sponsorship programme enables the event to keep its ticket prices down in order to continue to supply entertainment. In so doing it asks that fans of the event 'reward its title sponsor Mastercard along with its games sponsors with their patronage' (Alamobowl, 2006). The event has a title sponsor, an official telecommunications partner (at&t), a television partner (ESPN) and six games sponsors (American Airlines, Corporate Express, San Antonio Convention and Visitors Center, Express-News, Ticket 760 KTYR and Wells Fargo). In addition, on the event website, there are no less than 117 further firms that are acknowledged as sponsors. Whilst the supplies, services and fees that the event receives are no doubt required in order to run the event successfully, the event is in danger of providing its partners with a platform that is too crowded. For most events the dangers of over-commodification and the ensuing clutter are that sponsors' messages become diluted.

The opportunity to achieve greater revenue streams from sponsorship is an important aspect of sponsorship programme management, and the inclusion of levels of status in programmes is another way of differentiating sponsors in order that they may work alongside each other. An understanding of what structure to apply and how to bundle rights so that sponsorship potential is maximized is required.

There are three basic sponsorship programme structures (Masterman, 2004). If there is only one sponsor in the programme then this is a simple structure and may be referred to as solus sponsorship (see Figure 4.2). If there is more than one sponsor then the programme can be structured in one of two ways. The first of these allows the programme to have different levels of acknowledged sponsorship status and in a tiered hierarchical structure (see Figure 4.3). The second allows for sponsors that have the same status and for them to be acknowledged as such whether or not they have identical sets of rights. Its nature is therefore flat because there is no hierarchy involved (see Figure 4.4).

It is possible for a rights owner to maximize revenue by building a programme that consists of sponsors that sit comfortably and successfully together to achieve their objectives with either a tiered or flat structure.

The 2003 Toronto Pride event managed to combine 25 sponsors into its programme. In a tiered sponsorship structure it had two top tier 'diamond' sponsors, Labatt Blue beer and the Government of Canada. In all there were seven levels of sponsorship, diamond, platinum, gold, silver and bronze, supporting organizations and media partners (Toronto Pride, 2004). In 2005 the event reduced its number

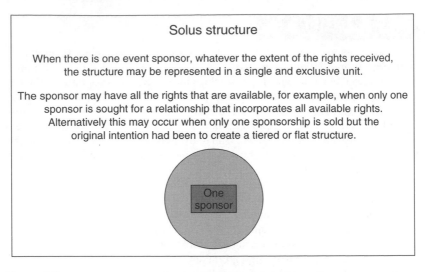

Solus structure

When there is one event sponsor, whatever the extent of the rights received, the structure may be represented in a single and exclusive unit.

The sponsor may have all the rights that are available, for example, when only one sponsor is sought for a relationship that incorporates all available rights. Alternatively this may occur when only one sponsorship is sold but the original intention had been to create a tiered or flat structure.

One sponsor

Figure 4.2 Solus Sponsorship Programme Structure (adapted from Masterman, 2004)

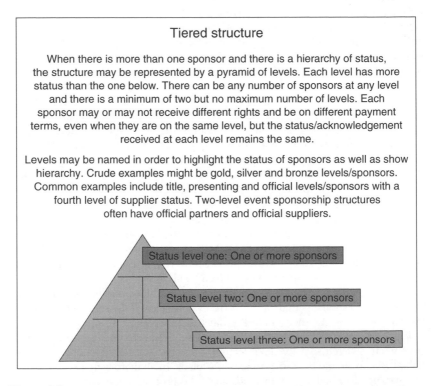

Tiered structure

When there is more than one sponsor and there is a hierarchy of status, the structure may be represented by a pyramid of levels. Each level has more status than the one below. There can be any number of sponsors at any level and there is a minimum of two but no maximum number of levels. Each sponsor may or may not receive different rights and be on different payment terms, even when they are on the same level, but the status/acknowledgement received at each level remains the same.

Levels may be named in order to highlight the status of sponsors as well as show hierarchy. Crude examples might be gold, silver and bronze levels/sponsors. Common examples include title, presenting and official levels/sponsors with a fourth level of supplier status. Two-level event sponsorship structures often have official partners and official suppliers.

Status level one: One or more sponsors

Status level two: One or more sponsors

Status level three: One or more sponsors

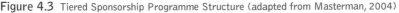

Figure 4.3 Tiered Sponsorship Programme Structure (adapted from Masterman, 2004)

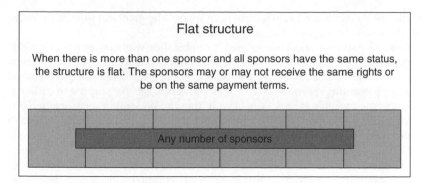

Figure 4.4 Flat Sponsorship Programme Structure (adapted from Masterman, 2004)

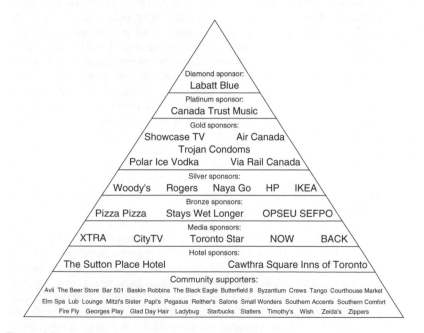

Figure 4.5 2005 Toronto Pride Sponsorship Programme (adapted from Toronto Pride, 2005)

of sponsors to 22, but continued with a similar seven-tier structure. Another level of support was created, 'Community Sponsors' and the event managed to recruit 32 partner retailers and suppliers in order to ensure the event was totally integrated with the community (Toronto Pride, 2005) (see Figure 4.5).

In tiered structures it is possible, as Figure 4.3 explains, to have more than one sponsor at each level. It is also possible to maximize revenue with more than one sponsor at the top level, where the sponsors might be referred to as joint sponsors or partners. The Cathay Pacific/Credit Suisse First Boston Hong Kong Sevens 2004 is more than a mouthful for any journalist to acknowledge but nevertheless this event provides an example of two 'title' sponsors. The dangers for such a strategy lie in a potential lack of user friendliness. Full verbal and written acknowledgements of this event title by media are likely to have been sparse. The graphical form of the event title logo was also cumbersome and cluttered.

Presenting sponsorship has been used in combination with title sponsorship rights in the past. It is less common now, but in the 1980s for example the Nabisco Masters Doubles (ATP Tour end of season world doubles tennis championships) managed to sell a presenting sponsorship as well as a title package. As referred to earlier in this text, the example is an unusual one in that the presenting sponsorship rights were bought by Nabisco UK. The rights owners, WCT Inc, had sold the title rights to Nabisco International and had kept the right to sell a presenting package whereby the Nabisco Masters Doubles would be 'presented by' another sponsor. The prospect of cluttering their 'title' message with that of another (even though non-competing) was so unattractive to Nabisco that its regional operational division, Nabisco UK, bought those rights ahead of interested party Mercedes. With the title and present-ing rights protected there was then no need to insist on an event title that would have appeared confusing, for example the 'Nabisco Masters Doubles presented by Nabisco (UK)'. The other presenting package rights of advertising, signage and cor-porate hospitality were, however, taken up and thus the result for WCT was a tiered programme with a title, and a presenting sponsor and the revenue that went with it.

The use of two-tiered sponsorship programmes has become popular with events more recently. The 2002 Commonwealth Games had a programme of official spon-sors (Asda, Imperial Leather, Microsoft, Cadbury, Adecco, Xerox, Manchester Airport and Guardian Media Group) plus official partners (United Utilities, Addleshaw Booth, Bruntwood, Guilbert, Claremont and First Bus Company). In this example the partners are depicted at a lower level in all acknowledgements, principally because they were mainly non-fee paying and in sponsorship-in-kind deals. The example only goes to demonstrate still farther that rights holders and sponsors can agree to use whatever terminology they deem wise; a partner being lower in the hierarchy than a sponsor in this case.

The owners of the stadium in Atlanta, USA sold their rights in two levels. Their 'naming rights partner' is Philips and the stadium was renamed as the Philips Arena. The next level of sponsorship in their two-tiered programme provided a status of 'founding partner' (Bank of America, Anheuser-Busch, Coca-Cola, Delta Airlines, The Home Depot, UPS, T-Mobile and WebMD). These eight founding partners do not though, as the acknowledgement might suggest, remain as 'founders' in per-petuity. In 2006, T-Mobile and WebMD were withdrawn and Georgia-Pacific was brought in. All of these sponsors receive sector exclusivity and supplier rights to the venue. They also provide different levels of function, some less obvious than others. The Home Depot, a hardware and home supplies retail group for example, has little function at the stadium and enjoys a package that is predominantly advertising.

The F.A's five 'pillars' mentioned earlier, have been formed around association with the governing body's main strands of football. This sponsorship structure appears flat. It consists of five sponsors, directly connected to the main strands of football in sponsorships that are made up of entirely different rights in order to achieve a fit with each sponsor. The idea is that each strand and its sponsor are synonymous and together they form a pillar, thereby achieving an appropriate fit. Each of the sponsors has access to the F.A's top two brands, the F.A. Cup and the England team. Whilst the pillars are all acknowledged in the same way, the F.A. does have another level of sponsorship, a lower level of official suppliers. The suppliers are also acknowledged in the same way and so this structure is in fact two tiered (see Figure 4.6).

The F.A. partners

Nationwide	McDonald's	Umbro	Carlsberg	Pepsi
Pillar: **Women's Football**	Pillar: **Community Football**	Pillar: **Elite Football**	Pillar: **Men's Football**	Pillar: **Youth Football**
The F.A's 'Growth Market'	The F.A's 'Classroom and Showroom'	The F.A's 'Showcase'	The F.A's 'Mass Market'	The F.A's 'Future Market'

Official Suppliers

Sainsbury's	Walkers	DHL	Ford	Giorgio Armani	Gatorade	Mitre	British Airways

Figure 4.6 The F.A. Sponsorship Programme (adapted from The F.A., 2006)

The F.A. aims to retain its sponsors on long-term contracts and for contracts to run over the same time periods. This is not always possible however and the result is a level of sponsors that can often be in a state of change. Ostensibly the F.A. has maintained long relationships with its partners McDonald's, Pepsi and Carlsberg whose contracts ran concurrently until after the FIFA World Cup, Germany 2006. Negotiations were at the time of writing being considered for a 2006 to 2010 period; a World Cup 4-year cycle in effect. Nationwide renewed as 'Lead Partner' for the England team after the 2006 World Cup, whilst Umbro renewed their sponsorship in late 2005, a deal that takes them through to 2014 with rights that include England shirt provision, 'founding' sponsorship of the new Wembley stadium, title sponsorship of the National Football Centre and for them to replace Mitre in 2007 as official ball supplier. The deal was reputed to have cost £200 million in fees alone (Kelso, 2006).

The IOC also has a two-tier sponsorship structure and because it currently (TOP VI) has a number of sponsors and suppliers it unsurprisingly has difficulty in maintaining deals that run concurrently (see Figure 4.7).

In 2005 Coca-Cola renewed their agreement as a TOP sponsor until 2020. They have been involved as a sponsor with Olympic Games since 1928. On the other hand, in 2006 there were TOP sponsors that were contracted only until 2010 (Omega). Three sponsors were contracted until 2012 (Atos Origin, GE and McDonald's). Despite the difficulties of managing a programme that has partners on different contracts, the IOC is building a number of key relationships. This group of sponsors is becoming quite a select club. Alongside long-standing partner Coca-Cola, Kodak has been involved with every games since the modern era began in 1896. The Swatch group has been involved since 1932 (missing only three Games) and now associates its Omega brand with the programme. Visa (1986) and Panasonic (1984) are also growing their relationship whilst McDonald's have been supplying fast food for athletes since 1976. In addition to Swatch, Atos Origin (previously Schlumberger Sema) and Manulife (previously John Hancock) have also switched their associated brand (IOC, 2006). Kodak are featured in Case Study 4.1.

The development of two-tiered sponsorship programme structures has evolved out of the use of flat structures. A 'flat' approach is an attempt to form fewer relationships but for a larger share of the rights and generally larger fees. It is an approach that is deliberately attempting to restrict clutter and the dangers of over-commodification. The F.A. believes this to be a 'more dynamic and less cluttered environment' for its partners (The F.A., 2006). The success of some early flat structures though has led to greater negotiating power and the creation of a second level.

It is therefore quite rare to find industry usage of flat sponsorship programme structures, particularly in large-scale and high-profile event sponsorships. However, individual endorsement-type sponsorship programmes (of sports, music stars) are often flat in structure. David Beckham's sponsorship programme is flat. No one sponsor, despite there being different levels of fees involved, is perceived as anything other than an official supplier to him. None of his sponsors are acknowledged as his main or title sponsor. Albeit some sponsors naturally receive more media exposure. Britney Spears provides a similar example from the music industry (see Figure 4.8).

A more unusual example of flat structures occurred in the summer of 2003 when a diver, Tanya Streeter, successfully broke one of the world's more extreme

TOP sponsors

Visa	Samsung	Atos Origin	Lenovo	McDonald's	Manulife	Kodak	GE	Coca-Cola	Panasonic	Omega
Consumer payment systems	Wireless communications equipment	Information technology	IT equipment	Retail food services	Life insurance annuities	Film photographics & imagery	Energy health care Lighting Security	Non-alcoholic beverages	Audio TV Video equipment	Timing scoring venue results services

Official suppliers

Daimler Chrysler	Mizuno	Schenker
Ground transport	Clothing	Freight forwarding & customs clearance

The Olympic Partner (TOP) programme is owned and managed by the IOC. Agreements with sponsors are based on an Olympiad or quadrennium, and therefore each sponsor commits to a 4-year deal. This is an important revenue stream for the IOC as sponsorship contributes more than 40 per cent of its marketing income. Sponsors are recruited in order to provide direct support, services and expertise at both the winter and summer games of each quadrennium – as can be seen from the categories, each sponsor is providing an important function. In return each of these multinational companies receives rights in global regions, category exclusivity and the use of designated Olympic imagery and marks including the five rings. In addition. TOP sponsors also support National Olympic Committees. A Games Organizing Committee will, in addition, also negotiate and recruit its own series of sponsors.

The Olympic Supplier Programme provides further support in vital areas for the IOC on a year-round basis and a Games Organizing Committee for their operations, but generally not for direct support for a Games.

Figure 4.7 IOC TOP VI Sponsorship Programme (adapted from IOC, 2005)
Source: IOC (February, 2006)

Case Study 4.1 Sponsorship function: Kodak – IOC TOP Sponsor

Kodak, as a provider of 'infoimaging' to individuals as well as a range of businesses, has interests in photography, health, commercial imaging, component supply and display.

Kodak is the IOC's most loyal supporter. It provided a supporting role at the first modern Olympics in 1896 and has been at every games since then and is claimed by the IOC to have recorded 'virtually every great moment in Olympic history'. Kodak became a charter member of the TOP programme in 1986 and is currently the supplier of film, photographics and imagery for Olympic Games. As can be seen below, this status affords the company a wide range of function at Olympic Games.

Kodak and Turin 2006

Kodak supplied a number of key functions for the 2006 Winter Olympics in Turin. These included services and equipment for photo journalists, security systems, health equipment for the medical care of all participants, and imaging services for all visitors and official recordings. Here is how they did it.

Imaging functions

Kodak digital products were available for purchase at the Olympic Superstore and retail outlets in the Olympic Villages. These products included films, cameras, batteries, memory cards and printer docks. At the 'Kodak Picture Maker Kiosk', in the Superstore, Olympic visitors could burn their pictures from their memory cards on to Kodak Picture CDs. The 'Kodak EasyShare Gallery' was an on-line photo service (via the Kodak website) that could be accessed to securely share digital photos with friends and family. Promotions were run on the site, for example for the best picture of the day. These functions were available for all visitors and participants and enabled new technology to be personally sampled. It also achieved direct sales for the company.

The Kodak Image Center

Kodak also created and serviced a 20,000 square-foot centre as part of the Games Main Press Center. From this centre the company was able to offer products and image services to all the games accredited photo journalists. Three million images were processed through this centre via high-speed Internet connections to editors all over the world. Some of the imagery was also used for display purposes around the Olympic sites for all to see.

Security functions

Kodak document imaging technology was used to produce 300,000 security badges and the 60,000 visa credentials that were required for athletes, officials, volunteers and sponsors for the games. In showcasing this technology, Kodak was able to state that each credential was produced in less than 10 seconds from paper applications in order to produce an electronic record. Their products, the Kodak EasyShare digital camera and the Kodak Professional ML-500 Digital Photo printer were used in the process. Lost credentials were re-issued via 23 Olympic sites. This function enabled Kodak to demonstrate new technology to target audiences.

Health functions

Kodak Health Group products supported three key medical facilities for the Games. State of the art equipment was therefore made available for the examination of injuries. X-ray, radiography and diagnostic services were provided via equipment installation as well as manpower including 21 radiographers, 20 consultants and 28 dental professionals. Much needed health care was therefore provided to target audiences.

Whilst all of these services were being showcased to target audiences at the Games, Kodak also communicated to its audiences what it was expertly providing. Providing function in a sponsorship is a key element for the achievement of communications objectives with both event audiences and in achieving reach further a-field.

Source: IOC (2006); Jurrien (2006); Kodak (2006)

records. She dived to a depth of 122 metres and held her breath for 3 minutes and 38 seconds. She was sponsored by Red Bull (energy drink), Tag Huer (watches/timing), Yamamoto (dive suits) and Club Med Turkoise (event venue). The story was covered by media around the world with a full-suited (with sponsor logos) diver in many photos (*The Times*, 2003). Flat sponsorship structures are also more readily found in the arts. The aforementioned Lincoln Center in New York for example, a multi-cultural provider, has two sponsors in Continental Airlines and Movado and a third in media providers WNBC/WNJU.

Sponsorship is not always used to generate revenue. In order to reduce expenditure and/or add value to the product, sponsorship-in-kind can be sought. Such sponsorships, also called contra deals or trade-outs, still involve mutual benefit but with no money changing hands. It is not a new form of sponsorship but it is becoming increasingly more important as it continues to grow (Mintel, 2000, 2002). The benefit comes in the form of product or services that are of benefit to the rights owner, such as in the delivery and management of an event in particular. For example, a sponsor providing resources such as people, equipment, product, decorations, printed materials and communications mechanisms, can receive sponsorship rights to the equivalent value.

The saving of expenditure is a prime driver in wanting to attract sponsorship-in-kind but a longer-term view is also to consider those organizations that can augment the event entertainment product, even when expenditure for this was not part of the original budget. 'Claridge's Night of Pure Indulgence' is an example of the fit being created, the sponsor gaining a showcase for its product and the ENB providing additional entertainment for its audience.

The eventual choice of sponsorship programme structure is a complex decision that involves the juggling of several solutions before finalization. The target for the rights owner is to achieve a successful programme whereby success is measured against objectives. Generally these objectives are focused on maximizing revenue and/or reducing expenditure with the recruitment of fee paying and/or resource supplying sponsor(s). In order to maximize this position, some decisions should not be made too early. Ideally a rights owner would firstly research and identify all its potential sponsors' needs in order to determine the packages of rights that would

David Beckham

Gillette	Adidas	Pepsi	Marks & Spencer	Snickers	Vodafone	TBC
Shaving	Sportswear	Soft drinks	Clothing	Candy bars	Communications	Cosmetics

Britney Spears

4 Wheelers	Got Milk	Pepsi	Mauli's	Proactiv
Roller skates	Health drink	Soft drinks	BBQ sauce	Skin treatment

Figure 4.8 Flat Endorsement/Sponsorship Programme (adapted from Duncan, 2006)

suit them whilst at the same time determining the structure that they then all fit into. They would then be able to go back to each sponsor with details of the overall programme and their role in that, knowing that they have exhausted all the opportunities and maximization has been achieved. This is obviously a tough task as rights owners cannot afford to keep sponsors waiting for decisions and not all rights owners have negotiating power to bring in who they want.

Audit process

Whilst rights owners need to adopt a bespoke approach when recruiting sponsors and therefore should be researching and then fulfilling sponsors requirements (as opposed to selling their own pre-determined packages) they can prepare for that process by producing an inventory of the rights they might have available. It is important to acquire knowledge about appropriate sponsors communications needs in order to identify and then offer them sponsorship solutions. At the same time, rights holders can also identify all the assets they have, or could have, for the required tailored sponsorship packages. An audit is required in order to achieve a thorough inventory.

An audit for many rights holders will begin with identification of advertising, corporate hospitality, joint promotions, sales and media opportunities. This might appear to be a straightforward task. However, in order to maximize sponsorship recruitment a more lateral approach is required. The process needs to also identify opportunities that perhaps are not available as yet but could be and how combinations of rights could be bundled more creatively. A car park one mile away from an event venue for example might be available for corporate hospitality, there may be spare time slots in a festival programme for additional spectator entertainment and a different view of how a music tour's programme is made up might reveal that it can have regional sponsors. By firstly considering eight general categories of assets, the process can be undertaken with an open and creative mind (Masterman and Wood, 2006) (see Figure 4.9).

Physical

By considering the physical nature of an event, a venue and even a group of individuals, it may be possible to identify assets that are of sponsorship value to the right sponsor. Naming rights are an example of rights that are associated with the physical, in this case a venue, stadium or concert hall for example. Further segmentation might also identify that a single venue might also be divided in to areas that may be assets, each hall, concourse or room for example. Even further segmentation might reveal advertising sites on walls, from ceilings and by projection rather than by fixed hoarding. An event may feature several 'fields of play' in action at any one time which may be identified as assets, such as adjacent football pitches, different music stages and exhibition zones.

Individuals and groups of rights owners can also have physical assets. The shoes and clothing Tiger Woods wears, the car he drives and the tools with which he does his job are all physical assets that have been identified as expensive sponsorship rights. At perhaps the opposite extreme a local sports club can secure

Sponsorship asset audits

A sponsorship asset audit consists of an internal evaluation by the rights owner of all possible assets in order to create an 'inventory' of possible sponsorship rights that can be combined to provide sponsors with tailored marketing solutions. The generic audit areas may be categorized as follows:

Physical

The division of rights into physical and geographical assets such as sites, zones, locations, venues, levels, indoor or outdoor.

Territory

The division of rights into local, regional, national catchment and geographical assets. This can include by round-of-competition.

Time

The division of rights into time frames, including by session, day or again by round-of-competition.

Programme

The division of rights into various running order components. This might include pre-event, mid-event and post-event ceremonies, entertainments and other associated and ancillary events.

Communications

Rights holders' direct communications that can also incorporate sponsors messages. Such as advertising, public relations and promotional activity via print, broadcast and Internet points of contact.

Status

The placement of one or more sponsors into a sponsorship programme structure that accords that sponsor acknowledgeable status and sector exclusivity. Such as via title, presenter, naming or official supplier rights.

Supply

The identification of supplier or services costs that can be reduced or replaced by getting sponsors to pay for or provide those supplies or services, or by getting the suppliers themselves to become sponsors and supply at no or reduced costs, thereby exercising supplier rights to the providers. Such as kit, transport, equipment, accommodation and food product. This might include the provision of media activity via the recruitment of media sponsors/partners.

Function

In addition to auditing by supply, rights owners need to identify existing assets or create new ones that are tailored for sponsors whereby any one sponsor can provide a function for or to the rights holder and in so doing showcase their products and/or services. Such as runner water stations in a fun run, air transportation for an opera company or satellite navigation for boats in a yacht race.

Figure 4.9 Sponsorship Asset Audit (adapted from Masterman, 2004)

sponsorship from a firm that might use the clubs shirts for advertising. Auditing for physical assets has indeed moved on from a time when snooker and equestrian sports people were not allowed by their respective governing bodies to bear such advertising.

Territory

Geographical territory may also be used as criteria for the audit. A sophisticated event may involve several locations for example. If it is an orchestral music tour, there are potential assets in each of the locations concerned, as local or regional sponsors may be attracted if each leg of the tour can be targeted to local or regional audiences. The Rolling Stones 'A bigger bang' 2005/2006 rock music tour was a worldwide project incorporating 35 North American dates and venues followed by tours of Mexico, South America, the Far East, Australasia and finally Europe. In the UK it was sponsored by American Express ('American Express presents The Rolling Stones – A bigger bang'). In the USA, however, it was identified that there were separate geographical assets and consequently similar rights were sold to Ameriquest.

If it is a singing competition such as an Eisteddfod or even an 'X Factor' television derived pop star search, the event may start at a local level and produce winners for the next level of regional competition, which may in turn produce winners for a national final. Each round of competition may also involve several locations and each is therefore an asset for the inventory.

Timing

In addition to the locations being assets in the example above, the rounds of competition are also possible assets. At this stage of the process you put both down as assets. Later, and after potential sponsors needs have been identified, these may or may not be realized as sponsorship rights.

It is possible that the timing involved lasts a numbers of years. The FIFA World Cup qualifying period lasts 2 years and is then followed by the finals. Therefore, it is possible that the period involved, rather than the round, be an asset. The IOC sells its TOP programme in Olympiad 4-year cycles and is therefore renegotiating with different sponsors such as Coca-Cola, McDonald's and Panasonic at different times.

It is also possible for an individual rights owner, if they have not signed over their rights to an event, to at least consider themselves as an asset for the period of one event at a time. Whilst this would not be a feasible asset for the likes of the commercially valuable Roger Federer whose agents can maximize his sponsorship worth more highly in contracts over longer periods of time, an up-and-coming performer from sport, the arts or music, might be of value for a short period of time, for example one event. The fit has to be right of course and a player who has unexpectedly qualified for the latter stages of golf's British Open may well be of value to a sponsor if advertising assets are available on the player. This is eased by the fact that logo patches can be stitched on to clothing very quickly. The asset may not be extendable over a longer period of time if the player does not consistently perform at this level.

Programme

The programme of an event may also be divided into attractive assets. 'The entertainment at half time is sponsored by', or the 'pre-banquet cocktail reception for VIPs is supplied by' are two ways to maximize sponsorship rights. SBC Southwestern Bell, as the telecommunications sponsor at the 2002 Alamo Bowl, agreed rights that saw it as the 'presenter' of several key ancillary occasions, the Alamo Pigskin Preview, the Alamo Bowl Golf Classic and the Alamo Bowl Fan Zone. At the same event, Corporate Express presented the 'Pre-Game Party' (Masterman, 2004).

Conferences, exhibitions and similar events can use this approach to divide assets into entertainment, ceremonies and seminars. The Pepsi Extravaganza in London provided its audiences with the adidas lazer battle arena, the Boots (the chemists) model competition and fashion walk and the Panasonic music zone all under one roof.

Communications

The rights owner's own communications can also be assets in that they may incorporate sponsors messages. Any advertising, public relations or promotional activity might bear a sponsors message of one form or another. It may be that one type of communication is associated with one sponsor or only one-off activities are of value. Alternatively it may be that this becomes a generic right for all sponsors. Therefore any advertising by the rights owner will bear all their sponsors' logos. This has been common practice for many events and in many cases this has resulted in a lack of integration in the messages put out. Event advertising bearing sponsor logos in 'flashes' have little synergy and are unlikely to be of as much value. A cluttering of logos is not necessarily going to meet a sponsors requirements and rights owners should not now make so much of such rights when they offer them.

The 2006 Great Yorkshire Show distributed its promotional leaflets via a number of methods including regional and local newspaper insertions. The leaflet was sponsored by the HACS Construction Group and carried a simple acknowledgement of that on the front and rear pages. HACS did not receive any other form of rights at the show but this was more than a simple advertising package as the costs of producing the leaflet were wholly met. The show organizers were successful in recruiting a number of organizations to supply or meet the costs of other event communications efforts, including estate agents Carter Jones as sponsors of the show catalogue.

Status

The sponsorship programme structure is an important collective asset. By designing a programme that evokes solus, hierarchy or parity in status, the programme itself can become a valuable vehicle. Acknowledgement of the status that is afforded to each sponsor in a solus, tiered or flat structure then becomes a valuable right. In theory a rights owner should remain flexible until they can identify the best way to maximize revenue and sustain a sponsorship programme, therefore all three types of structure are feasible at the start of the sponsorship recruitment process.

What materializes is a balancing of the opportunities in relation to the sponsors that can be attracted. On the one hand an exclusively occupied platform may be an attractive proposition for one particular sponsor, but will that sponsor be willing to offer/pay enough to the rights owner to exclude other sponsors? On the other hand will several sponsors be willing to share the programme and at what price? Offering equal status in a flat structure allows a limited number of sponsors a shared platform whilst a tiered hierarchy provides different levels of status and levels of payment for perhaps a greater number of sponsors.

Supply

By reviewing budget costs a rights owner can identify assets. Supplier and service costs can be reduced or replaced by getting the suppliers concerned in as sponsors and then supply at reduced or no cost. Alternatively other sponsors can be contacted and hopefully persuaded to pay for or provide those supplies. Whilst this does not improve income it can improve the bottom line. Kit, transport, equipment, accommodation, food and drink can all potentially be provided in exchange for rights. For those rights owners with greater bargaining power a sponsorship-in-kind arrangement may be converted into one that also has sponsorship fees attached to consequently allow the sponsor to provide a function within the sponsorship programme.

The importance of function

Auditing begins with as much lateral creativity as possible and by starting with the process that is detailed above, a comprehensive inventory can be identified. In other words it is prudent at this stage to exhaust all the possibilities even though some may be less feasible in the long run. This inventory is not yet a sponsorship programme or a set of sponsorship packages to sell and indeed it would be very unlikely for every single asset in the inventory to be offered as rights. The dangers of over-commodification are clearly an important test. What the inventory does provide though is a flexible set of assets that may be used to create sponsorship solutions once a potential sponsor's requirements have been identified.

The potential sponsor's requirements may of course not be so easily met and in order for a sponsor to finally agree to sponsor, the rights owner may well have to create fresh and new assets that provide a better fit. This is where function can provide the key to ensuring that a sponsorship is bespoke. Whilst any of the event assets may be bundled together to form a tailored set of sponsorship rights, it is the inclusion of rights that are intrinsically functional to the sponsor that will make a sponsorship unique (Masterman and Wood, 2006). For the closest of fits, the sponsor, its image or its brand need to be incorporated into a sponsorship, and the way to achieve this is to ensure that the sponsor and/or its brands, products and services provide a function. It is not always possible for this to be a basic function but the sponsorship should be a shop window for a sponsor's products or services. This is the window that is seen by mutual target markets and so as communications objectives are addressed, the sponsorship relationship can also grow.

Some functions are easier to identify than others, for example 'flowers presented by', 'the musical instruments were supplied by' and insurance was in association with'. Other functions may prove more difficult to identify and when put into practice may appear somewhat convoluted. Indeed the greater the creativity in the function the greater the need for careful attention in ensuring this function is perceived to be a good fit in order to dispel any perceptions of convolution.

As convoluted as it may appear, Lanson Champagne provides a function at the Wimbledon Tennis Championships. The 'official champagne' is served throughout the event to corporate guests and is also available for purchase in event bars to compliment the strawberries and cream. Mumm have previously supplied the winners podium bottles for the famous champagne spraying of spectators in F1 motor racing. The spraying alone is an important function within motor racing in general.

Wembley National Stadium Ltd (WNSL) secured a number of 'founding partners' during its construction of the new stadium. Amongst them are two examples of function. Microsoft signed a 5-year deal in October 2005 prior to the new stadium being completed, to provide technology support both during and after construction. NPower, the energy supplier, were signed to provide free lighting, including the arch that runs over the top of the stadium to provide floodlighting for matches and other events. In a bid to promote the relationship even before the rest of the construction was complete, the arch was lit on the day England's cricket team won the ashes in September 2005 (Goodbody, 2006).

Technology is currently a key area for the development of innovative and effective sponsor function. Ship-to-shore technology in yacht racing is proving to be a creative showcase for a number of sponsors. SAP, one of the world's largest software manufacturers, were the sponsors and suppliers of wireless function for a New Zealand entry in the Americas Cup and in return had their logo on the boat sails. This was potentially a life-saving function and SAP were able to showcase their technology in extreme performance via the event's media exposure as well as via their own exploitation of their association. The mobile/cell phone boom is also an avenue for showcasing products. FIFA recruited Swisscom in 2006 to broadcast all 64 matches of the 2006 World Cup live to mobile handsets (Gibson, 2006b).

Samsung and Swatch enjoyed functional showcases at the 2004 Olympic Games in Athens where they were the provider of 'Wireless Olympic Works' (WOW) and 'official timing', respectively. Samsung supplied much needed information services via the handheld devices they gave to event officials, staff and media (*Sunday Times*, 2004), something it had also done at the winter Olympics in Salt Lake City 2 years earlier. In providing mobile phones with free 3-minute calls for the public and athletes it estimated that it supplied 13,500 minutes of talk time in the 2 weeks of the event (Event, 2002). This function helped improve communication systems and provide a vital information service for those Olympics. Swatch provided timing for the sports competitions, but also a new 'On Venue Results' (OVR) service. This function was deemed to be fundamental following an audit of the previous games where accurate measurement and scores information services were provided by a number of sponsors and suppliers. Swatch was able to be a more effective and efficient supplier whilst introducing and demonstrating that its new technology could enable immediate competition results information at 35 different venues simultaneously (*Sunday Times*, 2004).

A more unusual example of function was provided by Motorola at Super Bowl XXXIX in Jacksonville, Florida, 2005. Instead of choosing to buy expensive national advertising on Fox Television (average cost of $2.4 million for a 30-second slot during the game with an estimated audience of 90 million viewers), Motorola decided it would get a more effective return by creating something that would get their products into its customers' hands. The function they provided to the event was an obstacle course for pairs of fans to engage with in the NFL Experience Pavilion. One fan would be blindfolded whilst the other guided him/her around the course via the use of new Motorola mobile phones or wireless headsets. At the same event Campbell's, the soup brand, built a 30-foot inflatable soup can and gave out 100,000 samples of their new 'hot and chunky' soup and chilli to fans whilst watching their 'Armchair Quarterback' game (Vranica, 2005). In both cases the event owners, the NFL, enhanced the fan experience whilst enabling their sponsors to provide credible functions that in turn enhanced their respective messages to the same fans.

Another unusual example of the application of function was the sponsorship of one of Alton Towers theme park's rides by the soap brand Imperial Leather. As part of a 3-year deal the park's log flume was renamed 'The Flume Unplugged by Imperial Leather'. The logs themselves were replaced with bathtubs and riders had to encounter water jets from giant shower heads and large floating branded ducks. The park used the ride as a focus for its television campaign and the sponsor produced on-pack promotions for 50,000 visitor tickets and 10 million discount offers. A website was used to promote themed competitions with prizes that included overnight stays at an Imperial Leather-branded room at the Alton Towers Hotel complete with oversized bathtub and bath-shaped bed (IEG, 2004).

Importance of media timing

There is one final area of consideration in the auditing of assets and the subsequent structuring of sponsorship programmes. The potential assets of communications as described above are clearly an important means of targeting audiences and therefore sponsors will assess the value of any rights that allude to achieving such exposure. However, if all that is on offer at the time of proposal is a list of where exposure might 'potentially be', as opposed to specific media mechanisms and schedules, there is clearly no basis for the sponsor to undertake that valuation. Thus they have no way of determining if there can be a return on investment. Media points of exposure therefore need to be already secured and guaranteed at the point of proposal.

Proposals that state that an event will be (and not 'are') undertaking a communications campaign but fail to provide details of media schedules and target reach are therefore not providing any base from which to assess whether the sponsorship proposal will meet a sponsors communications needs. Equally, a proposal that indicates that 'television schedules have not yet been determined', 'radio and Internet broadcasts are currently being negotiated', is also not providing a potential sponsor with the information it requires. The solution is to identify only agreed and guaranteed media-associated assets in the inventory. Of course they can come in later and of course sponsorship sales processes overlap with those for media, but in this case it is critical that any sponsorship proposals offer firm media rights and not just opportunities that are to be determined at a later point in time. There is one proviso to this. It may be that a sponsor is satisfied with the base agreement and any future media opportunities will be gratefully received, but unless they are to be separately paid for, the rights owner has been guilty of not previously maximizing its sponsorship rights. The key is to adopt an approach that determines all media assets that are to be offered as rights before the offer is made.

Summary

Whilst it is common practice for rights owners to approach potential sponsors with prescribed packages already in mind, this mindset is already starting to show that this will lead to demise in both the quality and the quantity of sponsorship use. For a return on investment, sponsors will be increasingly measuring against their objectives. It is therefore imperative that rights owners begin their recruitment process by being fully prepared to identify what a sponsor requires in order to tailor packages that meet communications objectives.

The tailored approach also requires the rights owner to prepare by considering what rights it can eventually offer any one sponsor. An audit of its assets and the compilation of an inventory will provide a base from which to eventually tailor packages. Further exploration of any one sponsor's needs, should then lead to an all important set of rights that allow it to provide a function in the sponsorship. The complex nature of the overall job of recruitment has to also simultaneously consider the best programme structure for numbers of sponsors to fit into, whilst ensuring that rights have been maximized. Will one sponsor, or several sponsors, provide a successful sponsorship programme? Will a tiered hierarchy of sponsors or a flat structure ensure that a rights owner maximizes its opportunities? These questions are discussed further in Chapter 7.

Tasks and discussion points

- Select a sponsorship programme and conduct an asset audit.
- Select a tiered sponsorship and critically analyse the programme by firstly identifying the levels of sponsorship status and types of sponsorship rights, and secondly by commenting on why this combination works or not.
- Select a flat sponsorship and critically analyse the programme by identifying the sponsors and the rights involved and secondly commenting on why this is successful or not.
- Identify and explain ways in which both these programmes might be developed for the future.
- Select a sponsorship that innovatively and successfully demonstrates why sponsorship function is important for return on investment.

References

Alamobowl (2006). www.alamobowl.com/sponsorship/current_sponsors (accessed 10 February 2006).

Duncan, A. (2006). www.advertising.about.com/od/beckhamdavid (accessed 21 February 2006).

Event (2002). In brief: Samsung provided the wireless, March 2002.

Gibson, O. (2006a). FA Cup/E.ON sponsorship deal. *The Guardian*, 9 February 2006.

Gibson, O. (2006b). How did that happen? *The Guardian*, 16 February 2006.

Goodbody, J. (2006). Rush for hot seats. *The Times*, 6 January 2006.

HCHSA (2000). Reliant names new Harris County Stadium and complex. www.hchsa.org/reliant/reliant_named (accessed 10 February 2006).

IEG (2004). IEG sponsorship report. *IEG*, June 28, 2004. Vol. 23, No. 12.

IOC (2006). www.olympic.org/uk/organisation/facts/programme/index (accessed 23 February 2006).

Jurrien, I. (2006). Kodak imaging sponsor at Olympic Winter Games, 9 February 2006. www.letsgodigital.org/en/news/articles/story (accessed 23 February 2006).

Kelso (2006). England shirt is a nice fit for Umbro. *The Guardian*, 16 December 2005.

Kodak (2006). www.kodak.com (accessed 23 February 2006).

Masterman, G. (2004). *Strategic sports event management: An international approach*. Oxford: Butterworth-Heinemann.

Masterman, G. and Wood, E. H. (2006). *Innovative marketing communications: Strategies for the events industry*. Oxford: Elsevier/Butterworth-Heinemann.

McCarthy, L. and Irwin, R. (1997). Names in lights: Corporate purchase of sport facility naming rights. *The Cyber-Journal of Sport Marketing*, www.cjsm.com/Vol2/mccarthyirwin23 (accessed 4 April 2002).

Mintel (2000). *Sponsorship Report*. UK: Mintel.

Mintel (2002). *Sponsorship Report*. UK: Mintel.

NLL (2004). www.nll.com/sponsorship (accessed 27 September 2004).

Sunday Times (2004). Section: Engineering in sport, 4 July 2004.

The F.A. (2006). www.thefa.com/TheFA/FASuppliers (accessed 10 February 2006).

The Times (2003). News, 22 July.

Toronto Pride (2004). www.pridetoronto.com/sponsors (accessed 26 April 2004).

Toronto Pride (2005). www.pridetoronto.com/sponsors (accessed 10 February 2006).

Vranica, S. (2005). Super Bowl XXXIX: Obstacle courses vs. 'Potty Palooza.' *The Wall Street Journal*, 24 January.

5

Endorsement

The objectives for this chapter are to:

■ Define endorsement and its use in sponsorship
■ Critically examine the value of endorsement as a marketing communications tool
■ Analyse why endorsements can fail and the
extent of the risk that can be involved
■ Identify a process for the successful implementation of endorsement

American Express and Andre Agassi

American Express posters at the nearest subway station to the US Tennis Open, Flushing Meadow in 2004, featuring Andre Agassi and Andy Roddick and the company's endorsement-based sponsorship programme used to exploit its involvement in the Open

Introduction

The importance of brand endorsement and its role in the evolvement of sponsorship is reviewed in some depth in Chapter 1. This chapter adopts a different focus by discussing the contemporary use of endorsement in general and also as a set of sponsorship rights as used by sponsors. This consists of a review of what endorsement is in the sponsorship context and focuses on how it is, and how it should be, implemented in the industry.

What is endorsement?

To endorse, or indorse, is to give or declare public approval or sanction (Oxford, 2006). So how is endorsement viewed in the sponsorship context? Having established, in Chapter 2, that sponsorship is a mutually beneficial arrangement, and that sponsorship fit is critical, it is reasonable to perceive that both sponsor and rights owner can endorse, and be endorsed. This requires further consideration.

Sponsorship was defined in Chapter 2 as consisting of communications that are for the 'achievement of objectives for commercial gain'. For endorsement to work as a communications tool then, the endorser needs to be recognizable within the targeted publics and markets. This is how and why celebrities have been so critical in the development of endorsement. A celebrity endorsement, such as that by a film actor or athlete, uses a publicly recognized star and that public recognition assists the other party (the endorsee) to gain commercially (Charbonneau and Garland, 2005). An unknown endorser cannot provide this to the same extent. For example, endorsement of adidas products by footballer David Beckham, Breitling watches by actor John Travolta, T-Mobile communications by rock singer Robbie Williams and OneTouch Diabetes meters by jazz musician B. B. King.

These are examples of high-profile brands and high-profile celebrities, but world renown is not always necessary. Depending on the nature of the targeted public/market, endorsement can be used in focused communication programmes. John Tisch, owner and chief executive of Loews Hotels, for example, continues to use his own family name, rather than his brand's, to endorse the Tisch Center for Hospitality, Tourism and Sports Management, an academic school at New York University. In analysis, Jonathan Tisch, and his father Preston Robert before him, is approving the Center's work. Whilst this is not so easily a defined endorsement arrangement it is nevertheless a successful one. Jonathan Tisch, is an important businessman in New York with significant international recognition in the hotel (hospitality) industry, an important voice for New York City tourism and is treasurer for the New York Giants football club.

Recognition might also derive out of credibility. Emphasizing the point that communications need to be targeted, a relatively unknown medical practitioner might be an appropriate endorser of a product. Dr Colin Crosby, MA FFSEM MB BS LRCP MRCS, for example, endorses Yoga-ez fitness 'minimal bounce' bras for women. The endorsement is simply a website placed letter that states that the brand is the 'best in the market' and that the doctor's credentials are that he is Director of Sports Medicine at the Garden Hospital, London, and that he has a range of personally gained qualifications (Yoga-ez, 2006).

It is not just individuals that can be successful endorsers; organizations, institutions and groups can all provide endorsement for brands. On the same Yoga-ez website, the brand is endorsed by the Women's Sport Federation, the International Rugby Board, the International Women's Boxing Federation and the British Board of Boxing Council. A further example is the British Olympic Association and the endorsement it gives to its Team GB sponsors, B&Q, Blue Arrow, Microsoft, Easynet and Michelob Ultra and their brands.

It is also possible for an organization to endorse a brand, where the 'brand' might be another organization. For example, in 2 years of activity prior to the opening its Architecture Gallery in 2004, the Victoria and Albert Museum (V&A) developed promotions with the Royal Institute of British Architects (RIBA, 2002). Another example, in Case Study 5.1, shows how the Royal Warrant is an

Case Study 5.1 Endorsement: The Royal Warrant

The Royal Warrant is a formal recognition for tradesmen who supply goods and services to Britain's Royal Household. The process for getting the right to use the royal crest on packaging and wrapping takes a minimum of 5 years – the right is given free of charge on application.

There are 800 British companies that are warrant holders.

For those that have the Royal Warrant, there is a seal of approval that is an institution endorsement. It is arguably a mark of excellence. There are four crests that can be acquired, awarded by the Queen, the Duke of Edinburgh, the Prince of Wales and the late Queen Mother and they represent endorsement not just by an individual but also the British Royal Household as a whole.

A warrant is an implicit endorsement in that the application of a crest to a piece of packaging implies that the said member of the household uses the product. The Royal Household forbids advertising and promotion and so there is no mutual endorsement for commercial gain, but it is clear that there is a great deal of kudos to be exploited by those that are awarded the warrant.

There is a view that the warrant can be both a positive and negative endorsement, thus highlighting the importance of target audience perception. Celebrities gain their attributes through achievement and behaviour. A member of the Royal Household has attributes mainly through position and behaviour and for some consumers this may not be as credible a source for endorsement. Consumers also seek brands that can match their aspirations and may also therefore identify more closely with celebrities than they might with a Queen or a Prince.

The prestige of the Warrant does though come at no cost and as such is not a 'bought' endorsement and unique in that fact.

The warrant holders vary considerably, here are three examples:

1. Gibson Saddlers are suppliers of racing colours (Queen)
2. Yardley and Co are suppliers of soaps (Queen, Queen Mother and Prince of Wales)
3. Wolseley (Build and Plumb Centres) are suppliers of plumbing (Queen)

Source: King (2006)

unusual and effective endorsement, by the institution of the Royal Family, of various organizations.

In sponsorship, it is possible for both sponsor and rights owner to be both endorser and endorsee. Each party can gain from the recognition the other has with their targeted publics/markets. For example, the V&A and its Architecture Gallery are being endorsed by RIBA, and RIBA and its 'Architecture for All' campaign that year, also gained a valuable endorsement from the V&A. Ralph Lauren is a recently added sponsor to the Wimbledon Tennis Championships sponsorship programme and it is clear that the sponsor wants to use the endorsement of the All England Lawn Tennis Club's (AELTC) eminent tournament in its future communications strategy. Its initial advertising describes itself as the 'official outfitter of Wimbledon'. Whilst the AELTC has sufficient negotiating power to be able to select from a number of would be sponsors much of the time, it still has the luxury of being able to benefit from its sponsors endorsement too. The sponsorship of Leeds United by Nike, when the team was in the English Premiership in 2002, was described by the club at the time as an upgrading of its sponsorship programme thus indicating that they regarded the deal as a mutually beneficial endorsement arrangement. There is clear value in using endorsement in sponsorship programmes and even more benefit to be gained if the fit is sufficiently exploitable for mutual endorsement.

Puma, the sportswear manufacturer, provides another example of mutually beneficial endorsement. Its strategy has been to extend into fashion markets and produce shoes that are for fashionable leisure wear and in so doing has formed alliances with significant designers such as Philippe Starck and Jil Sander, as well as super model Christy Turlington. The designers have also benefited from a reverse endorsement.

Based on the work of other commentators, a definition of endorsement in this context is that it is 'the use of fame or renown to help enhance and/or sell a product or image' (Charbonneau and Garland, 2005; Daneshvary and Schwer, 2000; Kamins, 1989; McCracken, 1989).

The role of endorsement

Having established what endorsement is, it is important to analyse how it is used, for example there are four modes of endorsement to consider.

Endorsement by 'association'

By placing a celebrity into an advertisement, or other setting, and alongside a product, the connection between the two can be described as being 'by association' in that one endorses the other because they are seen to be together. This might also be described as 'co-presentation', especially if a mutually beneficial endorsement is sought. An example is provided by computer manufacturer Lenovo and a number of newspaper advertisements the company ran in the UK during the 2006 FIFA World Cup. The advertisements carried its endorsement of Microsoft software with a simple statement, 'Lenovo recommends Windows XP Professional', and of Intel by carrying a pictorial Intel Centrino logo, in a not uncommon approach within that industry. In addition, the advertisements also carried pictures of World Cup footballers. One version used the tag line, 'I need mobility, I need speed, I need to connect, so do you'. This was not in quotation marks and nor did it carry the signature of Ronaldinho. However, it did carry the Brazilian and FC Barcelona star's picture, in his club kit, holding only a football. The only other picture of a Lenovo laptop was on the other side of the quarter page advertisement (*The Guardian*, 2006). In analysis, Ronaldinho's endorsement of Lenovo was by association via a simple placing of the two together on the page.

'Implicit' endorsement

If an endorser is in a setting and is using the product, or is interactive with the endorsee in someway, then the endorsement is more than 'by association'. The use is an implicit indication that the endorser is endorsing the endorsee. Ralph Lauren's use of its right to acknowledge itself as the 'official outfitter of Wimbledon' and a picture of a fashion model wearing a shirt emblazoned with a new logo ('The Championships – Wimbledon – Polo Ralph Lauren') shows that the manufacturer is implicitly endorsed by the Wimbledon Championships. A more humorous example in 2004 is provided by Apple computers and a television advertisement where it showed its 17- and 12-inch laptops from its Aluminium Powerbook range, in use by NBA basketball player Yao Ming and the actor that played 'Minime' in the film 'Austin Powers 2', Verne Troyer. There were no words used, just a play on the fact that Ming is 7 feet 2 inches and considerably taller than Troyer at 2 feet 8 inches.

John Travolta's endorsement of Breitling watches, utilizes printed advertisements and pictures of the film star wearing one of the manufacturer's watches and dressed ready for piloting an aeroplane. There is synergy in the use of a celebrity that is known for his keenness for flying and Breitling's aviation focus for its brand positioning. This is an implicit endorsement as it uses pictures of the usage of the product (a watch on the wrist). A less common approach was used by car manufacturer, Ford, in the late 1990s. The image of the late Steve McQueen was superimposed into scenes using the car manufacturer's new Puma model. McQueen's celebrity clearly lived on sufficiently well enough for this advertisement to win an award and for Ford to claim that not only had the car sold out, but second-hand models had also sold at a premium above the original price (Erdogan and Baker, 1999).

'Explicit' endorsement

More explicit is a verbal or written acknowledgement by an endorser of the endorsee. Using celebrities to verbally acknowledge, as opposed to just stand alongside, wear, or use a product, can cost more in fees. In practice they are doing more work via explicit endorsement that involves making a statement and enhancing the endorsement. Early examples of this were Faberge's Brut aftershave television advertisements featuring boxer Henry Cooper, and footballer Paul Gascoigne, where they put the Brut on themselves whilst verbally saying that they often 'splash it all over'. More recently, former heavyweight boxing World

Champion, George Foreman has been used as a 'spokesman' for manufacturer Meineke and McDonald's and its product, the 'Lean Mean Fat Reducing Grilling Machine'. The company claims that this explicit form of verbal endorsement helped achieve sales of over US $375 million in 2002 alone (Brandchannel, 2006).

'Imperative' endorsement

It is one thing for an endorser to say that they use a product themselves, but it is an enhanced message if they recommend that someone else should use it. Imperative endorsement will usually involve an endorser using and then recommending the endorsee. An example is the 'because you're worth it' campaigns by L'Oreal and their use of endorsements by actresses Andie MacDowell and Scarlett Johansson.

Richard Branson has recognized the value of self-promotion and uses it often to good effect. His verbal recommendations whilst sitting in the cockpit of one of his own Virgin Atlantic aeroplanes in television advertisements are an attempt at using his endorsement. However, it is important to understand the difference, this self-promotion involves no third-party endorsement.

The value of endorsement

It would appear that consistent and evolved use of endorsement in marketing communications since the mid-1800s is testament to it being successful. But how valuable is it?

Many companies have claimed that endorsements have had a direct influence on product sales. In 1960 the American Dental Association was used by Proctor and Gamble to endorse its toothpaste brand, Crest, and sales rose sufficiently for it to become the best seller in the USA only 2 years later (Longman, 1997). In addition to the impressive sales of George Foreman's grill mentioned above, Nike too claims that endorsement works. As discussed in Chapter 1, the sports manufacturer signed golfer Tiger Woods in 1996 and by 2002 golf ball revenue alone grew by US $50 million to US $250 million. Nike's use of implicit, explicit and imperative endorsement has though been at significant costs. In 1996 the Woods fee was US $40 million but rose to US $125 million in 2000 (Vemuri and Madhav, 2004) In spending these amounts on fees, it might be reasonably assumed that Nike believes this to be good value and as such probably demonstrates that a much improved sales performance is considered to be at least partly due to the endorsement by Woods.

Endorsement is reported as having played a significant role in a number of impressive sales results. The use of The Simpsons cartoon characters to endorse Domino's Pizza helped produce £13 million in incremental revenue, but even more impressive is Sainsbury's reported £1.12 billion incremental revenue via the assistance of television chef, Jamie Oliver's endorsement. Compare that with competitor Tesco's £2.2 billion using the actresses Prunella Scales and Jane Horrocks (Sylt and Reid, 2006).

A key factor is that campaigns that use the famous are strong in holding target public and market attention and as, perhaps, ever increasing media interest in celebrity might suggest, there are many people that want to see and learn more about the famous (Charbonneau and Garland, 2005; Dyson and Turco, 1998). Furthermore, the more familiar the endorser, the more likely consumers will buy the endorsed product (Gardner and Shuman, 1986; Kahle and Homer, 1985; Kamins, 1989; Miciak and Shanklin, 1994; Ohanian, 1991). There are a number of theories relating to the social influence network in the literature that attempt to explain the effectiveness of endorsement (Daneshvary and Schwer, 2000). These are explained below.

Identification process of social influence

This theory maintains that a person is more likely to be influenced by and adopt an attitude or behaviour of another person/group if the former can identify with the latter. This being the case, celebrities would be most effective in demonstrating the positive, or negative, assets of a product or service (Friedman and Friedman, 1979).

Internalization process of social influence

On the other hand the internalization process is when a person is influenced because of congruence with their value system. In this way consumers are more likely to purchase, in particular complex or expensive, products that are endorsed by expertise (Friedman and Friedman, 1979).

Credible source

The theory behind credibility, is that consumers are more likely to adopt behaviour that is endorsed by an association if they can identify with it and that furthermore, if the association is perceived as credible because of the expertise they have in using the endorsed product/service, then consumers are more likely to purchase it.

Ohanian (1990) produced a Source Credibility Scale that incorporates the themes from the literature. The scale can be used to identify how strong a potential endorser might be and therefore utilized by practitioners making the decision of whether to use a particular endorser or not. Ohanian (1990) maintained that attractiveness, trustworthiness and expertise were the key criteria by which to measure suitability and so created a scale that consisted of five points of attractiveness (unattractive or attractive, not classy or classy, ugly or beautiful, plain or elegant, not sexy or sexy), five points of trustworthiness (undependable or dependable, dishonest or honest, unreliable or reliable, insincere or sincere, untrustworthy or trustworthy) and five points of expertise (not an expert or an expert, inexperienced or experienced, un-knowledgeable or knowledgeable, unqualified or qualified, unskilled or skilled). The purpose then is for practitioners to assess where on the scale a potential endorser might be by canvassing appropriate target markets. The scale has been further tested on the general public by others and is thought to produce reliable data on the value of potential endorsers (Charbonneau and Garland, 2006).

The scale is clearly dependent on a subjective view of what each of these points actually means and then a subjective view of how the endorser fits each of the points. Additionally, it is also important to highlight that the key to any use of attractiveness as a criterion, or a scale that uses attractiveness, is that the assessment is dependent on what the endorsement is to achieve. A sexy image, for example, may be an important factor for one product but not for another. Tennis player Gabriella Sabatini was one of the first endorsers to be used in the famous 'white moustache' advertising campaigns in the USA for milk in what was clearly an attempt to create sex appeal. In contrast, the selection of non-human endorsers such as cartoon characters Bugs Bunny and Fred Flintstone to endorse USA breakfast cereals involved the targeting of audiences where the use of sex appeal was clearly not appropriate. Sexiness is not always a requirement and indeed the opposite might be preferable. The same goes for the other points of attraction. For example, the use of actress Joanna Lumley and the perception of her as elegant, in contrast with ex-footballer Ian Wright and the perception of him being more down to earth, was deemed important for Privilege Car Insurance in its 'You don't have to be posh' television advertising campaign in June 2006.

Research does indicate that customers are more likely to choose goods or services that are endorsed by celebrities than those that are not (Agrawai and Kamakura, 1995). Daneshvary and Schwer (2000) for example, found in their study, that the identification and internalization processes of social influence were likely to affect behaviour change and that would result in increased purchases from endorsements. They specifically researched the effect of endorsement of the Professional Rodeo Cowboys Association (PRCA) and found that frequency of attendance at rodeo events positively affects purchase intention. Their results demonstrated that those individuals that attend often are more inclined to be influenced by a PRCA endorsement than individuals who attend every other year. They concluded that endorsement is most effective when consumers have the opportunity to interact with the Association.

There are similar findings from research into the success of endorsement by NASCAR motorsport drivers in the USA. Performance Research (2000) found that 72 per cent of NASCAR fans would almost always or frequently choose the brand they associate with NASCAR over one that is not. Significantly they also found that as many as 46 per cent of fans would also pay up to 10 per cent more for a NASCAR-associated brand in making that choice and 43 per cent of NASCAR fans are influenced enough to switch from their normal brand of grocery store item to try a NASCAR-associated brand.

There has been a tendency to find that consumers believe in the purity of the motives of celebrity endorsers, however, endorsement is dynamic and not only dependent on the celebrity or renown of the endorser, but also on the social conditions surrounding the endorsement at any one time (Silvera and Austad, 2004). For example, celebrities that endorse several products are viewed as less credible (James and Ryan, 2001; Swerdlow and Swerdlow, 2003; Tripp et al., 1994), and celebrities that are associated with negative events can have a detrimental effect on the performance of products they endorse (Louie and Obermiller, 2002; Swerdlow and Swerdlow, 2003).

There are also examples of 'matches' that have become mismatched resulting in critical decisions for communications. This can be entirely accidental. For example, an injury to a sports endorser can limit the latter's exposure and performance and consequently affect the success of the endorsement (Irwin et al., 2002). A team player that becomes out of favour with the coach and as a consequence loses a place on the team can also lead to less exposure and a less successful endorsement. Oliver Kahn, the highly rated and successful German footballer was arguably perceived by many fans to be his country's number one goalkeeper. So high was this rating that adidas created an advertising campaign around him for the FIFA World Cup in Germany in 2006. One expensive and giant advertisement was mounted on a bridge so that it looked like Kahn was diving across the road to save a shot. Unfortunately, Jens Lehmann was preferred in goal for each of Germany's regular matches in the tournament (Kahn played in the third place play-off).

There are also those endorsements that can fail due to endorser misconduct. For example, there are some well-reported endorsements where the endorsers have had their contracts reviewed and/or cancelled as a result of activity that has been perceived as being damaging to the endorsee. For example, whilst PepsiCo continues to enjoy successful endorsements with David Beckham in particular it has also had its share of negative associations. In 1989, pop singer Madonna, an endorser for Pepsi, released her controversial video and song 'Like a Prayer'. Under pressure from church groups, the company discontinued its Madonna related advertising campaign (Swerdlow and Swerdlow, 2003). In 1993, Pepsi again had to deal with a negative association when its endorser pop singer Michael Jackson was charged with various sexual offences. The association between Jackson and Pepsi had begun nearly 10 years previously, in 1984, yet it was deemed appropriate to end it.

Sainsbury's appears to be content to continue to use Jamie Oliver especially considering the success in incremental revenue referred to above. This loyalty was tested however when his wife, Jules, who has appeared in Sainsbury's advertisements, was pictured in newspapers carrying a Waitrose shopping bag only 200 yards from a Sainsbury's store (Sylt and Reid, 2006).

Even with these examples of the highest of endorser profiles there is still a risk in endorsement and in particular in who is selected to do the endorsing. The image, reputation and credibility of an endorser are clearly important at the time of making the decision to contract them, but it is also important to note that the risk of these qualities being diminished is prevalent throughout the contract (Erdogan and Kitchen, 1998; Ohanian, 1990; Swerdlow and Swerdlow, 2003). Conditions can start well enough but can become critical.

Swerdlow and Swerdlow (2003) alert endorsees to consider cost versus benefit in selecting endorsers due to the high fees that can be involved. A risk is also taken regularly in sport by sponsors when they invest in bright but young talent. The fees can be high even for the associations with teenagers, yet the outcome becomes a gamble because the talent might not fully achieve the identified potential or may also be cut short by injury. Nike, for example, has invested US $90 million in Le Bron James, a 19-year-old basketball player in a 7-year deal. The same company spent US $1 million on sponsoring Adu, a 13-year-old footballer. The risk for Nike is in not knowing whether there will be a return on these investments.

Similarly, the bottled water brand Highland Spring has weighed up the costs and benefits of sponsoring Andrew Murray, the Scottish tennis player. Like all professional tennis players, Murray is contracted to be seen to drink the sponsored water at each tournament he plays in as event promoters are allowed to contract the sponsors of their choice. Highland Spring is therefore taking a risk but it is in the full knowledge that their endorser may be seen drinking a competitive brand. Their strategy is that the television exposure of the logo on Murray's sleeve and the press coverage their own exploitation will achieve, will outweigh any negativity. The brand has paid £1 million for Murray's endorsement (Lewis, 2006). Clearly an evaluation of their return on their investment is required in order to measure this.

Endorsements need not always involve high fees. In 2006, Jaguar Cars launched a new XK model and produced an endorsement strategy involving no fees. Unlike most car sponsorship deals, including that of Jaguar Cars and its association with footballer Michael Owen, the manufacturer arranged to loan out 10 XKs to some of 'Britain's beautiful people' (Gadher, 2006). The intent was to have their selected 'brand ambassadors', including designer Carlo Brandelli, DJ Vernon Kay and *GQ magazine* editor Dylan Jones, stimulate demand by being seen at the right time, in the right places, driving and parking Jaguar cars. These were finely segmented target audiences for these endorsement communications but with a car that was priced at £60,000, the endorsements were cost effective as the loan arrangements were only for 6 months. Associated and placed media exposure also included supporting statements by the endorsers in order to endorse the brand. For example, *GQ magazine* claimed to have reviewed the car 'as the best car Jaguar had ever made' but editor, Jones, claimed that this was done prior to the start of his endorsement arrangement and that the review was completed by another unbiased commentator. All in all this endorsement was imperative, explicit, implicit and by association for numerous audiences and very innovative on Jaguar Cars' part.

'Vampirism' is also a possible disadvantage of endorsement. This is becoming more common and is where the endorser is perceived to be bigger than the endorsee in endorsement communications (Swerdlow and Swerdlow, 2003). A classic example is when Cinzano, the alcohol drink producer, ran several television advertisements in the 1970s using actors Leonard Rossiter and Joan Collins to endorse their drink. The theme played the non-elegant Rossiter off against the sexy Collins in a series of advertisements that proved to be very popular and consequently ran for a long time. However, it was found that too few of the target audience could recall the product and indeed confused it with a competitor's brand.

Another endorsement pitfall is that whilst the use of an endorsee's products or services by an endorser is an implicit endorsement, misuse or even non-use can be an implicit way of demonstrating a lack of credibility. Unfortunately, this is not always that easy for endorsees to control. Catherine Zeta Jones was contracted to endorse Sainsbury's recipes on television and yet she was photographed shopping in a shop belonging to rival supermarket chain, Tesco. Similarly, Paul Gascoigne, referred to above as an endorser of Faberge's Brut aftershave, was alleged to have said, whilst under contract, that he would not use the product in his personal life. Avoiding such pitfalls might be addressed via tighter clauses in contracts and/or policing, but is still dependent on selection of the right endorser.

It is apparent, that, endorsement is seen as a positive additional value to a product or service in that it can transfer positive qualities such as physical attractiveness and likeability to a brand (Ohanian, 1990). McCracken (1989) developed a Meaning Transfer Model to help explain how an endorsement works in this way. The theory is that an endorser transfers values to an endorsee that enhances consumer perception of the latter. The model consists of a three-stage process that begins with public perception and the forming of an image of a particular celebrity. The celebrity image thus has a 'meaning' to consumers. The endorsement matches the celebrity with a brand in stage two and the 'meaning' transfers to the brand and in stage three the new 'meaning' for the brand transfers to the consumer. For example, Roberto Carlos, the Brazilian footballer, despite being a defender, has an image as a regular scorer of goals. Consequently, Nike, as part of its overall sponsorship of the Brazil national team, utilized Carlos in an advertising campaign for its football merchandise under the tag line, 'attack is the best form of defence'. Another example is Indian cricketer Rahul Dravid who has an image of being 'Mr Dependable'. His endorsement of Castrol attempts to create the perception that the oil brand also has dependability (Sarkar, 2006). If the model is applied in both these cases, it demonstrates the importance of selection of an endorser that has an appropriate image.

Erdogan and Kitchen (1998) agree that endorsement can help develop brand personalities and as a result can also contribute in order to achieve brand name recall. Dyson and Turco (1998) further suggest that this can be even more the case when the product or service is also seen to contribute towards the endorser's success. The sales success of several sports endorsements demonstrates this. The endorsement of Nike products by Michael Jordan and the development of the Nike Air brand in particular are attributed to the technological assistance the brand gave to the basketball star and his success on the court. The increased sales of Puma tennis rackets when endorser Boris Becker won his first Wimbledon and of adidas 'predator' football shoes endorsed by David Beckham are two further examples. The key is to make it known that the endorser has had technical input into the design of the product.

The literature generally appears to agree that there are three key advantages of endorsement:

1. *Audience attention capture*: Celebrities can cut through advertising clutter and hold viewer attention (Charbonneau and Garland, 2005). An easily recognizable figure or group can work well to draw attention and more so than unknowns or more generic communications (Dyson and Turco, 1998; Miciak and Shanklin, 1994; Swerdlow and Swerdlow, 2003).
2. *Increase product awareness*: Communicating brand messages will assist in the achievement of product awareness. However, associating a celebrity endorser will increase the likelihood of that product's recall still further (Erdogan and Kitchen, 1998; Friedman and Friedman, 1979; Swerdlow and Swerdlow, 2003).
3. *Influence product purchase decisions*: The expertise of the endorser has a direct effect on the consumer's decision to purchase (Ohanian, 1991). If the endorser is seen as credible or as an expert on the product, then that target market can be influenced by the infusion of the product with the success and appeal of the endorser (McCracken, 1989).

Endorsement works better when there is an inherent match or congruency between the endorser and endorsee, and when the communications are targeted appropriately (Charbonneau and Garland, 2005; Chung-kue and McDonald, 2002; Erdogan and Baker, 1999; McCracken, 1989; Miciak and Shanklin, 1994). There are however, examples of endorsement that appear to lack congruency. For example, Michael Jordan and WorldCom Communications, Bruce Willis and Seagrams, Whitney Houston and AT&T. Toyota's signing of young pop singer Britney Spears to endorse its 'family car' the Soluna Vios model also appears mismatched (Vemuri and Madhav, 2004). However, there are many examples of endorser/endorsee matches that are perceived to be better suited. For example, Michael Jordan and Nike, Elizabeth Taylor and White Diamonds perfume, and Cindy Crawford and Revlon are successful associations that are perceived to match well (Till and Busler, 1998).

Match-up hypothesis suggests that endorsers are more effective when there is a fit between the endorser and endorsee (Till and Busler, 1998). Much of the research on matching has previously been framed within the context of physical attractiveness, whereby attractive endorsers are maintained to be more effective when promoting products that are used to enhance one's attractiveness. However, there has been some research that has looked at the importance of other factors. For example, Till and Busler (1998) and Ohanian (1991) found that expertise is more important than physical attractiveness for matching a brand with an appropriate endorser. The former reinforce the point that careful selection is required in order to maximize the value of endorsement and as such there needs to be more criteria for doing so. They also suggest that the role of image as a match-up factor requires further research.

The implementation of endorsement

Many endorsements fail because the endorsers' characteristics and image are not researched and they are then used in contrived communications that are attempting to 'force the fit' (Vemuri and Madhav, 2004). The result is a harmed brand, possibly lost endorser credibility, and no return on investment. To avoid this, a company, once it has decided to use endorsement as a method of communication, needs to follow a selection process. A number of practitioners and researchers have looked at this and the result is a well-accepted group of criteria for the assessment of potential endorsers.

The Young and Rubicam advertising agency conducted a survey of 30,000 people and 6000 different brands to see why endorsement succeeds or fails (Swerdlow and Swerdlow, 2003). The results were developed into a set of guidelines for the selection of endorsers, summarized as FRED, an acronym which stands for familiarity, relevance, esteem and differentiation (Dyson and Turco, 1998; Vemuri and Madhav, 2004). Miciak and Shanklin (1994) took this model further and added another 'D' for decorum, thus renaming the guidelines FREDD. Whilst it is no guarantee of success, this tool is at least an approach that can identify effective matches when used alongside individual endorsee objectives.

Familiarity

This is the first essential component of an effective endorser (Dyson and Turco, 1998). There must be consumer awareness of the celebrity or organization. The perception also needs to be positive where the endorser is likeable, friendly and trustworthy and not offensive. It is important to note that this need not be world-wide or even national recognition. The recognition need only be by the intended target audience. Research is required in order to establish the nature and extent of familiarity.

Relevance

There should be a meaningful link between the endorser and the endorsee. This should be in the form of a consumer perceived matched fit (Swerdlow and Swerdlow, 2003). There also needs to be a fit between the target audience and the endorser as consumers will feel more comfortable accepting and purchasing the brand if they can associate with the endorser (Dyson and Turco, 1998). This too needs research in order to identify that target audiences have favourable perceptions so that endorsee decisions and assessments of potential endorsers are substantiated.

Esteem

The target audience needs to be able to respect the endorser and this needs to be enough to develop credibility in the association between the endorser and the endorsee. The respect can derive from the success in an endorser's life, possibly through winning, heroism, social standing and values. The confidence an audience has in the endorser is then transferred to the endorsee (Vemuri and Madhav, 2004).

Differentiation

An endorser also has to stand out from the crowd (Dyson and Turco, 1998; Vemuri and Madhav, 2004). Endorsement can cut through advertising clutter (Charbonneau and Garland, 2005) but it also has to cut through other endorsements and so the endorser must be distinct enough to catch the eye of the target audience. If there is no perceived distinctiveness then an endorsement strategy will not work.

Decorum

Miciak and Shanklin (1994) added this important element. There are an increasing number of failed endorsements and whilst it is not always possible to control an endorser once contracted, the research conducted prior to contracting needs to establish the nature of past behaviour and wherever possible assess the likelihood of misconduct. An assessment and prediction of external forces, whilst difficult, can also assist in the selection of an endorser that needs to be a sustainable asset (Swerdlow and Swerdlow, 2003).

Knowledge Networks completed research in the USA in 2004 for *Advertising Age* in order to determine the intangible sports endorser qualities that are perceived to be of value to target audiences (Tenser, 2004). The key findings below might also be used as specific criteria in the selection of endorsers:

- 66 per cent felt that it was very or extremely important that endorsers should not use drugs.
- 64 per cent felt that it was very or extremely important for an endorser to be a good role model.
- 62 per cent felt that the private actions of endorsers in their personal lives were just as important as accomplishments in their work (sport).
- 44 per cent felt that it was not at all important for the endorser to be stylish or attractive.

These findings are in agreement with some of the literature discussed earlier in this chapter, in that being attractive is not as important as it was once perceived to be. The key findings in this research are in the need for respectable and socially credible endorsers to be used.

FREDD and other selection criteria are useful tools that need to be slotted in to an endorsement selection process. The selection of endorsement as a communication tool can only be agreed once it has shown that it has the capacity to achieve an organization's wider marketing, communications and possible sponsorship objectives, but achieve them more effectively and efficiently than other forms of communications. Pitts and Stotlar (2002) consider the use of Martin's (1996) process that consists of firstly researching the image perception, then measuring image factors, selecting endorsers that most closely match the endorsee and then finally evaluating the capacity of the matches to enhance the endorsee. Whilst this process does provide for an assessment of potential endorsers it does not address the wider implications or ensure that endorsement is an effective and efficient communications solution. The following process is a more comprehensive approach.

Endorsement selection process

1. Evaluate the image and perception of the endorsee – how do target audiences perceive the endorsee product or service? A match cannot be identified without this prior knowledge.
2. Identify potential matching industry images. Which industries are perceived well by target audiences? For example, sport, music, arts.
3. Identify potential matching sector images. Which sectors are perceived well by target audiences? For example, tennis, football, surfing, pop, rock, classical music.
4. Identify potential matching specific images. Which images are perceived well by target audiences? This is where selection criteria such as those provided by FREDD can be utilized, so long as they are used in conjunction with the specific requirements of the endorser. For example, tennis players Agassi, Roddick or Federer? Tennis organizations, the ATP Tour, Wimbledon or International Tennis Federation.

5. Shortlist the appropriate matches, evaluate each one for their effectiveness and efficiency against other communications solutions in a costs versus benefits exercise, in order to then...
6. Select and contract the endorser.

Targeting is a key element in achieving successful endorsements. The endorser has to match with the target audience and this is clearly where individual organizational objectives are important. In identifying whether endorsement is an effective and efficient communications route to take, as part of the endorsement selection process, it is critical to firstly research the image and perception of the endorsee as perceived by target audiences. Age alone, for example, is an important consideration. ICM Research (2002), in a random sample, interviewed 1000 adults and found that whilst on average 32 per cent said that endorsement makes them feel more positive towards retailers, that rose to 59 per cent among those who were 18–24 years old and dropped to 9 per cent among those who were 65 years plus.

At any stage during this process, there may be an assessment that endorsement is not an appropriate communications selection. In particular, a suitable specific image might not be available or may cost too much to contract and this will then be a time to abort endorsement plans.

Whilst this is a selection process and is ostensibly over once selection has been made, post-selection and the endorsement lifecycle are obviously important periods for review and evaluation in order to realign to objectives via enhanced communications or discontinue the endorsement where necessary.

Finally, finding a formula for successful endorsements is not easy and multinational organizations like PepsiCo can get it wrong as reported earlier. However, there are a number of issues that are worthy of consideration by practitioners when contracting endorsers (Quinn, 2004).

Pre-existing obligations

Most sport stars have restrictions of some kind in their existing contracts with clubs, a national team or governing body. Music recording artists might have similar conditions via their promoters and record labels. Endorsees should therefore seek full disclosure of these before making endorsement selection decisions. Typical restrictions, for example, might be a cap on the number of endorsements an individual can undertake or a prohibition on the individual getting involved with competitors of a team sponsor.

Services to be performed

It is important to ensure that all of the services that the endorser is to perform are specifically contracted. For example, the number of days in the photo studio (shoot days) and arrangements in the event of cancellation.

Brand usage

Usage of the endorsee's products or services in question should not start and finish at the photo studio. It is important to ensure that contracts stipulate if there is to be usage (and non-usage of competitive brands), where and when it is required and for what period. For example, careful attention is required to get contracts to end when advertising campaigns have had sufficient time to conclude.

Careful attention is also required in stipulating which territories are in operation. The Internet now allows for global activity for many endorsees and so non-competition clauses may be required.

Sports stars that represent their country at international competitions are clearly attractive endorsement prospects but they may also have restrictions on what they can endorse whilst on international duty. They may be required to wear a competitor's clothing (via a national team sponsor) or use a competitor's equipment (via an international competition) and so before an endorser is contacted, these conditions need to be identified and considered carefully.

Disrepute

No endorsee should enter into an agreement expecting their endorser to harm the brand, accidentally or through misconduct. However, it happens, and in order that the damage can be limited it is advisable to ensure contracts allow as easy a discontinuation as possible. The endorser needs to try and retain the final decision on whether the brand has been harmed and be able to affect an exit from the relationship. This might apply equally to the endorser's general behaviour as it does adherence to any work or appearance requirements.

Summary

Endorsement is the use of fame or renown in targeted communications to help enhance and/or sell a product or image, and as such can utilize the famous and celebrity to good effect. The fame of organizations as well as individuals can be used for endorsement.

Research does show that celebrity endorsers have more effect than non-celebrities. However, this is not to say that the very famous and those that have the highest of profiles are the only effective endorsers. Successful endorsement depends on the target audience or market involved and if an endorser has sufficient renown with even a local audience, then an effective endorsement can be achieved.

Familiarity though, is not all that is important in the selection of endorsers. Research shows that an endorser must also be credible. Audiences look for a credible match between endorser and endorsee and as such an endorsement is susceptible to a number of factors that can reduce that credibility. There is a risk in the selection of an endorser if their credibility can be at threat after a contract has been executed. Credibility can be affected by non-performance, for whatever reason, and if the endorser brings the endorsee into disrepute in some way. Credibility can also be affected if an endorser has too many endorsements and the endorsee can also suffer if the endorser overshadows them (vampirism). The extent of these risks needs to be much reduced in order to effect successful endorsement.

Endorsement works by transferring positive values from the endorser to the endorsee and then on to the consumer. As such an endorser can transfer a 'personality' to the endorsee. Equally, if the endorsee and endorser, and the endorser and target audience/market, are a good match, then the endorsement can provide a return on investment as successful sales results for many endorsed products can testify. In sponsorship, an endorsement can also be a mutual benefit, whereby both rights owner and sponsor can endorse, and be endorsed by the other.

Endorsement can cut through communications clutter and capture audience attention. It can also increase awareness and as a consequence influence consumer product purchase decisions. However, for this to happen, the match between endorser and target audience, and endorser and endorsee, is critical, just as sponsorship fit is. This highlights the necessity for the use of effective endorser selection and contracting processes that can reduce the extent of risk. Assessing FREDD, aligned to specific objectives, and as part of a thorough approach to selection, followed by a comprehensive review of contractual limitations can provide a successful route to successful endorsement.

Tasks and discussion points

- Identify and analyse examples of the use of endorsers from sport, music and arts for each of the following modes of endorsement:
  - By association
  - Implicit
  - Explicit
  - Imperative
- Identify one endorsement that you consider to be mismatched and explain why.
- Using the endorsement selection process, including the FREDD tool, develop appropriate endorsement choices for the following brands:
  - Hummer cars
  - Prada Sport
  - Red Bull
- Identify one endorsement by each of the following and examine the risks the endorsees need to pay heed to for the future:
  - David Beckham
  - Kate Moss
  - Madonna
- Select one local business from the region where you live and prepare a short-list of endorsers for its key product or service and fully explain why the company can expect to achieve a return on its investment.

References

Agrawai, J. and Kamakura, W. (1995). The economic worth of celebrity endorsers: An event study analysis. *Journal of Marketing*, Vol. 59, No. 3, pp. 56–63.

Brandchannel (2006). Celebrity endorsements: Reach for the stars. www.brandchannel.com (accessed 2 June 2006).

Charbonneau, J. and Garland, R. (2005). The use of celebrity athletes as endorsers: Views of the New Zealand general public. *ANZMAC 2005 Conference: Sports, arts and heritage marketing.*

Charbonneau, J. and Garland, R. (2006). The use of celebrity athletes as endorsers: Views of the New Zealand general public. *International Journal & Sports Marketing & Sponsorship*, Vol. 7, No. 4, pp. 326–333.

Chung-kue, H. and McDonald, D. (2002). An examination on multiple celebrity endorsers in advertising. *Journal of Product and Brand Management*, Vol. 11, No. 1, pp. 19–29.

Daneshvary, R. and Schwer, R. K. (2000). The association endorsement and consumers' intention to purchase. *Journal of Consumer Marketing*, Vol. 17, No. 3, pp. 203–213.

Dyson, A. and Turco, D. (1998). The state of celebrity endorsement in sport. *Cyber Journal of Sport Marketing.* www.ausport.gov.au (accessed 23 May 2006).

Erdogan, B. and Kitchen, P. (1998). Getting the best out of celebrity endorsers. *Admap*, 17–20 April.

Erdogan, Z. and Baker, M. (1999). Celebrity endorsement: Advertising agency managers perspective. *Cyber-Journal of Sport Marketing.* www.ausport.gov.au (accessed 2 June 2006).

Friedman, H. and Friedman, L. (1979). Endorser effectiveness by product types. *Journal of Advertising Research*, Vol. 19, No. 5, pp. 63–71.

Gadher, D. (2006). Beautiful people push new car. *The Guardian*, 2 July.

Gardner, M. and Shuman, P. (1986). Sponsorship: An important component of the promotions mix. *Journal of Advertising*, Vol. 16, No. 1, pp. 11–17.

ICM Research (2002). Celebrity endorsement. www.cmmol.net/celebrity_endorsement (accessed 2 June 2006).

Irwin, R., Sutton, A. and McCarthy, L. (2002). *Sport promotion and sales management.* Champaign, IL: Human Kinetics.

James, K. and Ryan, M. (2001). Attitudes to female sports stars as endorsers. *Proceedings from the ANZMAC Conference*, Auckland, November.

Kahle, L. and Homer, P. (1985). Physical attractiveness of the celebrity endorser: A social adaptation perspective. *Journal of Consumer Research*, Vol. 11, pp. 954–961.

Kamins, M. (1989). Celebrity and non-celebrity advertising in a two-sided context. *Journal of Advertising Research*, Vol. 18, pp. 34–42.

King, E. (2006). Does royalty lead to brand loyalty? www.brandchannel.com (accessed 2 June 2006).

Lewis, P. (2006). Record-breaking deal that could turn And Murray into £80m man. *The Guardian*, 3 December.

Longman, P. (1997). Endorsements for sale. *US News and World Report*, Vol. 123, No. 8, pp. 11, in Daneshvary, R. and Schwer, R. K. (2000). The association endorsement and consumers' intention to purchase. *Journal of Consumer Marketing*, Vol. 17, No. 3, pp. 203–213.

Louie, T. and Obermiller, C. (2002). Consumer response to a firm's endorser association decisions. *Journal of Advertising*, Vol. 30, No. 4, pp. 41–52.

Martin, J. (1996). Is the athlete's sport important when picking an athlete to endorse a non-sport product? *Journal of Consumer Marketing*, Vol. 13, No. 6, pp. 28–43.

McCracken, G. (1989). Who is the celebrity endorser? Cultural foundations of the endorsement process. *Journal of Consumer Research*, Vol. 16, No. 3, pp. 310–321.

Miciak, A. and Shanklin, W. (1994). Choosing celebrity endorsers. *Marketing management*, Vol. 3, No. 3, pp. 51–59.

Ohanian, R. (1990). Construction and validation of a scale to measure celebrity endorsers' perceived expertise, trustworthiness, and attractiveness. *Journal of Advertising*, Vol. 19, No. 3, pp. 39–52.

Ohanian, R. (1991). The impact of celebrity spokespersons' perceived image on consumers' intention to purchase. *Journal of Advertising Research*, Vol. 31, pp. 46–54.

Oxford (2006). *Oxford English Dictionary*, 11th Edition. Oxford: Oxford University Press.

Performance Research (2000). Viagra and Lycos outperform first year sponsors to NASCAR. www.performanceresearch.com (accessed 10 September 2003).

Pitts, B. and Stotlar, D. (2002). *Fundamentals of sport marketing*, 2nd Edition. Morgantown, WV: Fitness Information Technology.

Quinn, L. (2004). Finding a formula for successful endorsements. *Sport Business International*, Issue 96, October.

RIBA (2002). HLF endorses RIBA/V&A Architecture for All initiative. www.riba.org/ go/RIBA/News/Press (accessed 9 June 2006).

Sarkar, S. (2006). Impact of celebrity endorsement on overall brand. www.mastermindss. blogspot.com (accessed 2 June 2006).

Silvera, D. and Austad, B. (2004). Factors predicting the effectiveness of celebrity endorsement advertisements. *European Journal of Marketing*, Vol. 38, No. 11/12, pp. 1509–1526.

Swerdlow, R. and Swerdlow, M. (2003). Celebrity endorsers: Spokesperson selection criteria and case examples of FREDD. *Academy of Marketing Studies Journal*, Vol. 7, No. 2, pp. 13–23.

Sylt, C. and Reid, C. (2006). Secrets of Beck's appeal. *Business Life – British Airways*, October.

Tenser, J. (2004). Endorser qualities count more than ever. *Advertising Age*, 8th November.

The Guardian (2006). Lenovo advertisement, 14 June.

Till, B. and Busler, M. (1998). Matching products with endorsers: Attractiveness versus expertise. *Journal of Consumer Marketing*, Vol. 15, No. 6, pp. 576–586.

Tripp, C., Jensen, T. and Carlson, L. (1994). The effects of multiple product endorsements by celebrities on consumers attitudes and intentions. *Journal of Consumer Research*, Vol. 20, No. 4, pp. 535–547.

Vemuri, K. and Madhav, T. (2004). *Celebrity endorsement through the ages*. Hyderabad, India: ICFAI Business School Case Development Centre, The European Case Clearing House.

Yoga-ez (2006). Report statement from Dr Colin Crosby. www.yoga-ez-fitness-wear.com/ Awards (accessed 9 June 2006).

6

The media and sponsorship

The objectives for this chapter are to:

- Identify and examine the nature of broadcast sponsorship
- Determine whether broadcast or other forms of media opportunity are sponsorship or simply forms of advertising
- Evaluate the role of product placement
- Evaluate the critical role media partners play in sponsorship

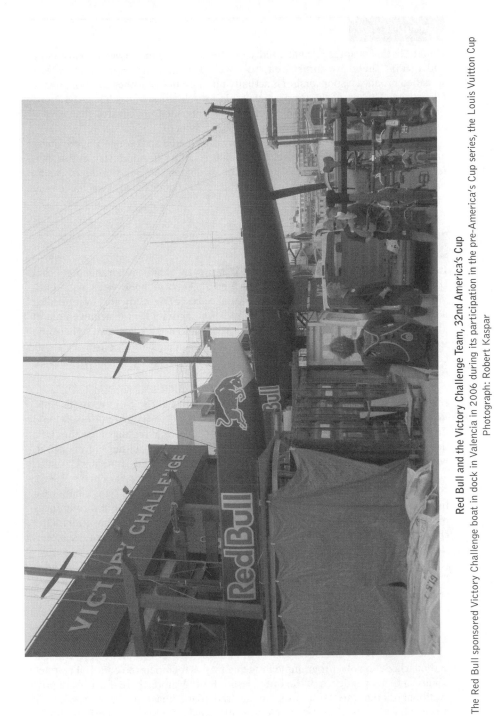

Red Bull and the Victory Challenge Team, 32nd America's Cup

The Red Bull sponsored Victory Challenge boat in dock in Valencia in 2006 during its participation in the pre-America's Cup series, the Louis Vuitton Cup

Photograph: Robert Kaspar

Introduction

Generally this chapter is concerned with the relationship between sponsorship and media. There are three areas to cover. The first task is to explain why so-called broadcast sponsorship is actually no more than another form of airtime advertising. The use of the term sponsorship for television and other programme bumpers is misleading and detrimental to a sponsorship industry that is cognizant of the fact that sponsorship is for mutual benefit.

The second task is to consider other forms of media sponsorship opportunity and the role of product placement, particularly in the film industry, and how it relates to sponsorship. Finally the chapter evaluates the importance of media partners and the role they play to successfully act as conduits for the achievement of sponsorship objectives.

Broadcast sponsorship

In Chapter 2, sponsorship was defined as a mutually beneficial arrangement that consists of the provision of resources of funds, goods and/or services by an individual or body (the sponsor) to an individual or body (rights owner) in return for a set of rights that can be used in communications activity, for the achievement of objectives for commercial gain. A television or radio broadcaster can sell airtime in packages that comfortably meets these requirements and therefore by rights call it broadcast sponsorship. However, this demands further investigation and comment.

The first point to make about television and radio sponsorship is that the resource that the sponsor gives to the broadcaster is in the form of funds only. What they get in return is a short slot of airtime that is trafficked at the start and finish of programme credits. Ofcom, the broadcasting regulator in the UK, defines a sponsored programme as being advertiser funded, either in full or part, with a view to promoting the sponsor's, or another's, name, trademark, image, activities, services, products or other direct or indirect interests (Ofcom, 2006). A sponsor of a 30-minute UK television programme that has one commercial break in the middle, gets four 'bumpers' or 'idents' (visual and verbal references on both front, mid and end programme credits). These bumpers do not contain the sponsor's product. For example, Cadbury's are a long-term sponsor of the television soap 'Coronation Street' on ITV, with a deal that has lasted since 1996 (Cadbury, 2006). A number of their brands are referred to in their slots (Cadbury's Crème Egg, Cadbury's Caramel, Celebrations) and because there are up to two and a half hours of first-runs of the soap in any one normal week on ITV1 (there are reruns on other ITV channels) the sponsor utilizes up to 20 slots per week that refer verbally and visually to their product and its association with the programme. No actual Cadbury's brands are featured in those slots.

The second point is that a broadcast sponsor must not influence the content and/or scheduling of a programme in such a way as to impair the editorial responsibility and independence of the broadcaster. Furthermore, there must be no promotional reference to the sponsor (name, trademark, image, activities, services or products) within the programme. Non-promotional references are permitted only when they are editorially justified or incidental (Ofcom, 2006). So a sponsor may not place its products into the programme it sponsors. For example, 'Coronation Street' (ITV) has no Cadbury's products in its programming. There was no Jacob's Creek wine in 'Friends' (Channel 4) nor was there any of Electricite de France's (EDF) energy services utilized in ITV's FIFA 2006 World Cup programming. The sponsorship of the USA produced 'Desperate Housewives' on UK television by the shampoo brand Herbal Essences is an even more disparate relationship. This is a critical point because the sponsor is not contributing in any way to the broadcaster's production. Significantly the brand can play no 'function' in the sponsorship, despite the increasing importance of functionality as previously highlighted in this text. To be credible, sponsors need to show that they have helped make it happen (Durden, 2006).

Ostensibly, broadcast sponsorship bears little difference to advertising space. Whilst a sponsored slot cannot feature the actual product and make calls to action/encourage purchase or rental (an advertisement can) but can make reference to its association with the programme (there are no such links between advertisers and programmes), they are both paid-for measured slots of time that are designed to promote brands. Whilst broadcast sponsorship credits must be clearly separated from advertising they must also be clearly separated from programmes by temporal or spatial means (Ofcom, 2006). In effect broadcast sponsorship is nothing more than advertising airtime (Durden, 2006).

Television and radio sponsorship has developed in a short space of time and there are some media in industry that believe broadcast sponsorship does work (STV, 2006). The media-related recruitment pages in the UK press also indicate a still growing market for 'sponsorship sales' roles particularly for printed publications and website media. However, is it sponsorship?

Critically there is no integration of the sponsor into the programme production and other than the creation of a new bumper and the payment of higher rates, there are no opportunities to develop the relationship, as is increasingly the need and the benefit within sponsorship. Scottish Television plc encapsulates this one-way relationship by describing that broadcast sponsorship works due to the relationship between the sponsor and the programme, where the relationship is wholly dependent on the creative approach 'by the sponsor to the programme' rather than also the programme to the sponsor and its brand (STV, 2006).

Is it successful? There are indications that it has become a tired medium as critical media comment has also become increasingly prevalent. The innovation has come and gone in a short space of time (Durden, 2006). Whilst there are examples of creativity, such as the use of animation and chocolate streets, houses and characters in Cadbury idents for 'Coronation Street', there are more examples of it being unoriginal and possibly poorly targeted. The matching of EDF, the company that took over the London and Eastern Electricity company, with World Cup coverage and UK football television audiences, at a time of the French team's success and the England team's failure at the quarter final stage of the competition, did appear somewhat incongruent (Ramchandani, 2006).

A similar case can be made for other forms of media opportunity. The use of sponsorship on the Internet and within publishing, of special newspaper or magazine supplements or sections for example, also protects editorial independence although the use of competition mechanisms can allow more integration for products.

Product placement

Another related form of opportunity is with product placement, particularly within the film and television industries. Since the 1950s the placement of products into television programmes and films has become common practice. One of the earliest examples of identifiable products in a film was in 'The African Queen' starring Humphrey Bogart and Katherine Hepburn when the latter tossed Gordon's Gin over the side of the boat. A milestone though is possibly the use of Ray Ban sunglasses by Tom Cruise in the 1983 film, 'Top Gun'. Since the 1980s this form of communication via television broadcasting and the cinema has become more creative.

In UK television, an early use of a car in the 1960s productions of 'The Saint', starring Roger Moore, began a trend that has in some cases become iconic. Originally Jaguar were approached to provide Moore's character, Simon Templar, with his on-screen car. However, the deal was done with Volvo when the Swedish manufacturer seized the opportunity to provide the car, on loan, for free (New Media Group, 2006). The placement of cars into film in particular has gained some manufacturers considerable brand awareness. The use of a fairly obscure car, the DeLorean, in the 'Back to the Future' films gained that firm almost cult status, even now, but in fact did not help them stay in business for long. There have been several car brands used in James Bond films including Lotus and BMW, but 'the' Bond car is arguably an Aston Martin.

Almost any product can be 'placed' and it can be an actual product, its image or a reference to it. It can occur in three ways. The first is for it to happen incidentally. For example, for a product to be in a television show but with no arrangement having been made by the manufacturer. The placement in this case has been done by the producers of the programme for no recompense. They have done this to add realism to their show, rather than use a bland non-descript product. The ant killer product Raid was quite recently used by the producers of 'The Sopranos', the hit USA television show. There was no arrangement made with the manufacturers but the scene and the use of the product, not for killing ants but for aggressive intent to cause human harm, was arguably better understood by the audience because of the pre-conceived perception of the product.

The other two ways for product placement to occur are both via an arrangement between a manufacturer/supplier and a media producer. The arrangement can either be for the supply of an agreed amount of free product and/or a fee may be charged. Steven Spielberg, the Film Producer and Director, is reported to have recouped a significant part of the £103 million it cost to make the film 'Minority Report' starring Tom Cruise in 2002 via product placement revenue. Nokia mobile telephones, Reebok shoes, Burger King catering, Guinness, Gap clothing and Lexus cars were all placed in the film with the latter reportedly paying £3.2 million for that privilege (Merrett, 2002).

For product placement to work, the product needs to be visible within a scene but not be the focus. The product needs to fit the scene, almost seamlessly. The key word here is 'almost'. If it were a totally seamless fit then it would go un-noticed and yet there is a fine line between overkill when any credibility for the use of the product is lost and appears convoluted and underplay where the product goes unnoticed. For example, a billboard is seen to say to Tom Cruise's character in 'Minority Report', 'you look like you could use a Guinness' (Merrett, 2002).

There may be one or two exceptions where the seamlessness is not always required. For example, in an attempt to achieve parody there have been a number of films that have overplayed the use of product. The film 'Josie and the Pussycats' was a send-up of the music industry and specifically set out to satirize name branding. The 2-minute 25-second trailer alone featured 26 different brands, including American Express, America Online, Billboard Magazine, Bebe, Campbell's Soup, Evian and Pringles.

Product placement has clearly been a successful communication for many brands. Ray Ban were at a low sales point prior to their placement of their 1952 design sunglasses in 'Top Gun', but when the film came out sales rose to 360,000 pairs of 'Aviators' in 1983 (New Media Group, 2006). Red Stripe beer sales increased by more than 50 per cent in the USA market in the first month of the release of the film 'The Firm' in 1993 (Business Week, 1998). Sales for Reece's Pieces rose by 65 per cent after their placement in the film 'ET' (Business Week, 1998).

It now appears as if the majority of films use product placement and no doubt do so to improve the budget conditions. Some have appeared to have been very close to or succeeded in affecting editorial independence. The film 'Castaway', starring Tom Hanks, for example, featured the actor as a Fed Ex (couriers) employee intent on escaping the island he had been marooned on to do his job and deliver his package no matter what. Also in the film was his fictitious best friend, a Wilson produced oval football with painted face, called 'Wilson'. The animation film, 'Toy Soldiers', featured toys by Hasbro, Gorgonites and Commando Elite, that were available on shelves at the time of the films launch (Business Week, 1998).

Product placement can clearly be for any form of product. More unusual cases might require the services of an agent. For example, Hasbro Games have been placed in television programmes over a number of years, Buckaroo and Pictionary in 'Randall and Hopkirk' (BBC2), Monopoly in 'Bernard's Watch' (ITV) and Twister in 'Mr Charity' (BBC2) as part of a 2-year campaign that achieved 800 seconds of coverage (New Media Group, 2006). However, it need not necessarily be a hard-good. It can be a service, for example between 2001 and 2003, the charity Scope was placed in 'EastEnders', 'Doctors' and 'My Hero' (all BBC1) and 'Dream Team' (Sky) via verbal references and signage. Across a 6-year campaign the charity gained 2040 seconds of coverage (New Media Group, 2006).

Richard Branson, an expert at using self-promotion for the good of his Virgin brands, has also used product placement well. In the 2006 Bond film 'Casino Royale', Branson himself is briefly seen being searched at a Miami airport security gate. Several airport and runway scenes then follow with a host of aeroplanes but only one non-fictitious brand is featured, Virgin Atlantic. Branson is featured first in order to 'lead' cinema audiences to the brand.

Is product placement sponsorship? It meets the definition, in that there is a mutually beneficial arrangement for commercial gain, involving the supply of product, services and /or funds in return for rights. Many product placers also exploit their brands' associations too, Omega being very active in this in its promotion of its supply of watches to James Bond. The products also provide a function. The function is critical for both the supplier and the producer. If the fit does not appear credible then the placement will be unsuccessful. However, if there is a fit then placement can achieve a number of benefits, brand familiarity, endorsement by those that use the products, exclusion of rival brands and support for sales staff. There are similarities with sponsorship here and clearly, product placement, as part of wider marketing campaigns, can work well as an integrated marketing communications tool and in particular as part of and alongside sponsorship activity. We therefore, should not view product placement as so different from or separate from sponsorship.

The role of media partners

A regulation that limits broadcast sponsorship opportunities is that the sponsor's name can only be used in the programming title if the sponsor is also the event sponsor and already has that integration. This should be viewed as an opportunity rather than a restriction however. An event sponsor that works with appropriate media to provide a wider but integrated set of communications that are focused on a sponsorship, has a greater chance of success. As an integrated communication tool, generally, broadcast and other forms of media sponsorship, are of great value. Whilst the specific sponsorship of a television programme is arguably only an advertising activity, it can play a significant role in helping wider sponsorship led communications achieve success. For example, Ernst and Young, the financial services firm, have used television broadcast associations in combination with other sponsorship activities. In 2000 the firm formed an association with PBS (public television) in the USA and an arts programme production called 'Great Performances'. The affiliation on screen, with operas like La Traviata, supported the sponsorship of the 'live' event alongside other related print and radio advertising, website activity, and significant internal communications activities, for 78,000 employees worldwide, throughout the USA and internationally (Sponsor Thirteen, 2006).

Media partners can be important from four perspectives:

1. *Broadcast rights revenue*: Those sponsorship rights owners that have greater negotiating power have the advantage of being able to secure media partners that pay a fee for broadcast rights. In particular an event can sell broadcast rights to television or radio. This can extend to sales for various territories so that even terrestrial rights may be sold separately from cable or satellite rights, and for international as well as domestic provision. Internet broadcasting rights are generally an individual agreement.

   In some cases, it might be an advantage for a rights owner to receive no fee from the media partner or even to pay them to produce the programming so that media sales, for other territories, can then provide decisive revenue.

2. *Sponsorship rights revenue*: Media partners, such as publishers, can also pay a fee to those rights owners that have sufficient negotiating power.

   For many more sponsorship programmes however, media partners are more commonly secured on an 'in-kind' arrangement.

   In return for sponsorship rights that are similar to those for any other type of sponsor (see Chapter 4), whether for a fee or not, a media partner provides the rights owner with media exposure.

3. *Media exposure*: A media partner provides valuable communications activity for a rights owner. An event for example, can agree with a television partner that it can run promotions to attract a television audience for its broadcast, and if the event has more than one session of activity, provide pre-event promotions that

can also lead to calls for action for ticket sales by incorporating sales contact details.

The Tate Modern used two print media partners in 2006 in order to promote several art exhibitions. For its showings for Constable and Howard Hodgkin it appointed The Sunday Telegraph as its media partner. For its Pierre Huyghe and Kadinsky exhibitions it partnered with The Times, where the broadsheet featured various editorial pieces and promotions such as 'Reader Evenings' and exclusive ticketed opportunities for readers to apply or enter competitions for limited numbers of tickets. For the Huyghe showing this included a tour with the artist.

In addition, a media partner can provide important exposure both directly and indirectly for other sponsors associated with the same sponsorship programme. For example, a radio station can not only acknowledge a title or presenting sponsor in the promotions it produces, it can also work directly with other sponsors on promotions for them in association with the sponsorship programme. A printed newspaper event promotion, produced as a result of an agreement between the rights owner and the print media sponsor, can bear the logos and messages of other sponsors.

This is a critical provision for most rights owners. So much so that, again, it might be an advantage for a rights owner to receive no fee from the media partner or even to pay them to produce the programming. This allows other sponsors to achieve the kind of exposure that can help the rights owner to secure higher sponsorship fees and recoup the cost of their media investment.

4. *Sponsorship function*: Like all other sponsors, a media partner can, and should, provide a function. In addition to their provision of exposure, they may also provide valuable 'content'. A radio broadcaster for example, can provide a stage, music acts and celebrities that can add value to the production of an event. Even a newspaper, with dedicated and specific coverage, can provide a 'daily' report for an event to be given out to audiences. Similarly, a website provider, with linked or dedicated pages, can provide pre-, during and post-event functions.

Most rights owners offer sponsorships that provide sector exclusivity benefits. Operating a media partnership programme alongside can work in the same way, with a partner from the sectors of television, radio, the Internet, magazine and newspaper publishing for example, although this does depend on the negotiating power of the rights owner. Associating with a number of media from different sectors can prove very beneficial for rights owners. An event for example can work successfully without there being too much competition between the partners. For example, Urban Gardens, a gardening exhibition, has previously been sponsored by Volvo and has recruited media partners in The Observer newspaper and UK Style the television channel. Both the newspaper and the television channel were able to promote each others association with the event as well as promote the event itself.

The capacity to have a range of partners is a clear way of potentially securing all the benefits of revenue and exposure as indicated above. However, there are dangers in this. In securing an exclusive arrangement with a media partner in one sector will mean that are limitations to what is achievable with the other media producers in that sector. Again, depending on how much interest an event generates in the public domain, will determine how much interest and then exposure a non-associated media provider will give it.

Timing the recruitment of media partners is critical. A rights owner needs to be in a position to prepare a sponsorship proposal, and have all points of media exposure agreed and clearly defined in order that the recipient potential sponsor can make a wholly accurate valuation of the offering. Proposals need to provide details of media schedules and target reach. Anything less than this, for example an indication that media partnerships, television, radio and other schedules are still 'to be decided', will be inadequate. The key is to adopt an approach that determines all media assets that are to be offered prior to making any proposals. This way, potential sponsors will have a proposal to say yes to.

The following examples are of two very dissimilar but successful media partnerships:

Litter Fairy

In 2002, the Greater London Authority (GLA) identified that litter was a serious issue in London with 260,000 tonnes being dropped yearly at a cost to clear up to the taxpayer set at £51 million. The GLA proposed to tackle this by educating Londoners to stop dropping litter and hired the marketing agency Euro RSCG to deliver an appropriate campaign. They came up with the tag line 'A cleaner London is up to you' and a non-existent 'Litter Fairy'. A sponsor, in recycle-more.co.uk, and London Broadcasting Corporation (LBC) radio stations, LBC 97.3FM and LBC News 1152AM as media partners were recruited. Other integrated activity included local press and bus shelter advertising, poster and post-card distribution to a target audience of 4 million 15–34-year-old Londoners.

The arrangement between the GLA and LBC was mutually beneficial. The GLA was able to reach 900,000 listeners whilst LBC was able to associate and interact with its target audiences by addressing key London issues. The stations ran advertisements and five features on LBC News on the subject of litter and utilized London Mayor, Ken Livingstone, in live studio discussions with listeners. In addition a roving 'Litter Fairy' (a reporter) was sent out on to the streets of London to 'name and shame' litter droppers in an aggressive slant to the campaign.

Cherry Creek Arts Festival

In 2006 the Cherry Creek Arts Festival, Denver, Colorado, USA, celebrated its 16th anniversary and sought the assistance of no less than four separate media group partners (Cherry Creek Arts Festival, 2006). The Rocky Mountain News (RMN) was a founding media partner for this nationally important arts festival for visual and performing arts. Each year the RMN, the official newspaper of the Festival, produces a Festival special section and the official catalogue and walking guide.

The Festival also has a magazines group partner and the support of two titles, Colorado Homes and Lifestyles and Mountain Living Magazine. The magazines have special sections and promotions on a year-round basis.

KMGH Denver's 7 is a local television station and an official media partner. It recruits the Festivals' volunteers via promotions for the 'Denver's 7 Volunteer Corps'. As well as pre-event promotions the station also reports from the event live on each of the 3 days. Entercom Radio Group has four local stations, KOSI

101.1, Alice 105.9. 99.5 Mountain and Studio 1430KEZW, each of which target different and local audiences that are also important targets for the Festival. All four stations have been media partners and official radio stations for the Festival for 8 years and each broadcast live from the event.

This array of media partners works because each of the stations or publications targets a different audience. Because the audiences are all important Festival attendees, their promotional activity pre, during and post the event, are all important Festival communications, not just for the event itself but also the event sponsors. All of the partners also occupy booths at the event, some broadcasting live and others distribute event guides and other information and as such provide important event functions. In addition, these functions can also be seen to be providing the event audience with valuable experiences and are therefore greatly adding to the event's programme content.

Summary

Whilst broadcast sponsorship has evolved rapidly, and with some success, it is a greater opportunity if it is part of a wider and integrated communications programme. As a form of sponsorship, it fails to allow brands to play functional roles within programming and as such brings little more than advertising revenue for the programme producers. Product placement on the other hand can utilize a product, or a service, within the content of a film or a television programme for a credible form of sponsorship. Either can be integrated with other sponsorship activities for successful marketing communications.

Media partnerships are an essential element of most sponsorship programmes. Media partners may provide fees that contribute to either sponsorship or media rights revenue but even when exposure is given in-kind, media partners provide a necessary function through the exposure they supply for the rights owner and its sponsors. In addition, an even more valuable media partner is one that can enhance audience experience with functions that add value to the content of the rights owner's property.

Tasks and discussion points

- Identify an innovative use of broadcast sponsorship and explain how it might achieve greater success as part of a wider integrated sponsorship programme.
- Identify a sponsoring brand and the communications that are utilized. Choose an additional and appropriate product placement opportunity that could be integrated into this communications programme in order to further achieve sponsorship objectives for the brand.
- Select an event that has no significant set of media partners. Identify which media partners you would approach and explain the activities that would benefit them and the event.

References

Business Week (1998). www.businessweek.com (accessed 4 July 2006).

Cadbury (2006). Coronation Street sponsorship www.cadbury.co.uk (accessed 24 January 2006.

Cherry Creek Arts Festival (2006). www.cherryarts.com (accessed 4 July 2006).

Durden, J. (2006). Brash sponsorship is an outdated bore. *The Guardian*, 26 June.

Merrett, J. (2002). How firms jump on brandwagon. *Daily Mirror*, 5 November.

New Media Group (2006). Product placement history – and in the UK? www.newmedia-group.co.uk (accessed 7 July 2006).

Ofcom (2006). Rules. www.ofcom.orh.uk/tv/ifi/codes/bcode/sponsorship (accessed 28 June 2006).

Ramchandani, N. (2006). EDF bravely enters the three lions' den. *The Guardian*, 3 July.

Sponsor Thirteen (2006). Great Performances. www.thirteen.org/homepage/sponsorship/national/pop_case_gp (accessed 25 January 2006).

STV (2006). Sponsorship. www.stvsales.tv (accessed 28 June 2006).

7

Recruiting sponsors and developing sponsorship programmes

The objectives for this chapter are to:

- Further understand the process by which sponsorship rights are developed
- Evaluate the role research and targeting play in the recruitment process
- Further understand the importance of, and approaches for achieving, sponsorship fit
- Evaluate the importance of relationship building for a long-term approach

Piazza Di Siena

A training day at the 2004 Piazza Di Siena equestrian event, held in the Borghese Gardens in Rome, where sponsors AAMS, UNIPE, Longines and Loro Piana enjoy various points of arena signage

Introduction

Chapter 4 refers to the process that rights owners should undergo for the development of their sponsorship programmes. One key issue was highlighted; in order to maximize their revenue and/or reduction of expenditure via the recruitment of fee paying and/or resource supplying sponsors, rights owners would have to have all their potential sponsors lined up before deciding on a programme structure. This is clearly a dilemma as rights negotiations with individual sponsors are hinged on the placement of any one sponsor into a programme structure. For example title rights cannot generally work in a flat structure consisting of several sponsors and a two-tier structure might suit some sponsors' requirements but not others. If a potential sponsor is wanting an agreement and there are still other potential sponsors to see, either in the same category or others, then the rights owner is faced with making either a decision too early and losing other sponsors, or too late and losing the first one. Some rights owners have rights that are in high demand and therefore have some negotiating power in order to manage such issues but the majority of rights owners do not and therefore need an approach that will maximize, rather than wholly solve, their dilemma. This chapter considers such an approach.

Firstly, the importance of research and its role in a targeted approach is discussed, followed by the need to provide tailored rights. The overarching approach for this process is one that seeks continuous development of sponsor relations in order to nurture, develop and grow individual sponsorships and the programme as a whole. This discussion begins with an overview of the process involved.

Sponsorship programme development process

The development of sponsorship programmes is intrinsically linked with the recruitment of individual sponsors. Ideally rights owners would negotiate with all of their possible sponsors and then decide on how they would all sit together in a sponsorship programme structure. However, it is rare for this to happen. Sponsors generally do not wait patiently whilst rights owners make their minds up on which sponsors they will go with. However, whilst the process is normally multi-tasked as most negotiations will be at various stages of the process at any one time, there is a process by which most opportunities can be maximized (see Figure 7.1). The process is in stages and is as follows.

Stage 1: Inventory

The process begins with a compilation of the rights owner's inventory, a listing of sponsorship assets that may be available for sponsorship packaging. This inventory is compiled following a comprehensive auditing of the assets as discussed in Chapter 4. As this is the first stage of the process there have been no discussions with sponsors thus far and so the 'function' assets that need to be developed for each sponsor will not necessarily be obvious at this point. There will still be those 'function' rights that will be uniquely pertinent to each sponsor to identify and agree.

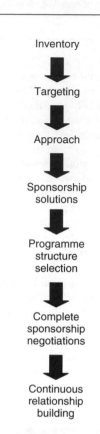

Figure 7.1 Sponsorship Programme Development Process

Stage 2: Targeting

The next stage in the process is identifying the sponsors that are to be targeted. Those rights owners with the capacity to attract sponsors on their terms clearly have an amount of bargaining power at their disposal. Their rights are generally in high demand because they can effectively reach target markets and do so more efficiently than other forms of communications. For example, sponsorship has often been perceived to be better value for money than advertising by sponsors. This is partly due to subjective individual assessment because sponsorship is both difficult to accurately measure and is seldom evaluated in the industry (CIM, 2004). Sponsorship is also one of the few forms of communications that consumers are not cynical about. In a Mintel survey, 90 per cent of the respondent advertising agency clients that were questioned felt that the traditional power of advertising had been eroded in the past 5 years (1999–2004) and sponsorship was a key area where marketers could reverse the trend towards consumer cynicism of marketing messages (CIM, 2004; Mintel, 2004).

However, not all rights owners, particularly those that are new, are able to demonstrate such a high level of demand and so the attraction of those sponsors that make the most successful communications partners is difficult. Ineffective targeting can make this task practically impossible.

The only way of credibly demonstrating any kind of pedigree in these circumstances is to present existing or new potential sponsors with evidence that identifies how their sponsorship objectives have been or can be achieved. Research data is therefore required in order to identify appropriate targets. This process involves two key steps (Masterman, 2004; Masterman and Wood, 2006).

Step One: Identifying target audiences

In the first instance, rights owners have to identify their own target audiences. Qualities as well as quantities are important here. In order to gain as much information in depth, a profile can be constructed via demographic, psychographic and behavioural research of all the audiences. Data on product preferences and buying behaviour will be useful in order to provide information of superior quality.

Determining the quantity (size) of each audience reached is also a key aspect of this process. For example at events the audiences that attend are important, but so are the audiences that are more widely reached via any event communications tools that are to be utilized. This is not just via television, it can also be via any of the marketing communications that are being utilized, for example direct marketing mailing lists, sales promotions and news media coverage.

Rights owners need to collect, analyse and use information from a variety of sources in order to gain knowledge of their target audiences' needs and behaviour. The cheapest and most accessible source of information is that which is generated on a day-to-day basis whilst running the organization. These secondary sources of information might be an event booking system where customer information has been garnered at the time of booking tickets. The contact address is usually collected, but it may also be possible to request other information if a suitable information system for storage and dissemination has been installed. Learning whether an advertisement generated the enquiry and generally building customer records can therefore be an important element of the targeting process.

The rights owner can also find further external secondary sources useful. For example, quantitative data such as government statistics, industry surveys, market research reports, trade or association data and published financial data as well as qualitative information from news reports or articles, trade journals and directories, competitor sales literature and websites can all be used alongside the internal customer information to form profiles. It is important to note that if this information is to be useful in the targeting of new sponsors, it is critical that this is an ongoing process of continual monitoring and updating.

In addition to the secondary sources there is also primary data. By also researching specific audience information first hand, a rights owner can provide a richer and more accurate profile and in so doing present a more comprehensive case to potential sponsors. Different research tools may be used to collect this information and whilst observation is common, market research techniques such as surveys and focus groups may be used more reliably. Figure 7.2 identifies the tools that are available.

Rights owners should aim to use the data they collect to then profile their audiences so that they can be later matched with those of potential sponsors' audiences. Research shows that the need for rights owners to do this is bearing more pressure. Most sponsors rely on their own internal sources and the respective

Secondary research		Primary research (external)	
Internal Quantitative or qualitative	**External** Quantitative or qualitative	**Quantitative**	**Qualitative**
Box office sales	Government reports	Surveys	Interviews
Costings accounts	Syndicated surveys	Test market	Focus groups
Prior reports and evaluations	Market research reports	Experiment	Case studies
	Trade press	Observation	Observation
	Websites		
	Media Directories such as BRAD, JICNARS		

Figure 7.2 Types of Audience Research (adapted from Masterman and Wood, 2006)

rights owners for information when making a decision to sponsor. Under a third (29 per cent) of respondents in the Redmandarin European Sponsors' Survey (2004) indicated for example that they used market research provided by their sales agencies or independent researchers to aid their decision. If this is the case, then the majority of sponsors are not identifying the total extent of their opportunity to reach audiences. They are also clearly relying on rights owners to provide them with audience information and therefore use this to ascertain whether there is a match worth pursuing.

The Wilmington Blue Rocks Baseball team plays in the minor leagues in the USA and provides a refreshing example of the use of audience research, albeit at a local level. Based in Delaware on the east coast they have identified that they draw fans from their home state as well as Pennsylvania, New Jersey and Maryland. Their average game attendance is around 5000 with capacity for up to 7500 at their Frawley Stadium and they actively seek team- and game-related sponsors as well as other commercial use of their facilities in order to increase revenue. Their approach is sometimes blunt in that they provide an eight-page download marketing brochure from their website that contains many communications opportunities together with prices. For example, there are 11 different ways to advertise and several ways to promote such as via 'Diaper Derbies' and 'Daddy Dashes'. They also link up with two radio stations and offer priced packages that include on-air spots. Whilst this does appear at first glance to be another example of predetermined and priced marketing opportunities, it is nevertheless an approach that does at least offer different elements to be pieced together in sponsorship packages. What is more impressive is that they have researched their audience. They are aware that 96 per cent of their fans rate their promotional activities as excellent, very good or good and that 91 per cent of fans rate in-game entertainment similarly. They also know that between 1993 and 2006, the team hosted 320,000 to 330,000 fans at games each season, a total of over 4.3 million (Wilmington Blue Rocks, 2006). So, whilst a single game with an audience of 5000 might appeal to a local sponsor, a season-long or more team-focused sponsorship might prove valuable to a state wide or North-East USA audience interested sponsor. The Blue Rocks use this kind of information plus other demographic data in their more targeted approaches to individual potential sponsors – individual fixture statistics on fans ages, gender, family and friends, and income, for example, are used to target sponsors.

Once data is collected and analysed the rights owner can then move on to step two and match their target audiences with those of potential sponsors. However, it is important here to acknowledge that the issue for most rights owners, and sponsors for that matter, is that research can be an expensive exercise and perceived as either prohibitive and/or unnecessary. This in part explains why this kind of preparation for sponsor recruitment is not common practice throughout the industry (AusSport, 2005; Redmandarin, 2004). There is also some doubt as to whether those sponsors that do research their target audiences are doing it to inform their decision-making or merely using it to post-rationalize a decision to sponsor (Redmandarin, 2004).

Audience research is an exercise in effectiveness and efficiency. The more comprehensive the data and analysis the more clearly defined the target audiences will be and therefore the more effective the targeting of the most appropriate sponsors. Equally, the more effective this targeting the less wasteful and therefore more efficient sponsorship recruitment becomes.

If this is not sufficient reason, and further justification, for rights owners to research is required, then there are other uses for the data that can be collected. For example, rights owners should at least be identifying their target audiences so that their own communications can be effectively targeted.

Sponsors have yet to demonstrate an understanding of the importance of research. The Redmandarin European Sponsors' Survey (2004) revealed that nearly half (48 per cent) of the respondents (decision-makers at sponsoring organizations) do not conduct primary research and 39 per cent do not conduct secondary research on target audiences prior to making a sponsorship decision. The survey indicated that even 39 per cent do not conduct primary research and 33 per cent no secondary research into the potential sponsorship property prior to making a decision. If this continues to prevail at the same time as an increasing requirement for positive return on investment, then it is a responsibility for rights owners to ensure that they at least research in order to target those sponsors that they can provide effective marketing communication solutions for.

Step Two: Matching organizational target markets

Sponsorship is an exchange of rights for benefits between a rights owner and another party for mutual commercial gain (Meenaghan, 1998; Sleight, 1989). Therefore the rights owner's target audiences need to match up to the sponsor's and if a rights owner wants to recruit a sponsor, particularly one that has all the bargaining power, they need to comprehensively demonstrate this match in any approaches made to potential sponsors.

The more research methods that are used in step one the better so that a comprehensive base for the formulation of the sponsorship can be built. Again, because individual sponsors' marketing requirements, activities and results are constantly in-flux rights owners must continuously monitor, collect and analyse data in order to present a credible case to a potential sponsor.

One of the issues with many of the sources that are used in research is that the information is old information. Most organizations have annual budgets and are therefore working ahead in order to formulate next year's targets and spend. That being the case many sponsorship agreements are negotiated a year or more in advance. It is therefore the future, rather than the past, that is of most importance. Observing trends is a key consideration. For example, knowing which industries will be the next critical users of sponsorship communications. Tobacco, Information Technology, Finance and Communications firms have all been important in the development of international sponsorship at different stages throughout the last 40 years. The ever increasing development of new technologies, not only for their use of sponsorship to achieve greater awareness, but also in the way they can provide new ways for sponsors to access audiences (digital media, wireless communications, advertising projection, web and pod casting) is a continuing trend that also requires close consideration.

It is therefore the potential sponsors, of any one recruiting rights owner, that are the most important source of information and whilst data and information on them from the public domain will assist, it is critically the information that emanates from investigative meetings with them that will prove the most valuable. So the next stage, having identified matches in potential sponsors, is to approach them and ask them for information.

Stage 3: Approach

That very first meeting then is of critical importance to the whole recruitment process. Rights owners have immediate credibility in making an approach if they have researched and demonstrated that there is a match between the mutual target audiences but rights owners should prepare much more besides for that meeting. The approach should not be made with pre-determined ideas, packages or inventories to present, but with key questions that will allow them to leave that meeting with sufficient information for them to then use their inventory to create packages, possibly consisting of new rights, and definitely consisting of 'functions', to form communications solutions for that potential partner. The areas of information ideally required from the potential sponsor are as follows:

- A detailed profile of the organization's target markets/audiences for pertinent brands and/or corporate communications so that mutual audiences can be confirmed. A lot of time and resources on both sides can be wasted if the approach does not demonstrate an already formed understanding of the types of needs the potential sponsor has. It is therefore critical for the credibility of the rights owner that the approach has been researched, prepared and therefore targeted.
- A comprehensive understanding of the organization's marketing objectives and hopefully their sponsorship objectives is required in order to set benchmarks for the creation of the sponsorship.

- An audit of all their marketing activity including results from past campaigns and particularly future plans so that any synergy with the rights owner's activities may be identified.

Stage 4: Sponsorship solutions

The aim here is to meet a potential sponsor's needs with a communications solution, in good time for their planning, so that they will be able to identify the value of integrating a particular sponsorship into their communications programmes. As previously discussed, this is by no means an easy task with so many other communications options on offer. The key is to present a sponsorship solution that can demonstrate a return on investment so that the sponsor can be effectively recruited.

The information that has been researched and supplemented by initial meetings with the potential sponsor can be used to formulate potential sponsorship solutions. As the rights owner considers which rights should be blended together into packages it needs to consider three critical factors. These factors form a checklist in order to ensure value in the proposition and demonstrate a return on investment for the potential sponsor.

Meet their objectives
In collecting information concerning the potential sponsor's communications objectives it is important to ascertain any measures they will be looking to use. The aim is to identify their specific, measurable, achievable, relevant and time-specific objectives (SMART objectives), so that there are built-in performance indicators and the sponsorship can be benchmarked for an evaluation of return on investment. This is not always possible however, as for example there are sponsors that fail to set objectives. This amounts to 12 per cent according to the 2004 Redmandarin European Sponsors' Survey, but there is an assumed larger number that do not set measurable objectives (CIM, 2004; Redmandarin, 2004). If these are not available, and this is more common than is desirable, then objective setting becomes the responsibility of the rights owner. It is in a rights owner's hands to ensure that their sponsorship offering is sufficiently attractive enough to be selected.

> The optimum approach in this case would be to identify areas where there could be measures and performance indicators built in. This includes the types of measures that could be used, how they fit in with existing/previous measures used by the potential sponsor and examples of similar and successful measures from other sponsorships.

Provide 'function'
It should now be possible to derive unique and functional rights if sufficient information has been collected from the potential sponsor. New rights that provide a sponsor with a functional showcase will sit alongside the rights that are already identified in the inventory. These are critical in providing competitive advantage.

A successful sponsorship relationship between a brand and an event, organization or individual can lead to a positive perceptual change towards that brand (Erdogan and Kitchen, 1988). In order to achieve this positive brand perception, sponsors need to be explicit. In other words the sponsorship has to have a credible meaning and it also has to communicate this so that target audiences see it clearly and understand the connection that has been made between a rights owner and a sponsor. Audiences must be able to make the connection between the sponsor and what it is sponsoring in order to make sense of it and when the connection is not so explicit then the sponsor has to inform its audiences of what meaning and connection there is. A functional role for the sponsor helps to achieve that.

Demonstrate 'fit'

The connections can also be made, or not, by audiences in their perceptions of the degree of fit that exists in a sponsorship. The phrase, 'sponsorship fit,' is used to generally describe the mutual appropriateness of entering into a sponsorship but refers to more than just the matching of target markets (Masterman and Wood, 2006; Erdogan and Kitchen, 1988). Firstly, it concerns the whole set of rights in any one sponsorship and how they collectively meet the specific objectives for both the sponsor and the rights owner. The relationship must function as a partnership where both the sponsor and the rights owner mutually receive benefits that can be exploited in order to meet objectives (Mullin et al., 2000). However, it also concerns the credibility and reputation with stakeholders and the ethos of each partner. Even if target markets match and objectives can be met, there may still not be a fit. Indeed an inappropriate fit may be dangerous. It appears very unlikely that two partners can interact with each other in sponsorship communications without the benefit of having shared conventions. Erdogan and Kitchen (1988) describe such a positive interaction as a symbiotic relationship.

There has always been some issues with the fit between health-related sports events and alcohol and tobacco. There has also been questions raised in music and arts-related sectors where artistic integrity has been in question in the seeking of sponsorship funding. Car manufacturer Audi sponsored concerts in 2003 and 2004 at the Royal Opera House (ROH), Covent Garden, London. The rights they received included an illuminated logo on the outside of the ROH, a historic and protected grade-one listed building, and they also took the opportunity to display Audi cars on the adjoining pavements. This was considered to be an attractive sponsorship by Audi in that it was seen to be able to help them reach their target consumer markets (Audi, 2002). However, the benefit to ROH appears somewhat nebulous and little more than a gain in revenue. All sponsorships have the potential of over-commodification and appearing to be too commercially exploitative. As a result there is the risk of alienating customers. This need not necessarily be just about the exuberant use of commercial messages however. In Audi's case this probably concerned a lack of congruity in that the listed building and high-brow arts institution had not been involved in such activity before and as such was possibly perceived as infringing on its artistic integrity, a common factor of resistance to sponsorship in the arts.

A more convoluted example perhaps demonstrates how there might be incongruity from both the sponsor's and the rights owner's perspective. It is unlikely that either the retailer Body Shop or any country sports organization would target each other for a potential sponsorship relationship. With Body Shop perceived as being actively against cruelty to animals there would be no fit and subsequently damage in the form of a loss of credibility on both sides.

More positively the provision of Rover cars to the Manchester 2002 Commonwealth Games provided the sponsor with the opportunity for increasing awareness of a new model. At the same time the event saved on transportation costs and served its participants and officials with courtesy travel services (Manchester Evening News, 2002). The fit was well founded in the function element of the sponsorship in this example.

Another example of this can be seen in Case Study 7.1 where Hewlett Packard provided an Athlete Search System for the Boston Marathon. The system was not a critical element of the event in that the event could be run without it, however the provision of this technology is seen to be highly beneficial to the runners and spectators alike and as such the perception is that Hewlett Packard are an integral part of the event (Boston Marathon, 2004, 2006; HP, 2004).

The English National Ballet's (ENB) recruitment of Mattel for its 2001/2002 Nutcracker season was quite contentious. Whilst the fees of £85,000 were clearly a welcome form of revenue, the involvement of a life-size 'Barbie' character, the Mattel owned child's toy, was seen by some as being somewhat too much of a commercial 'sell-out' by a cultural provider such as the ENB (Field, 2002). Clearly the family target audiences for a ballet season were seen as attractive for Mattel and their exploitation and timing of this as a promotion for the cinema film 'Barbie in the Nutcracker' was an innovative approach. This did do more for the ENB than was first perceived. Whilst the difficulty was that perceptions of over-commercialization were generated, what should have been made more explicit was the approach that was being used to develop awareness in new target audiences for ballet. Interestingly, the ENB pursued this strategy and recruited HIT Entertainment with their brand 'Angelina Ballerina' and used it in a sponsorship of the 2004 Nutcracker season.

Fit can also be concerned with the relationships between the individuals that are involved in negotiations and then the ongoing management of the relationship between rights owner and sponsor. The capacity for people to work harmoniously together plays a large part in the success of a sponsorship.

Different examples of how sponsors have met their objectives and been provided with function and sponsorship fit are also provided in Case Studies 7.2–7.4.

If there is to be more than one sponsor in a sponsorship programme, the rights owner concerned needs to be able to undertake the process that has been described thus far with a number of potential sponsors at any one time. It is unlikely as well that any of the potential sponsors will be at the same stage of this process at any one time thus multi-tasking expertise is required.

The aim is to not make any decisions too early as sponsors may need to sit alongside others in a structure that cannot be determined straight away. With the checklist above achieved for each individual potential sponsor, a rights owner can then consider the overall structure of its sponsorship programme.

Stage 5: Programme structure selection

The options that are to be pitched to potential sponsors have been devised whilst considering where a particular sponsor might sit in an overall sponsorship

Case Study 7.1 Sponsorship relationship development: Boston Marathon

On 17th April 2006, the Boston Athletic Association (BAA) staged its 110th Boston Marathon. The first race was in 1897. The race is not surprisingly the oldest annual marathon in the world and in recent years the organizers and rights holders have demonstrated equal fortitude in developing a number of key relationships with sponsors. For example, Gatorade has been a sponsor of the race for 14 years.

The 2006 race lists 18 sponsors and three media partners in a tiered sponsorship programme structure. It is enlightening to look at John Hancock Financial Services, adidas and Hewlett Packard in particular to demonstrate how the BAA has developed relations for stronger and increasingly more successful sponsorships.

John Hancock

John Hancock Financial Services has supported the race since 1986 when it provided the first ever prize money. It continues to provide a prize fund that has grown to over US $600,000 including performance bonuses. In addition the company provides a wide range of financial services to the communities that form the race course, namely Hopkinton, Ashland, Framlingham, Natick, Wellesley, Newton, Brookline and Boston.

John Hancock is a Boston firm and has been 'principal' sponsor throughout the relationship – the top sponsor in a tiered sponsorship programme structure. In order to grow the relationship though, a number of initiatives have been developed over the 21 years. The sponsor now provides media support with media guides, press material and accreditation co-ordination and it manages the pressroom. In order to achieve this, it utilizes its own Boston-based buildings by transforming them into race centres and 1900 of its employees are recruited as volunteer race helpers. In the last few years the firm has also provided a giant television screen near the finish line for public viewing.

The sponsor has also been exploiting its sponsorship. A number of key initiatives have been developed with the BAA. The 'John Hancock Running and Fitness Clinic' is a national educational programme that brings the top race winners into schools for demonstrations and training. Notable athlete involvements have come from Kenyans Ibrahim Hussein and Moses Tanui and Portuguese Rosa Mota. More locally the 'Boston Marathon Kenya Project' has been developed. This is a year-round schools project that celebrates the fact that Kenyan athletes have been the dominant race winners. John Hancock employee volunteers and Kenyan race champions educate pupils on Kenyan culture, language and geography and do it based at the Boston Zoo's African Tropical Forest exhibit. Another local project was first developed in 1992 – the 'Adopt-a-Marathoner' programme brings the Kenyan elite runners each year together with school pupils in a pre-race rally. These new ideas were all jointly developed to grow the relationship year-on-year and were initiated as exploitation of the rights in order to further achieve John Hancock's objectives for developing corporate awareness and internal relations in particular.

adidas

adidas have been a sponsor of the race since 1987 and are now the 'Official Footwear and Apparel Outfitter', a position that ranks them singularly at the next level below John Hancock. After 17 years it increased its commitment by accepting new rights that saw them provide the runners' bibs and numbers. It had already provided the 7000 volunteers and 1100 media representatives with branded jackets.

In 1992 adidas sponsored the BAA as well as the Marathon. After 12 years of involvement in 1999, adidas and BAA launched the year-round project, the 'BAA Freedom Run' and also an annual seminar series based at the Boston Marathon Expo. Another new and major exploitation initiative was introduced in 2005 with an adidas advertising campaign, using its latest shoe 'adistar control', entitled 'It's what happens between runs'. This was a 2-week campaign that was exposed extensively across Boston prior to and during the Marathon and it was the largest campaign of any sponsor to date. Again these new ideas and exploitation have been introduced at key points throughout the relationship in order to see it grow.

Hewlett Packard

HP has been a sponsor since 1994 and sits on the next level down in the tiered sponsorship programme structure along with 15 other sponsors. In its 10th year it adapted its technology to provide an exciting new function at the event. It launched the 'HP Athlete Search System', a state-of-the art wireless network to provide data on race participants as they were running. By placing a chip into their shoes or on their wheelchairs, race participants could be tracked during the race. This meant that anyone anywhere in the world could track an athlete via their own personal computer if they logged on to the HP supported race website. Additionally, spectators at the race could stop any of 75 HP employee volunteers and ask them to use their hand-held HP iPAQ Pocket PCs to track an athlete. The technology was therefore providing a number of information providing functions for race organizers, media and spectators as well as being a piece of entertainment. It also served well in showcasing HP technology and brands.

In order to launch this technology, HP had to work with another sponsor, Verizon Wireless. Here the collaboration between sponsors provided both firms with cross-promotional opportunities and demonstrates the commitment of both to their relationship with BAA.

Source: Boston Marathon (2004, 2006); HP (2004)

programme. The questions raised here concern whether there should be one or more sponsors, how many there should be if it is to be more than one, should they sit in a tiered or flat structure and which structure will maximize revenue and/or reduce expenditure via supply of resources. These decisions should not be made until the first sponsorship is finalized and until that point in time a rights owner needs to stay as flexible as possible. In some cases this can be a difficult task as it is not always possible to refuse a sponsor if they are keen to come on board and

Case Study 7.2 A sponsorship solution: O_2 – Diwali festival

Diwali, the Festival of Lights, in London's Trafalgar Square, has importance for Hindu, Sikh and Jain communities but is also of wide appeal to many nationalities and race. The theme is victory of good over evil, light over darkness.

Around 15,000 people attend and the setting is at night against Nelson's Column. Asian foods are served under the light of masses of floating candles and strung illuminations.

The 2003 event was sponsored by O_2 and is owned and run by the Mayor of London's office.

Objectives

O_2 participated in a number of Asian events in 2003 through its 'O_2 in the City Programme'. This additional event was seen as an opportunity to further extend its message of support for the Asian communities and at an event that attracted sizeable live as well as media audiences.

They were able to achieve this via event branding and signage and a print run of 50,000 Diwali Guides. The Guide incorporated details of Diwali festivals throughout Greater London and links to various Asian retail and temple networks.

Function

O_2 provided a big screen next to the main stage for improved vision, entertainment and promotions for the event.

The sponsors also had staff roaming through the crowd with O_2 Media Messaging Mobile units taking photographs of individuals and groups that it then relayed to the screen.

O_2 promotional vehicles were also on-site with further products on display and for interactive use by members of the audience. Visits were rewarded with mobile phone SIM cards and free texts with the capacity to be displayed on the big screen. Over 3000 photographs and 1000 SMS texts were displayed adding to the entertainment of the event.

O_2 also offered free ring tones of popular Asian music, price reductions for overseas calls and created a Bollywood style website for information for all its Asian activities.

Sponsorship fit

The sponsorship fit between O_2 and Diwali exists mainly because of the values the sponsor stands for and expresses via its relations work with communities ('O_2 in the City Programme' and others). They have a strong community programme and also target Asian audiences for brand awareness as part of their marketing communications activity. As O_2 is a high-profile sponsor it also helps to raise awareness for Asian culture, and this festival in particular, both within those communities and beyond.

It was necessary for O_2 to ensure that audiences were aware of these links and that there is a fit. This can be a requirement for a number of sponsorships when the links are less obvious. It is only the target audiences that have to be made aware and this is done via an exploitation of the rights. In this case O_2 used the printed guides and its function activity at the event itself to demonstrate that there were strong links between it and Asian culture and communities.

Source: London (2006); Article 13 (2006)

Case Study 7.3 A sponsorship solution: NatWest bank – RSC regional tours

The Royal Shakespeare Company's (RSC) tours from 1995 to 1997 were sponsored by NatWest. Each tour involved 17 weeks on the road and the transformation of leisure centres, schools and halls up and down the UK. The objective for the RSC was to take world class live theatre to the country.

A sponsorship agency, Sponsorship Consulting, were instrumental in exploiting the sponsorship on the bank's behalf.

Objectives

NatWest wanted to reach new target audiences and at local levels by involving its local banks and their staff wherever the tour played. In addition it wanted to exploit this activity to wider audiences via various media at local and national levels for the bank as a whole as well as some of its specific services.

The sponsor was therefore seeking to achieve corporate as well as brand awareness, and in addition internal objectives of staff involvement and benefit.

Function

This sponsorship lacked any obvious function. NatWest services and financial products were not naturally providing any function for the tour. However, the event had partnered with a sponsor that comprehensively exploited the relationship to ensure that the sponsorship got wide coverage. NatWest was therefore providing an event communications function at its own expense that afforded the tour a wider target audience reach than it might otherwise have achieved.

The exploitation activity included the following:

- National and regional press, television and radio coverage of the sponsorship and supported by an advertising campaign.
- Event signage, merchandise and print featuring NatWest branding.
- Exclusive offers for NatWest customers at NatWest branches and via direct mail.
- Branded tour transportation for advertising.
- Provision of specially produced education programmes for wider knowledge of the performances including interpreted performances for the hard of hearing and special needs workshops.

- Local branch involvement, including photo-calls at each venue for the managers, ticket discounts for all staff and sponsorship exploitation manuals for managers to make best use of their involvement.
- The corporate hospitality rights given to NatWest were used to entertain 2000 corporate guests.

Sponsorship fit

The sponsorship fit between NatWest and the RSC was founded on their re-positioning strategies and their targeting of mutually significant local and new audiences. The sponsorship served to communicate the new positions.

Whilst NatWest is a nationally important organization it was striving to make impact at local levels, stressing its provision of services and benefits for local customers. Similarly, as a national and generally perceived high-brow provider of theatre, the RSC was re-positioning itself by reaching out to local communities. It also did this with some credibility by organizing tours over a sustained length of time.

The match was an attempt to show two partners reaching out to local communities whilst letting a wider national audience know that, that is, what they were doing.

Source: Sponsorship Consulting (2006)

Case Study 7.4 A sponsorship solution: Shell Fuel Economy World Record Challenge

In January 2006, John and Helen Taylor, holders of 34 fuel economy driving achievements ventured on their biggest challenge, to set a Guinness Round-the-World Record for fuel efficiency. The attempt was to cover nearly 29,000 kilometres one-way around the world, in 70 days and on 50 fuel tank fill-ups or less.

An approach was made to Shell with the proposal for the company to be their exclusive fuel provider and sole and title sponsor.

Objectives

Shell's objectives were to firstly road test their newest fuel economy petrol formula ahead of general introduction to service station forecourts. The formula was designed to offer improved engine efficiency by improving friction control and increasing engine cleanliness. The Taylors journey provided Shell research units with the data to assess the performance and effectiveness of the formula over the total distance as well as considering different driving practices and various road conditions. The sponsorship therefore served Shell in a research and development capacity.

Secondly Shell wanted to use the success of the venture to fully exploit media potential. This they achieved with the implementation of a public relations campaign that consisted of media-fed stories to television, newsprint and radio.

They installed 'calls to action' in order to drive audiences to dedicated website pages off their own website and that of the event. The results were used to bolster Shell's 'FuelStretch' principles – a set of driving tips that they disseminate to the public as part of their marketing communications.

Function

The function was obvious yet innovative as well as double edged. The provision of fuel ensures that the event can take place and that the challenge can be met. The fuel provides function to the event and the Taylors.

Shell is also able to test its formula in reliable and rigorous conditions. Exclusive provision also allows Shell to exploit and seek competitive advantage via the media. The media were attracted because this involved testing for environmentally sound reasons. The event therefore also provides a function to Shell.

Sponsorship fit

A sponsorship fit was achieved because Shell wanted a media savvy event that tested and demonstrated that its new fuel promoted driving efficiency, and that it is a clean and environmentally sympathetic formula. A successful team such as the Taylors was also of appeal to Shell as they are consistent and successful performers of reliable efficiency challenges. As an ordinary everyday pair of individuals, and not a larger more commercial organization, they are also appropriate for Shell to use in endorsing their product to similar target audiences.

That is congruent with the Taylors' requirements for a fuel supply from a company that wants to test for such efficiency and as proven efficiency driving experts they would also want the best performing fuel for their task.

Together, the Taylors and Shell extol an environmental approach to fuel economy and at a time when fuel efficiency has become a popular political as well as socio-economic concern.

Source: Fuel Challenge (2006); Shell (2006)

particularly if there is imminent payment involved. Wherever possible though, if a right owner is to truly maximize their opportunities, then that flexibility is important. Not until the first deal is struck and the structure therefore duly determined should it be fixed.

The guideline here is to conduct a cost versus benefit analysis on the options available. Consider this scenario. There is an opportunity to bring in a small number of sponsors in a flat structure and for a certain level of commercial return. There is little opportunity to add to this number of sponsors as the organizations concerned want to restrict the numbers of sponsors. On the other hand an alternative option is for a larger number of sponsors in a tiered structure for a lesser commercial gain but with the potential to add more to the programme at the various levels of the tiered structure and achieve a greater commercial gain than the first option in the long run. However, there are no potential sponsors in line yet for these opportunities. A cost versus benefit analysis might reveal that there is potentially more commercial gain in the second option but that it is a risk to wait. The decision to go for the second option therefore needs to be quantified. For example, by considering other factors such as what types of sponsorship opportunities might still be available and how feasible those might be to recruit to. Taking the first option might also be affected by other factors such as the state of cash flow and whether sponsorship fees that come in early are a more attractive proposition.

By conducting a cost versus benefit analysis on the options available it is possible to maximize revenue and/or reduce expenditure via supply of resources. From here it is then possible to complete individual sponsorship arrangements.

An example of a consistent strategy for sponsorship programme structure is provided by the IOC. The changes that have been made since 1985 to its TOP sponsorship programme structure are represented in Figure 7.3. The IOC launched The Olympic Partners (TOP) sponsorship programme with a strategy to recruit sponsors for a 4-year cycle. This first cycle was named TOP I. The cycle, or quadrennium, consists of sponsor rights for one Winter and one Summer Games, for example, the 11 TOP VI sponsors received rights from the end of the Games in Athens in 2004 covering their involvement with the Winter Games in Torino in 2006 and the Summer Games in Beijing in 2008 (see Figure 4.7 in Chapter 4 for an overview of the rights of the TOP VI sponsors).

Generally the same industry sectors have been represented in each of the cycles, for example from IT, Fast food, Financial services, Photographic, Soft drink, Audio Visual, Timing and Credit Cards. However, at times there have been one-off representations, for example Bausch and Lomb held vision care rights in the 1980s. Media/Publishing rights stopped at the end of TOP V when Sports Illustrated/Time did not renew as did reprographics when Xerox also decided not

IOC TOP Sponsorship – Sponsorship Programme Development		
Quadrennium cycle	Number of partners	Sponsorship revenue
TOP I 1985–1988	9	US $96 million
TOP II 1989–1992	12	US $172 million 79 per cent increase
TOP III 1993–1996	10	US $279 million 62 per cent increase
TOP IV 1997–2000	11	US $579 million 108 per cent increase
TOP V 2001–2004	11	US $663 million 15 per cent increase
TOP VI 2005–2008	11	US $866 million 31 per cent increase

Figure 7.3 IOC TOP Sponsorship – Sponsorship Programme Development (adapted from IOC, 2006)

to progress to TOP VI. These were replaced by General Electric (utilities) and Lenovo (IT equipment) who now sit alongside Atos Origin, also from the IT industry. The IOC recognized some time ago that the general health area was an important inclusion for their programme. In addition to Bausch and Lomb, Phizer had been involved as a supplier from 1994 to 2002 (IOC, 1993). Consequently discussions were conducted with several interested companies, including Johnson and Johnson in 1999 (New York Games, 2005). It has taken until TOP VI though to recruit in this area and it has been through a multi set of rights for General Electric (as Figure 4.7 in Chapter 4 also shows).

The IOC's strategy for the development of its sponsorship programme has clearly been to maintain a consistent number of sponsors, between 10 and 12, and a similar representation of industries to form its sponsorship programme structure. The chair of the IOC Marketing Commission, Gerhard Heiberg, has made it clear that reaching the required revenue via a consistent number of sponsors is in its best interests (IOC, 1993, 2004).

Equally consistent is the Toronto Pride's approach of a tiered programme. They have acquired negotiating power to an extent that they can recruit sponsors to a programme that consists of eight levels (see Figure 4.5 in Chapter 4). They have identified that one sponsor at the top level (diamond level) plus one sponsor at the next level down (platinum level) works alongside having a flexible number of sponsors from year-to-year at all the other levels (five gold, five silver and three bronze sponsors, five media and two hotel partners and thirty-one community supporters in 2005).

Stage 6: Complete sponsorship negotiations

Once a structure has been determined, the rights owner can return to its potential sponsors and finalize negotiations. As the recruitment of each sponsor is unique this can take various lengths of time to complete. The individual nature of selling sponsorships successfully is covered in Chapter 8.

Stage 7: Continuous relationship building

Arguably though, the recruitment process does not naturally end at stage 6. Even when the programme is full there is always the opportunity to work on the process for next time and start early to determine how new or existing sponsors and their rights can be grown. Sponsors also renew and depart at different times, and so there is possibly always at least one more sponsor to recruit and always a sponsorship to develop. The recruitment process should therefore be viewed as a long-term job which creates the ongoing stage of relationship building.

The work to establish a relationship has already begun, or should have done when it started with the targeting process. The greater the preparation prior to an approach to a potential sponsor, the more likely there will be a welcome reception. Companies give little credence to bland approaches that are not informed and knowledgeable, in other words not targeted. Those companies that receive large numbers of approaches on a regular basis will not consider those that do not demonstrate how the sponsorship will reach their target audiences and effectively and efficiently meet their marketing objectives. To further stand out from the crowd then, rights owners also need to ensure that they are willing to work with a company, perhaps for as long as it takes, in order to convince them that theirs is that unique opportunity. For example, even having received an initial negative response a rights owner might still develop a relationship over a longer period by continuing communications with them in order to eventually nurture a sponsorship. For credibility then, any approach must be tailored and bespoke. It must also demonstrate a commitment.

Unfortunately, many rights owners still make contact with potential organizations with offers of pre-determined sets of sponsorship rights. There is no demonstration of any willingness for commitment in this approach and as such sponsors are increasingly giving rights owners' proposals short thrift. The macro picture might prove to provide an even gloomier outlook. With more potential sponsors turning to other marketing communication solutions a worrying result may be the decreasing use of sponsorship. In 2000, Pringles, the crisps snack brand was a sponsor of Union of European Football Association (UEFA) and EURO 2000 but for the following EURO 2004 championships in Portugal the brand did not renew its sponsorship and furthermore decided to ambush market the event. By independently agreeing to use the imagery of several key European international footballers on Pringles packs at the time of the event the brand was seen to be making use of a non-official association with football and the event specifically. For example, Ruud van Nistleroy, a Dutch international, appeared on-pack wearing an orange football shirt. The shirt did not bear any insignia or logos and colour wise was not the exact orange pantone reference of the official Netherlands FA national team shirt. This association cost Pringles a reputed £1 million to achieve via a football agent who secured the players' imagery, this sum being far less than the amount it would have cost to have renewed its sponsorship with UEFA. The worry here is that if this was deemed a success by Pringles then that represents one less satisfied sponsor and a move away from sponsorship. Other major sponsors have also shown signs of adding to this trend. The Chartered Institute of Marketing (2004) reported for example that both IBM and Coca-Cola had stepped back their sponsorship spends with the reasons being a lack of justification and evidence of a return on their investment (CIM, 2004). Sponsorship evaluation is discussed in greater depth in Chapter 11.

An 'off-the-shelf' approach that uses pre-determined packages only supplies a set of rights that has been designed with no specific sponsors in mind and as a result is unlikely to meet any individual requirements. There is clearly no bespoke tailoring or commitment to the development of a relationship in following such an approach but unfortunately it is still used in industry. The Catholic Youth Organization, for example, displays one line sponsorship titles and prices on its website (The National Lacrosse League referred to in Chapter 4 uses a similar approach). There were over 50 sponsorships ranging from $60 to $7000 available for one of its 2006 events. Whilst this was a local event in Portland, USA, and the prices were small there were no indications of what any sponsor would get if they took one of these offers (CYO, 2006). As recently as 2001, the fourth edition of Arts and Business's (2001) Sponsorship Manual contained its recommended process for selling and developing sponsorship in the UK. This process suggested 'developing a sponsorship package and proposal' unfortunately before recommending that rights owners 'identify companies to approach'.

Conversely, a tailored or bespoke approach that is researched and knowledge-able is demonstrating that a rights owner would like to get to know a sponsor and develop a relationship. It shows a willingness to commit.

The great value of relationships is that they can be developed for greater effect-iveness and have the potential to be more efficient because it is less costly to develop an existing relationship than it is to recruit a new one. This is the case whatever the stage of the relationship and so it is equally relevant at the start of or during a sponsorship. Lachowetz et al. (2003) have conducted research that demonstrates those events that focus on developing closer ties early in the sales process go on to earn more loyalty when it comes to sponsorship renewal. This also means that maintaining and developing existing sponsor relations is likely to be a more effective and efficient sponsorship approach. The closer a partner is, the easier, for example, it is going to be flexible and adjust to changing needs and objectives over time. This highlights the importance of making the renewal of sponsorships a priority (Lachowetz et al., 2003).

Demonstrating a willingness to build a relationship at the earliest stages in the recruitment process can establish footholds for rights holder/sponsor relations but clearly the process does not finish there. It is important that this approach is applied throughout the life cycle of the sponsorship. It can even be developed beyond that. For example, the continued relationship with an ex-sponsor may encourage that organization to return. This can be the case even at the highest of profiles. For example, Coca-Cola sponsored the Football League's League Cup (Coca-Cola Cup) from 1992 to 1998 and then agreed with the same rights owner to sponsor the Championship and Divisions 1 and 2 in 2004.

How are relationships nurtured? Relationship marketing literature highlights the importance of trust and commitment (Baker and Sinkula, 1999; Mavondo, 2000) and communication (Mohr et al., 1996). Relationships can only be main-tained over long periods when there is trust between the parties involved and this is achieved via effective communication between event and sponsor. Meenaghan (1998) and Hoek (1998) both maintain that partnership and co-operation is crit-ical to sustaining effective communications. Sponsorship is an ideal tool for this as it is essentially based on there being a mutual benefit, a benefit that goes beyond the receipt of funds, goods or services and similarly beyond the receipt of rights. Effective communication involves the development of the relationship jointly and from a rights owner's perspective this could mean allowing a sponsor to have some input into key event decisions. The trust can therefore come from a confidence in the other party knowing that they are focused on mutually benefiting objectives and that promises will be honoured. Trust is an outcome of previously successful interaction (Farelly et al., 2003), and consequently something that is built over time. A long relationship is therefore desirable. Trust, can also come from the knowledge that there is a degree of flexibility on both sides for change. A degree of flexibility, even when it comes to honouring promises and adhering to con-tracts, will be needed as the relationship grows because the need for change can occur at any time. There is an important relationship between the duration of a sponsorship and the flexibility that is allowed. Many sponsorships last up to 4 years and are then not renewed. This raises a worthwhile research question. Why do so many sponsorships peter out after this sort of time, and so few go on for so much longer and yet remain successful? The assumption is that degrees of flexi-bility that allow change from year-to-year, especially in meeting new objectives are critical. A common reason given by sponsors that have enjoyed a sponsorship of a number of years and yet not renewed, is that they are taking a different strategic direction to meet different marketing objectives.

The Gillette Cup, the limited-overs knockout cricket tournament, was sponsored by Gillette from 1963 to 1980. The sponsor pulled out when it researched and identified that target audience brand awareness was low; the majority did not know that the company made razor blades. Do such sponsorships simply grow tired because they have not adapted to changing needs? Stella Artois, the beer brand, has sponsored the Tennis Championships at The Queen's Club in London since 1979 and it is clear that the relationship between the rights owner, The Queens Club, and InBev, the brand owner, has been very effectively maintained over that time with flexible adaptation when required. This longevity has been assisted in no small way by the involvement of the Tournament Director, Ian Wight, since its inception. The climb to being the number one premium beer selling brand in the UK was a marketing objective that is also seen to have been assisted by this sponsorship.

Farelly et al.'s (2003) studies reveal that the more effective the communication process, the greater the commitment to the relationship. They found that greater communication allows partners to know where they stand and consequently feel a commitment to keep the relationship going. Both of these reasons can therefore lead to planning for the long term. What Farelly et al. (2003) also identified was that a strong market orientation has a positive association on the key factors of communication, commitment and trust. Sponsors and rights owners with high levels of market knowledge and focus are therefore more likely to display greater commitment to a relationship. The most attractive sponsors are therefore those that implement market research in order to devise and integrate sponsorships into their marketing communication strategies. The most attractive rights owners are therefore those that get to know what their sponsors want and then put effort in to providing that for them.

There are some key areas for consideration when building relationships and as an overarching guideline this should be an approach that 'gives them more than they expect' or over-delivering (Duff, 2004). These areas are as follows:

Personal communications

All organizational relationships are based on the personal interactions between the individuals on both sides. Taking an interest in a counterpart will help develop a personal relationship that in turn will help grow the relationship at the higher level. The advice for a rights owner here would be to get to know your counterpart at the sponsoring organization well.

Extra benefits

There are elements of the inventory that may prove beneficial if given away to sponsors even if they are cost items and especially if they are not a part of their set of rights. This can apply to potential sponsors, for example, by inviting them to an event they may then become interested in sponsoring. After some time, it may be of even more value to let sponsors have extra benefits. By giving their sponsor, MassMutual Financial Group, 2400 sport event tickets over and above their contracted allocation, the University of Massachusetts (UMass) was able to create further goodwill. At the same time this grew the relationship and gained more mutual success as MassMutual gave the tickets to its employees, thus extending the Umass reach to potential fans and raised revenue through merchandise and catering sales at the matches. The key is to recognize that the relationship can grow by sometimes giving away rights. That said, the rights owner needs to be aware of how much this activity with one sponsor might prove difficult with another. Wherever possible, transparency and parity should prevail across the sponsorship programme.

A simple 'thank you' to sponsors can be worthwhile. The US Tennis Association (USTA) took out advertising in *The New York Times* after the 2003 US Open that consisted of a 'sincere thanks' to players, fans, media partners (CBS, USA Network, Tennis magazine and *The New York Times*) and its 19 sponsors, each by name (*The New York Times*, 2003).

New ideas

New ideas can be presented at any time and by either side in order to grow a relationship. This can increase trust and commitment and achieve greater success if geared to key sponsor objectives. New ideas can provide new solutions and demonstrate flexibility in order to develop a sponsorship over time and adapt as necessary to major changes in requirements. However, minor changes can also be worthwhile as they can demonstrate a willingness to grow closer.

One idea that was developed at the aforementioned Stella Artois Tennis Championships was a hydraulic umpire's chair. The idea did not catch on at many other tournaments but for a time, it was used to effectively gain media coverage. The chair was of course predominantly coloured red, the brand colours of Stella Artois.

The ideas were also forthcoming when Leeds Metropolitan University sponsored Leeds Rhinos for the first time for the 2004/2005 UK rugby league season. Success came early and bearing the sponsor's Carnegie brand (Faculty of Sport and Education) the Rhinos won the Premier League. The Club then decided to ask its sponsor if they wanted to take advantage of another opportunity, sponsorship of the home-played World Club Challenge, which it won the right to play in following its championship win. The success kept coming with a Rhinos win in that sponsored match and as a result so did further ideas. The following season saw Bradford Bulls win the Premier League and the decision to continue to sponsor the Carnegie World Club Challenge was made as it gave the University an opportunity to extend awareness for 'widening education participation', a key Leeds Metropolitan objective, in new West Yorkshire target markets. The University then invested in the re-development of the Headingley Stadium and its re-naming to Headingley Carnegie Stadium, which it uses for teaching and research purposes whilst also hosting rugby league, Yorkshire county and test cricket.

Case Study 7.1 provides examples of how the Boston Marathon and several of its sponsors have developed stronger relationships via the consistent use of new ideas.

Cross promotions

Sponsors working with each other and the encouragement of that can also come from either side. It results in sponsorships that more effectively and efficiently meet objectives. For a sponsor this can mean extending target reach through partnerships with fellow sponsors that as a result allow an efficient economy of scale. For rights owners this can produce happier sponsors that then want to grow and renew. Hewlett Packard's partnership with Verizon for the delivery of its Athlete Search System for the Boston Marathon is one such example (see Case Study 7.1). The links can be quite simple but in so doing demonstrate a synergy that extends across the sponsorship. Toshiba, for example took out advertising across a number of target market territories in support of its sponsorship with FIFA and the 2006 World Cup. It pictured its own laptop products alongside adidas footwear and clothing.

From a rights owner's perspective, to grow a sponsorship relationship, the overall and critical aim is to ensure that the sponsor achieves its objectives. The types of objectives that sponsors seek to achieve have been previously identified in Chapter 3, but it is important to understand here that without knowledge of these a rights owner will be unable to begin or then maintain the relationship that is required. It is therefore important to consider potential sponsors objectives at an early stage in the recruitment process and then, in order to develop the relationship post-contract, continuous reassessment and alignment throughout the life cycle are required, including at the end of the sponsorship (Masterman and Wood, 2006).

Summary

In order to maximize sponsorship revenue and/or reduce expenditure using a supply of resources via sponsorship, the ideal approach for rights owners would be to negotiate with all possible sponsors and then decide on a sponsorship programme structure. However, this is an ideal and is an unlikely opportunity as rights owners will often be in negotiation with various sponsors at different times.

A more practical approach involves a process by which most opportunities can be maximized. This involves rights owners undertaking a number of stages. They need to firstly identify their sponsorship inventory. They then research and select (target) potential sponsors, contact them and identify their marketing requirements, and then provide them with a sponsorship solution that meets those requirements if they can. In preparing to return to the potential sponsor with a solution, the rights owner needs to ensure that the sponsorship opportunities they offer meet their client's objectives, provide a function(s) and can demonstrate a good sponsorship fit. The next stage in the process is to consider which sponsorship structure to adopt.

If there is to be more than one sponsor in a sponsorship programme, the rights owner needs to be able to discuss requirements and offer solutions to as many potential sponsors as possible. The aim is to remain flexible and not to decide on a final structure for them all to fit into by finalizing any of these negotiations too early. The rights owner needs to be able to analyse which sponsors in which type of structure will bring the most benefit. If a rights owner is to maximize its opportunities then that flexibility is important because as soon as the first deal is struck the sponsorship programme structure becomes fixed and from that point on should therefore remain unchanged. After the cost versus benefit analysis has been completed a rights owner can feel reasonably confident about which sponsorship structure will work best and can re-approach its potential sponsors to finalize agreements accordingly.

Recruitment should be considered to be a continuous process as there are always sponsorships to either newly create, renew or replace. The recruitment process should therefore be viewed as a long-term job and one that is focused on relationship building. This starts when the research to target appropriate sponsors is first undertaken. The resulting tailored approach can then demonstrate that a rights owner is willing to get to know and develop a relationship and a willingness to commit. This then continues after the sponsor has signed so that the relationship can become stronger by either lasting longer and/or growing. The value of strong relationships is that with commitment on both sides, they can be developed for greater effectiveness which will result in more benefits on both sides; sponsorship revenue for the rights owner and return on investment for the sponsor. Strong relationships also have the potential to be more efficient as it is less costly to develop an existing relationship than it is to replace it.

In order to develop existing sponsor relations, rights owners can look to encourage stronger and trustworthy personal communications with key people at their sponsor organizations and provide them with extra benefits that are over and above what are contracted. They should regularly instigate proposals for growth via new ideas for increasing the commitment of a sponsor and finally, offer sponsors the opportunity to cross promote with each other in order to maximize their linked sponsorship associations.

Tasks and discussion points

- Select an event and identify how sponsors' needs are being met via the development of tailored and bespoke relationships.
- Select an innovative example of sponsorship fit. Demonstrate your understanding of good and bad fit by analysing how the sponsorship might be perceived by the audiences concerned.
- Consider the Shell, O_2 and NatWest sponsorships in Case Studies 7.2–7.4 and propose ways in which the relationships can be further developed with new ideas.
- Figure 7.3 identifies how the IOC has developed its TOP sponsorship programme structure financially. Consider also Case Study 4.7 in Chapter 4 together with your own research.
  - Identify which other structure options the IOC might have considered.
  - Compare and contrast these other options with the current structure and identify the advantages and disadvantages for changing or continuing with the same strategy.
- Consider how Hewlett Packard and Verizon have collaborated in cross-promotions in Case Study 7.1. By researching and identifying other Boston Marathon sponsors for the current year consider what kind of further cross-promotions might be encouraged by the rights owner, the BAA.

References

Article 13 (2006). The Asian diversity success story. www.article13.com (accessed 27 March 2006).

Arts and Business (2001). *Sponsorship manual*, 4th Edition. London: Arts and Business.

Audi (2002). Fourth Phase at the Royal Opera House. www.fourthphase.co.uk/news/press21 (accessed 16 March 2006).

AusSport (2005). Measuring sponsorship's return. AusSport Sponsorship Register, 22 October 2005. www.aussport.com.au/sponsornews/sponsorshipinsights (accessed 25 January 2006).

Baker, W. and Sinkula, J. (1999). The synergistic effect of market orientation and learning orientation. *Journal of the Academy of Marketing Science*, Vol. 27, No. 4, pp. 257–269.

Boston Marathon (2004). www.bostonmarathon.org/BostonMarathon/Sponsors (accessed 7 April 2004).

Boston Marathon (2006). www.bostonmarathon.org/BostonMarathon/Sponsors (accessed 3 March 2006).

CIM (2004). The measure of success: Is sports sponsorship worth the whistle? *The Chartered Institute of Marketing*, April 2004.

CYO (2006) Catholic Youth Organisation, Camp Howard. www.cyocamphoward.org/sponsorship (accessed 19 February 2006).

Duff, M. (2004). Give your sponsors more than they expect. *Sports Business Journal. Street and Smith*, 31 May–6 June, 2004.

Erdogan, Z. and Kitchen, P. (1988). Getting the best out if celebrity endorsement. *Admap*, April 1988.

Farelly, F., Quester, P. and Mavondo, F. (2003). Collaborative communication in sponsor relations. *Corporate Communications: An International Journal*, Vol. 8, No. 2, pp. 128–138.

Field, J. (2002). Ballet: Another advertising hoarding. *Ballet Magazine*, April 2002. www.ballet.co.uk/magazines/yr_02 (accessed 22 February 2006).

Fuel Challenge (2006). www.fuelchallenge.com (accessed 8 March 2006).

Hoek, J. (1998). Sponsorship: An evaluation of management assumptions and practices. *Marketing Bulletin*, Vol. 10, pp.1–10.

HP (2004). HP technology keeps pace for 2004 Boston Marathon. www.hp.com (accessed 6 April 2004).

IOC (1993). The TOP programme. www.globalink.org/tobacco/docs/misc-docs/ioc1 (accessed 23 March 2006).

IOC (2004). *Olympic Review*, May 2004. Lausanne: IOC.

IOC (2006). 2006 Marketing fact file. IOC. www.multimedia.olympic.org/pdf/en_report_344 (accessed 28 March 2006).

Lachowetz, T., McDonald, M., Sutton, W. and Hedrick, D. (2003). Corporate sales activities and the retention of sponsors in the NBA. *Sport Marketing Quarterly*, Vol. 12, No. 1, pp.18–26.

London (2006). www.london.gov.uk/sponsoprship/diwali (accessed 25 January 2006).

Manchester Evening News (2002). Manchester news: Rover's & 163; 2m car is a winner. www.manchesteronline.co.uk/news/s/16/16101_rovers (accessed 16 March 2006).

Masterman, G. (2004). *Strategic sports event management: An international approach*. Oxford: Butterworth-Heinemann.

Masterman, G. and Wood, E. H. (2006). Innovative marketing communications: Strategies for the events industry. Oxford: Elsevier/Butterworth-Heinemann.

Mavondo, F. (2000). Measuring market orientation: Are there differences between business marketers and consumer marketers? *Australian Journal of Management*, Vol. 25, No. 2, pp. 223–245.

Meenaghan, T. (1998). Current developments and future directions in sponsorship. *International Journal of Advertising*, Vol. 17, No. 1, pp. 3–28.

Mintel (2004). *Sponsorship, Special Report*, May 2004.

Mohr, J., Fisher, R. and Nevin, J. (1996). Collaborative communication in inter-firm relationships: Moderating effects of integration and control. *Journal of Marketing*, Vol. 60, No. 3, pp. 103–117.

Mullin, B., Hardy, S. and Sutton, W. (2000). *Sport marketing*. 2nd Edition. Champaign, IL: Human Kinetics.

New York Games (2005). IOC: Johnson and Johnson potential TOP sponsor. www.newyork games.org/news/archives (accessed 23 March 2006).

Redmandarin (2004). *The 2004 Redmandarin European sponsors' survey*. Full Report. In Association with The Sponsorship Research Company. London: Redmandarin Sponsorship Consulting.

Shell (2006). www.shell.com/home/Framework?siteId=media-en&FC2=/media-en (accessed 8 March 2006).

Sleight, S. (1989). *Sponsorship*. Maidenhead: McGraw-Hill.

Sponsorship Consulting (2006). www.sponsorshipconsulting.co.uk/case_natwest (accessed 25 January 2006).

The New York Times (2003). Advertisement: You will always remember your first kiss. USTA. 14, September.

Wilmington Blue Rocks (2006). www.bluerocks.com/06_brochure.pdf (accessed 23 March 2006).

8

Selling sponsorship

The objectives for this chapter are to:

- Review the sponsorship selling process
- Identify the parties involved in the sponsorship selling process
- Evaluate key factors for successful sponsorship sales
- Review the role of sponsorship proposals
- Identify a successful approach for the development of sponsorship proposals

Bellhaven Best and the Wickerman Festival
A poster for the Bellhaven Best sponsored Wickerman Festival is displayed in the field where
the event takes place in East Kirkcarswell, Scotland

Introduction

Chapter 7 considered the approach required for the successful development of sponsorship programmes. The development of a sponsorship programme is intrinsically linked with the recruitment of individual sponsors and so rights owners are constantly juggling separate negotiations, each at different stages of completion, whilst determining their sponsorship programme structure. This sponsorship programme development process is now presented here again in more detail in order to demonstrate how individual sponsorships are developed (see Figure 8.1).

Stage three of this process, the 'Approach' is concerned with the first and subsequent meetings that are required in order to identify the needs of a potential sponsor. This is followed by the provision of sponsorship solutions (stage four) that are designed to meet those needs. The key factors for this are to meet a sponsor's identified objectives, provide them with functions within the sponsorship programme and demonstrate why and how they are a good fit with the rights owner, its programme and other sponsors. At these two stages there are a number of important aspects that need identification and discussion in order to examine how individual sponsors are recruited and particularly how sponsorship is sold. These factors are identified and discussed in this chapter and with the premise that whether a sponsor is recruited for a fee and/or in-kind for goods and services, the process is nevertheless a 'sale'.

---

1. **Inventory**
   Identification of all assets that may be used in the sponsorship programme

2. **Targeting**
   Targeting individual potential sponsors
   > Step 2.1: Identify target audiences
   > Step 2.2: Matching organizational target markets

3. **Approach**
   Approaching individual sponsors separately

4. **Sponsorship solutions**
   Providing solutions and opportunities for individual sponsors to fit into the sponsorship programme, by:
   > a. Meeting objectives
   > b. Providing function
   > c. Demonstrating 'fit'

5. **Programme structure development**
   Identifying where and how individual sponsors fit in the sponsorship programme

6. **Complete sponsorship negotiations**
   Conclude deals with individual sponsors

7. **Continuous relationship building**
   Build relationships with individual sponsors and assist in developing inter-relationships between sponsors

---

Figure 8.1 Sponsorship Programme Development Process

Use of intermediaries

Principally there are two parties involved in a sponsorship, the rights owner and the sponsor they provide rights to. Rights owners can directly recruit and sell their own sponsorships and many experienced organizations have marketing, even sponsorship departments with specialists for conducting this work. The extent of the human resources that are put in place to accomplish this depends on the scale of sponsorship operation. Whilst smaller operations might involve even dedicated or responsible executives, maybe with administrational support, a more complex sponsorship programme will require various tiers of executives and management.

In many cases sponsorship revenue is a lesser priority for rights owners and the role of sponsorship recruitment is therefore managed by executives, and non-executives, that have other responsibilities. For example, the Tate Modern arts organization manages sponsorship through a New Business Manager, the UK Premiership Rugby Union Club, Newcastle Falcons do it through two Business Development Executives and Leeds Grand Theatre uses a Head of Marketing supported by a Marketing Officer. Each of these personnel has other responsibilities. A more sophisticated example and one that demonstrates the complexities of an international and multi-tiered sponsorship programme, is provided by the London Organizing Committee for the 2012 Olympic Games (LOCOG) which was allowed to commence its sponsorship recruitment from September 2006. For the launch of that operation, the organization employed both a Director of Commercial Negotiations and a Marketing and Sponsorship Director. The Commercial Department employed several commercial managers with responsibilities for financial valuation and research to cover specific industry sectors whilst the Marketing and Sponsorship Department recruited various account managers. There were two points of focus for this human resources strategy, on the one hand there was sponsor and supplier research, valuation, recruitment and contracting and on the other relationship development and implementation.

Sponsors have also become increasingly sophisticated with the employment of sponsorship specialists and the creation of departments, although this has not always been the case and even now there are examples of sponsors with little in-house capacity. Those sponsors that have developed expertise however, have helped to professionalize the industry. There are particular industry sectors that have become very competitive through sponsorship activity and on an international scale and as a consequence, dedicated sponsorship teams have been created and developed over a number of years. For example, Barclaycard and Mastercard, Coca-Cola and PepsiCo and Nike, adidas, Puma and Reebok have significant in-house sponsorship teams. The activities at each of these organizations now involves executives that manage event and endorsement activities, across sport, art, music and the community, and in separate national as well global initiatives through networks of national and regional offices.

Intermediaries can also be used in an outsourced attempt to bring in expertise in order to enhance the chances of sponsorship success. This can be implemented by either main party. Rights owners for example, can appoint agents to recruit some or all of their sponsors, whilst sponsors can appoint agents to find them appropriate sponsorship solutions, either by identifying existing opportunities or by creating new bespoke sponsorships. Indeed the global activities of the credit card, soft drinks and sports organizations above, despite the scale of their sponsorship interests, all use intermediary agencies, and often use combinations of agencies for different aspects of sponsorship management for national and international activity.

Agents now come in all shapes and sizes. They can be individual consultants or larger multi-faceted services and they can specialize in working with rights owners, sponsors or both by offering a 'full service'.

Working with rights owners

Rights owners can appoint an agency to wholly manage their sponsorship programmes or to solely recruit to specific briefs, to particular sponsorship opportunities for example. The scale and nature of the arrangement depends on the profile and value of the sponsorship programme. For example, those rights owners with high-profile sponsorship opportunities may be in a powerful position to receive proposals from contending agencies and appoint the one that brings the best value. The value can be in the expertise offered for sponsorship sales and/or post-sales management. Rights owners may ask interested agencies to bid. Powerful sports rights owners such as FIFA have put their sponsorship recruitment out to tender and received bids from agencies. In these cases the agency concerned needs to bid a competitive amount of guaranteed revenue for the rights owner whilst still ensuring their own profit margin. International Management Group (IMG) has made a success of this approach and achieved significant sponsorship programmes for, amongst others, the Association of Tennis Professionals (ATP) Tour and the US and European Golf Tours. There have been failures however, with ISL for example, going bankrupt in 2001 and not producing its contracted television revenues to FIFA for the 2002 and 2006 World Cups or fulfilling its 10 year $1.2 billion marketing agreement with the ATP Tour (O'Connell and Goodman, 2002). As with all bidding processes, there is a fine line between realistic and non-realistic revenue guarantees.

Working with sponsors

Sponsors can also appoint agencies to work to find them suitable marketing solutions. This can be via marketing or sponsorship-dedicated consultants or larger organizations. As indicated above, even higher profile sponsors with numbers of dedicated executives may still outsource in this way.

The advantages of working with consultants and agencies are that they can provide specialist knowledge and expertise that cannot be supplied in-house by either a rights owner or a sponsor. A full service agency may also be able to sell a sponsorship on behalf of a client rights owner to one of its existing client sponsors. For a price, the agency may not only recruit sponsors, but also manage them throughout the relationship in its contract for such with a rights owner. Generally speaking an agency can bid with guaranteed revenue for a rights owner, work to a fixed fee as agreed with the rights owner or work to a percentage of revenue results. A sponsor will work with agencies mainly on a fixed fee basis where the agency will identify, negotiate and manage the sponsorship for the sponsor.

There are disadvantages for both sponsors and rights owners in working with agencies. An agency's failure to provide guaranteed revenue for a rights owner is one. The main issues though concern the conflicting interests that may arise. A rights owner for example, may be one of several clients of an agency and as such will need to ensure that their representation receives sufficient attention and focus. It is the same for sponsors. In more complex arrangements where an agency represents sponsors and rights owners there are also potential conflicts of interests, and as such rights owners and sponsors may insist on single representation. There are also agencies that only work as consultants with one side of a sponsorship arrangement.

The importance of personal contact

Building relationships in the sponsorship programme development process is a key success factor and it begins at the very earliest stages of recruitment and essentially even before contact is made with a potential sponsor. For example, knowledge of a potential sponsor, gained via comprehensive research, is likely to be a more successful route to convincing them to buy in. The building of trust and commitment are key to longer-term relationships (Farelly et al., 2003) and as these are attained via personal communications, it is important to reiterate the importance of such in the sponsorship sales process. The resulting organizational relationships that develop as a result of sponsorship negotiations are based on the personal interactions of the individuals on both sides. Therefore, a rights owner that takes an interest in its counterparts at the sponsoring organization will help develop personal relationships that will achieve a sale and in turn will help grow the relationship (Duff, 2004).

Role of sponsorship proposals

There is no way around it, a sponsorship proposal is required. There have been cases when these have been minimal and on occasions, even limited to verbal propositions, but essentially, a sponsorship proposal provides a focus for the selling process and ultimately forms the basis of any eventual agreement. As such, it plays an important role in the sponsorship selling process.

There is no absolute need for a proposal to be in hardcopy form. It can be presented electronically and never printed off. However, it is critical that whatever the format of presentation, the proposal needs to provide a record that can be referred to. A verbal proposition does not achieve this. Any part of a negotiation that is only verbally executed does not achieve this. Even when there may be a number of proposals for one sponsorship that have been made, each one must be available as a record in order to track changes and provide a focus for negotiation.

There may be several stages of negotiation that require a number of proposals to be prepared.

Initial proposal: 'To create interest'

This might be a fairly generic presentation of the entity that is to be sponsored. It will be descriptive of the history, background, successes, programme, people, locations, venues and existing sponsors involved.

It can be used at the first meeting or possibly to accompany any targeted approach but only as a means of support. Too often in the past and also even now, bland generic proposals are sent out, even to named recipients, instead of initiating personal contact. Proposals that are used as the sole recruitment tool are ineffective even at initiating interest. On the other hand, leaving a proposal that contains general descriptions and broad sponsorship parameters following initial personal contact, by whatever means, is a record for the potential sponsor to refer to and hopefully enthuse over.

Draft sponsorship solution: 'To provide sets of rights but without price'

There may be several versions that propose solutions and they may become more detailed as negotiations progress. It is not essential for a rights owner to provide a final, full and complete solution at the first attempt. In fact by not applying any prices, but still demonstrating an understanding of the potential sponsor's needs, a number of proposals can be used to actually progress the negotiation through to conclusion.

By not applying prices until the final stage, a rights owner is essentially delimiting its opportunities for maximizing its revenue potential. By applying price too soon, a rights owner can be left with no way to increase price and when a number of negotiations are underway, it is important to maintain as many options for achieving overall sponsorship revenue targets as possible.

Sponsorship solution: 'To provide sets of rights, that can be valued easily'

The ultimate proposal needs to contain sufficient detail for the potential sponsor to be able to value what is on offer. This does involve an overall price and where appropriate prices for various elements that may be taken as options.

It is essential that the sponsorship solution contains all the details that are required in order for the potential sponsor to quantify the offer. Full descriptions of the rights, with any appropriate supporting data, are therefore required. Full details of all potential parts of media exposure for the sponsor are required and the level of detail needs to be comprehensive so that sizes, quantities, quality and colours are specific. The detail required is as finite as is needed to place a monetary value on the rights on offer. Only this way can a potential sponsor quantify that offer and then determine whether it is good value or not and consequently identify what their potential return on investment will be.

The valuation of a sponsorship proposal is dependent on the provision of accurate and comprehensive supporting evidence. Detailed schedules for media activity, promotion campaigns and public relations together with specifications for sign-age, corporate hospitality and tickets in particular are required. A common error for example, is to be too vague regarding media exposure. Stating that an event communications campaign 'will be' implemented or that television coverage 'will be' via a particular broadcaster, but without providing details of the schedules involved, is not sufficient enough information for a potential sponsor to place a value on the offer. This is why it is important to secure media partners and such schedules beforehand, as explained in Chapter 6. Similarly, proposals that contain bland offers of a 'VIP box for ten', '100 tickets' or courtside signage are insufficient. Details on how many courtside signs, at what size, in what locations and using whose artwork at whose expense is the level of specification that is required.

Price

Schedules and specifications are fundamental requirements, but the proposal also needs to explicitly explain where the value is in taking the sponsorship. The potential sponsor is looking to compare this communication solution with others and so the rights owner is in competition with other rights owners and also sell-ers of other communications options. Therefore, researching and providing evi-dence that demonstrates value for money and why a return on investment can be achieved is critical.

It is difficult to provide one specific route for rights owners to follow when it comes to pricing a sponsorship. Every sponsorship sales proposition is unique and there is no exact science in determining prices for sponsorships. However, there is a multi-faceted approach that can be used in order to more successfully go about this task. There is no substitute for sponsorship sales experience and market knowledge, but for rights owners that are new to market, an approach that uses a number of methods, in an attempt to triangulate, is more effective than using any one individual method. The fundamental elements to this approach are the determination of all costs, the amount of sponsorship-in-kind involved, the use of market knowledge, the value placed on the offering by the sponsor itself and media equivalency. These key elements are now discussed one by one.

Costs

There are those commentators that suggest that, once costs have been calculated, a minimum 'profit margin' should then be added. A margin of 100 per cent (Bowdin et al., 2006; Grey and Skildum-Reid, 1999) though is too arbitrary. Why not 99 or 101 per cent? Determining a price that exceeds all the costs that are involved is essential, unless there is a loss-leader strategy that includes increased prices over a period and the initial loss can be borne for a longer-term gain. It might appear to be fairly clear to most that the determination of costs should be done prior to the presentation of a priced proposal. However, there are cases where this is not a common practice.

The price is dependent on the finer detail of the deal, as referred to above. For example, if it is not clearly stated that the sponsor provides the artwork for signage

at its cost, then it can likely fall to the rights owner to pick up that cost. If this
~~t identified until after a proposal has been presented, then the 'full-costing'
~~~~ is required has not been achieved. Forethought and thorough preparation of
this cost are essential because costs such as these may not be that clear at the outset. The sponsor in this case, for example may deliver the fully finished signage,
but it may come on a day too late for the rights owner to assemble or place it.
Further costs in ensuring that happens, with a newly contracted implementation
team may be necessary.

There are costs in the sponsorship that the rights owner will not be able to
accurately identify so easily. For example, the cost of supplying the indeterminable amount of media exposure the sponsorship might achieve on television,
radio or in the press (see 'equivalency' below), the provision of space on the concourse for the sponsor, even the cost of supplying tickets when they might not
have been sold. However, these cost elements need to be identified before an
amount of profit can be added in order to set the price.

Rather than being guided by an inflexible rule of thumb, such as 'plus 100 per
cent', the determination of the extent of the profit margin, the amount that is
added to the full costs, will require consideration of the other elements that form
this multi-faceted approach for sponsorship pricing.

Sponsorship-in-kind

Linked to the calculation of total costs is the identification of the amount of the
deal that is to be 'in-kind'. The general principal behind sponsorship-in-kind is
that it is agreed at an amount of value that is provided on both sides so that a
sponsor will supply a range of services or goods to the same value as the rights
owner's supply of sponsorship benefits, dollar for dollar, pound for pound. In
some cases it is difficult to put a cost and therefore a price on certain aspects of
sponsorship-in-kind as indicated above, and it is then that either party might like
to try to negotiate an upper hand in the deal. For example, a rights owner may
decide to cost all those elements of the package that have a price (tickets, advertising, hospitality) at face value. If they do, they should be aware that if they then
add on a further profit margin it is open to challenging negotiations from a sponsor that can easily identify those elements of the price. On the other hand, the
provision of services, that a sponsor might not ordinarily sell, will also require
careful pricing. In these circumstances market knowledge of prices for similar
services is required.

Putting a value on a service or a product on either side of the deal is always
going to be dependent on what the other party would or is willing to pay for it.
The guide for sponsorship-in-kind is to agree on a value that can be at cost or at
selling price, but whichever it is, it is advisable for it to be the same for both parties otherwise negotiations can become protracted. If there is also a sponsorship
fee in addition to the sponsorship-in-kind then this element of the overall price
needs to be determined separately by the rights owner, and similarly treated in
value estimation by the prospective sponsor.

There is one further consideration on the part of the rights owner here. One
advantage of sponsorship-in-kind is that it allows sponsors to come in with smaller
or no cash payments and therefore creates a sponsorship that can be easier to sell.

Another advantage is that it allows a rights owner to receive critical services or goods that it otherwise would have spent cash on attaining. Events in particular have found sponsorship-in-kind to be beneficial in this way. There is though a danger in giving away too much value in the deal. If the rights owner requires services/goods to a certain value, say telecommunications equipment for example, then they may secure that from such a provider and give them a range of sponsorship benefits to the same value in return. This would be of benefit to both parties and an equitable arrangement. However, if the rights owner budgets to spend a certain amount on such but then agrees to a larger provision of telecommunications services/goods to improve its event still further, the range of benefits given in return will have a value that is beyond that budgeted amount. The rights owner therefore needs to be aware that this may then limit the overall revenue it might receive for those extra benefits (Masterman, 2004).

Market knowledge

Knowledge of other sponsorships, how much they cost and sell for, is an important factor for both rights owners and sponsors. The value of experience in setting prices and buying sponsorships can therefore be critical. This is why rights owners and sponsors alike are increasingly employing and/or outsourcing the expertise they require and why it is an important consideration for those that are freshly moving into using sponsorship.

Whether an organization (rights owner or sponsor) is new to sponsorship or not, there is a requirement to gain and use market knowledge consistently and continuously in order to be current. Trade associations, periodicals and mass media can and do now provide a wealth of information on how a sponsorship has been negotiated, even on how negotiations are progressing, prices and all. Such information is important for staying current. *Sports Business Journal* in the USA, Marketing Week in the UK and Sportbusiness.com are all regular and reliable sources. The proviso is that this is historical information, even if it is news that day.

Value to the sponsor

The rights owner's knowledge of market prices may be useful, but a sponsor places its own valuation on the sponsorship proposition and so the price that is set is dependent on what that individual sponsor will pay, not what they might pay or what a rights owner wants them to pay. This is why it is so important to start building a relationship with a sponsor, even as early as from the initial tentative talks with them. Getting to know what they are prepared to pay, and for what kind of value in return, is exactly what the rights owner has to glean prior to preparing the final sponsorship solution. Presenting a potential sponsor with a price that is way beyond what they have paid for any previous sponsorship may appear to be a barrier (Grey and Skildum-Reid, 1999), but the closer the relationship and the greater the knowledge of what the sponsor wants, the greater the chances of the rights owner being able to demonstrate value and return on investment.

This becomes paramount when it comes to assessing what a potential sponsor is going to spend on exploiting its sponsorship, if it takes it. This is the extra and supporting spend on communications that the sponsor undertakes, and because it is not the rights owners direct concern, the exact amount of additional spend, indeed intended spend, is always going to be difficult to identify. This knowledge and understanding is important however. If a sponsorship is priced too close to the prices of the other communications options the potential sponsor has at its disposal, then there is little room to add exploitation spend and then show value over those other options. It is therefore important to know what other options there are and at what prices they are available.

Media equivalency

The rapid rise in the use of sponsorship, particularly sports sponsorship, was linked to a lack of understanding of what it was and why it worked. As advertising became increasingly more expensive throughout the 1970s and 1980s, marketers turned to sponsorship solutions. Sponsorship was, and still is in many cases, offered as a cheaper option by rights owners because of the difficulty in showing return on investment.

In an attempt to show value, sponsorship media exposure is calculated using the 'equivalent' prices that might have been paid had that media been purchased separately. So any broadcast airtime is counted up in seconds and print exposure in column inches/pages so that a comparison can be made. For example, all the seconds a title sponsor's name/logo are seen or heard by television viewers are counted up and totalled. A price for how much that amount of time of advertising with that media is then identified. In order to show value, it can then be demonstrated that the sponsorship can achieve, or has achieved, that amount of media time in addition to the further value of the other benefits the package has to offer. If the price of the sponsorship is less than the cost of the equivalent media, then the price also represents superior value.

The use of 'equivalent media value' (EMV, also referred to as 'equivalent advertising costs' (EAC)) as a calculation in this way became, and remains, an overused method by which to demonstrate value. For many rights owners and agencies it has become the predominant way to demonstrate value in both selling and evaluating sponsorship. However, the method is now being increasingly discredited, in particular by sponsors who are far from convinced of its accuracy. It is not that there is no merit at all in using EMV, there is, but it needs to be recognized for what it is. Firstly, because actual media space is not being bought, it is never possible to get an absolutely accurate price for what that space might actually have cost. In many cases advertising rate-card prices are used, and yet in industry, rate-card prices are seldom the final prices that are paid. Secondly, the communication points of exposure that are achieved in the media via a sponsorship are often not comparable with advertising because they are not bought space. The method does not therefore compare like with like (Masterman and Wood, 2006). Sponsors have begun to 'discount' the offer they receive via this method of calculation, in other words, assuming that the value is less than what it is claimed to be by reducing it by a percentage. This is no more scientific, however, as sponsors are using there own individual and subjective percentage of discount. The difficulties of using EMV are covered in more detail in Chapter 11.

The sole use of EMV to calculate sponsorship prices is not an accurate or reliable approach but it has yet to be replaced by any more objective methods. The merit in considering equivalency in determining price then, is where it can be used alongside the other elements in this multi-faceted approach in order to arrive at an appropriate price.

Presentation

There are a number of general guidelines that need to be observed when it comes to the preparation of proposals. Whatever the format (hard or electronic copies) the proposal should unfold as a narrative in order to build the picture and the opportunity. Figure 8.2 contains general guidelines and also a sample generic sponsorship proposal.

Whilst any one of the illustrated pages may be used, and in the order they appear, it is for the individual rights owner to determine which are appropriate. The rationale for each page is as follows.

General guidelines:

- Use professional presentation – for example, corporate proposal cover boards for front and back, audio-visual graphics, bespoke electronic designed templates
- Identify which pages are required for any one stage of the relationship with the potential sponsor – not all of the generic pages (one to ten) below may be required
- Use one page per topic where possible so that each page has one main title – use an appendix if schedules and detail are extensive
- Use pictures/graphics to show the exact nature of key opportunities, but ensure they are fully explained
- Different stages of the relationship may require the use of different tones – for example, 'will be implemented', 'are available', 'to be discussed', 'as agreed'
- Do not use an executive summary that detracts from the impact of the proposal – the proposal should unfold and build page by page
- Only use indexes and contents pages when there is an extensive use of pages and detail
- Use page numbers, these will make referencing easier in negotiations
- Use colour and mono, size of fonts and graphics for effect but so that the content is highlighted rather than diluted or obscured
- Only insert and use logos or the potential sponsor's marks with their agreement
- Get colleagues to edit and scrutinize the proposal for a flawless presentation

The following sample proposal pages do not contain detail and are intended to represent the key elements only. A rights owner (The ATP Tour) and potential sponsor (Nabisco) have been used for illustrative purposes only.

Figure 8.2 (Continued)

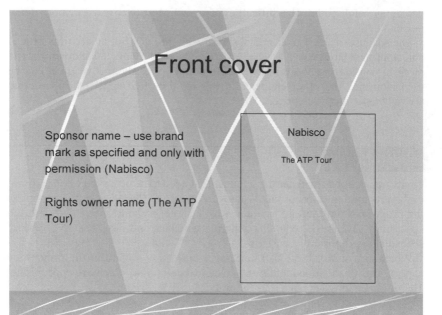

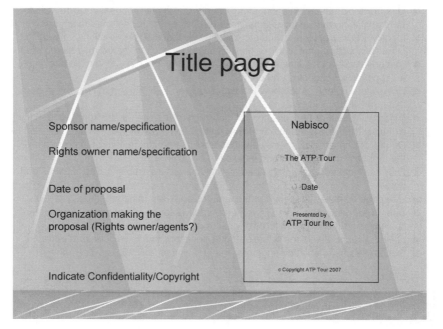

Figure 8.2 (Continued)

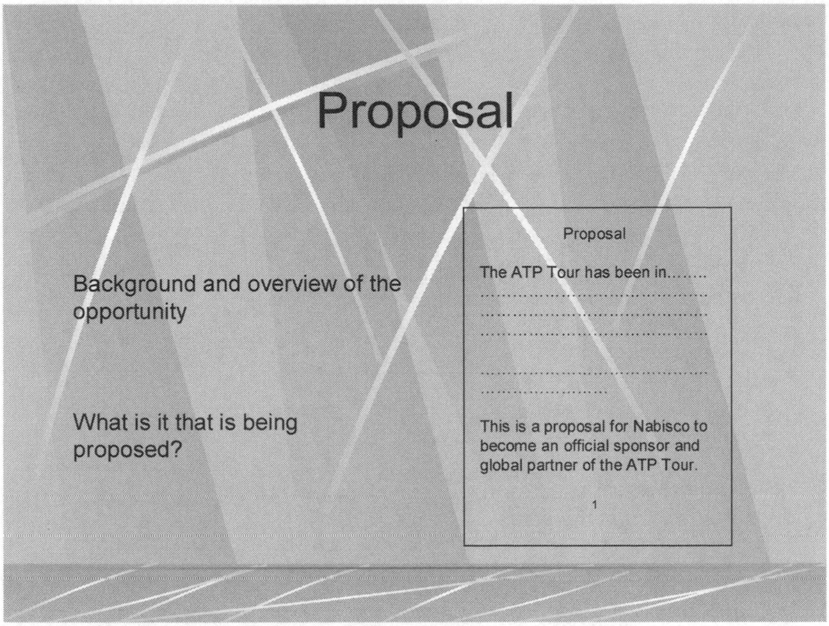

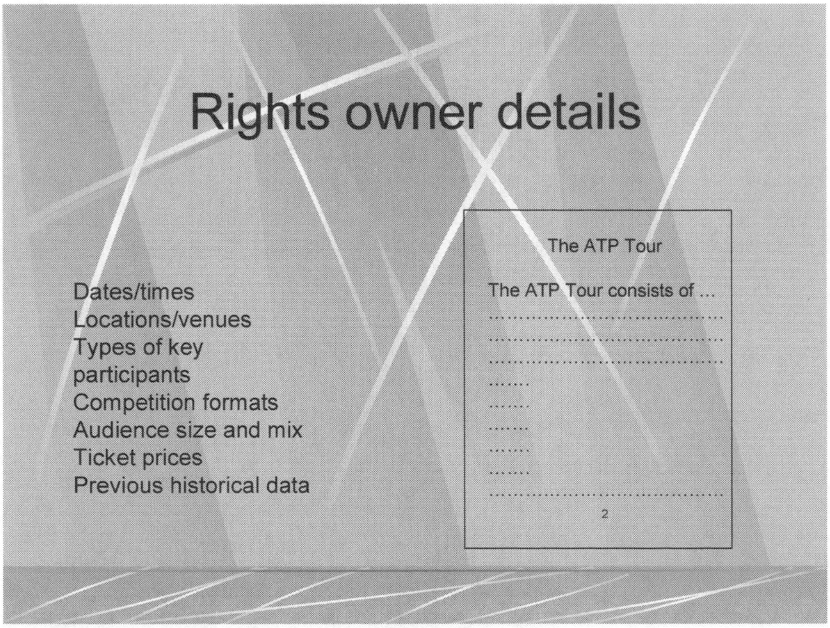

Figure 8.2 (Continued)

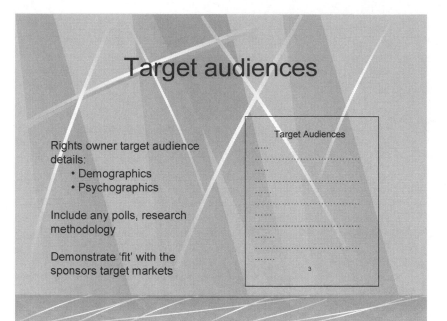

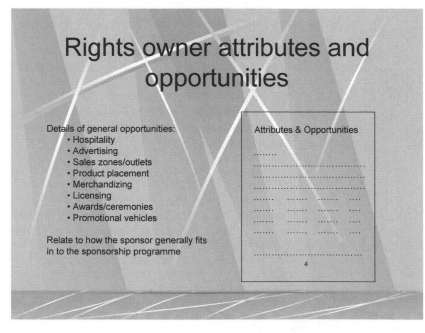

Figure 8.2 (Continued)

Marketing schedule

Rights owner marketing activity:
- Television
- Radio
- Newspapers
- Magazines
- Internet
- Direct mail
- PR

Include media partner details

Include any agencies involved

Communications Schedule

5

Partners

Details of the role played
by any third parties: agencies,
event management
organizations, linked
bodies, authorities

Partners

Sponsorship Agency

6

Figure 8.2 (Continued)

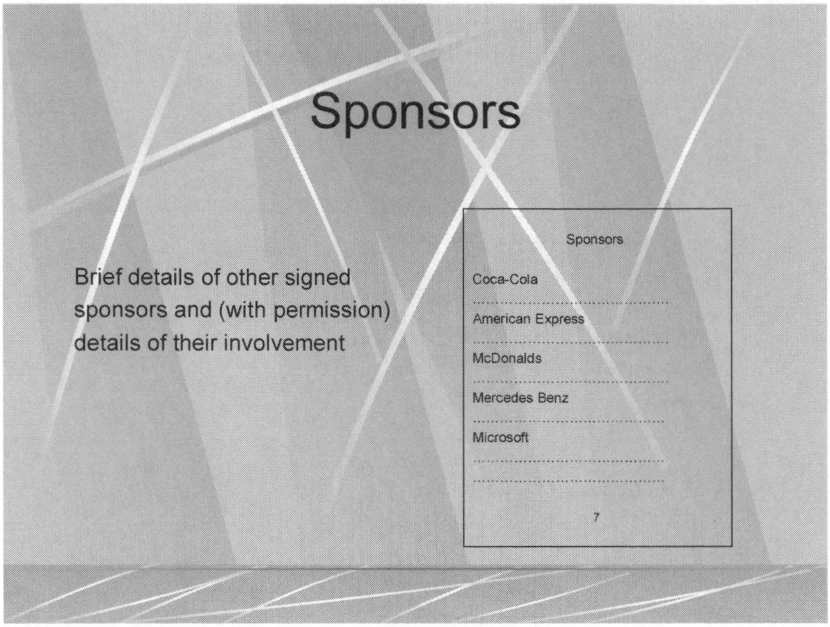

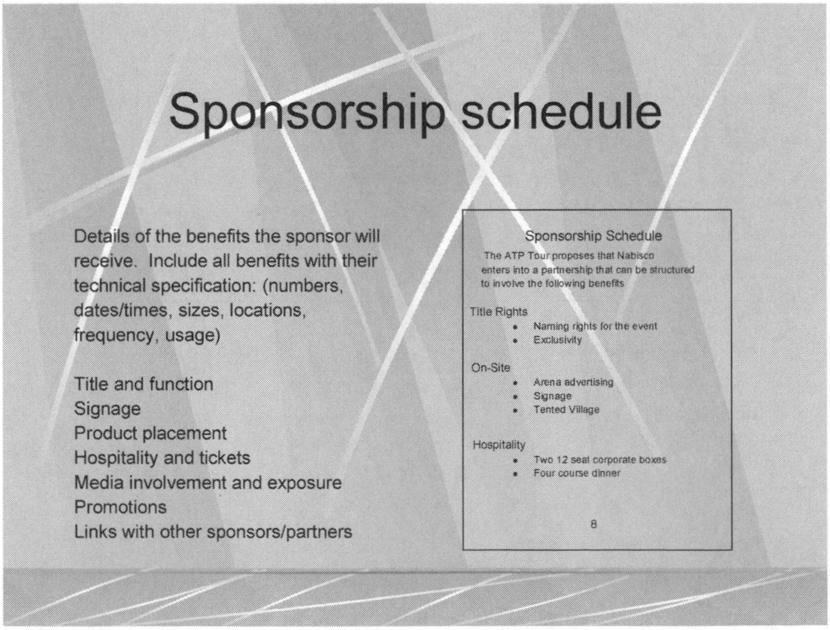

Figure 8.2 (Continued)

Finance/deal

Details of the sponsor's investment

Fees in appropriate currency
and/or details of:
Services/product provided in-kind

Payment schedule; include details of
instalments and timings

Only include finance details following
the thorough establishment of
sponsor's needs, this depends on the stage
of the relationship!

Renewal options

Investment

Nabisco's investment for this
opportunity will be:

- $
- Payment Details
- Product supply
- Service supply
- Renewal Options

9

Evaluation

Details on how the rights owner intends to
evaluate its sponsorship programme

Details of how this evaluation will benefit the
sponsor

Evaluation

Sponsorship evaluation will be
undertaken as follows:

10

Figure 8.2 (Continued)

Figure 8.2 Sponsorship Proposals

Front cover

This contains the names of the potential sponsor and the rights owner. It may also refer to the title, nature or categorization of the relationship that is proposed. So the rights owner might be the ATP Tour, the potential sponsor, Nabisco, and the cover might also carry 'Title Sponsor' or 'Founding Partner'. If the rights owner is directly making the approach and the nature of the attributes on offer are self-explanatory, the cover might also carry the name of the sponsor and an event title, for example, 'The ATP Tour'. In essence though, this is a cover that titillates and is entirely brief.

Title page

The title page can repeat the names used on the front cover, and as such can do that so that they are also located in exactly the same positions on the next page. A date for the proposal, the name of who is writing the proposal and any copyrights are added. Copyrights can also be applied page by page if appropriate.

A date is required as this may be one of several proposals made. The name of the writer might be an in-house executive, and as such their contact details are required here. If there is an author agency involved, then this is the point where their details are supplied. Further information on the agency appears on the 'partners' page/section. If several authors are involved it is usual for the leader of that group to be named, but if the leader changes for whatever reason, and there are further proposals, the new leader's name should be used. All of this information is required so that when there is more than one proposal and/or there are long periods involved, easy references can be made in negotiations and changes can be tracked.

Proposal

It is important to identify what the intent of the proposal is. The stage of the relationship, whether it is an initial or a final and priced proposal that is on offer, should be made apparent. If there is a title involved or if the relationship can be categorized in any way it should also be explicit here. For example, let title sponsors know that this is a sponsorship proposal for a 'title sponsorship'. If the proposal is for the sponsor to associate with an event as one of six partners then this too should be clear.

This is achieved with an opening gambit that introduces the rights owner, the nature of its business and the reasons why it is approaching the sponsor. It is more of a narrative than a long drawn or sub-sectioned piece.

Rights owner details

This is an opportunity to provide more detail on the rights owner and in particular the nature of the offer. For example, if it involves sponsorship of an individual person then there will be a brief historical background that features in particular recent successes and future potential. Similarly, if the sponsorship rights are event focused, there will be a potted history that highlights previous winners, types of audience, venues, dates and media interest in order to show how the event has developed in to what it is. Details of what is intended of it for the future then follow. This can be a mixture of narrative and bulleted detail with the use of sub-headings.

Target audiences

The opportunity here is to introduce why an approach is being made to the sponsor in question. This is where details and analysis of the rights owner's target audiences are provided and as data is required, the presentation needs to be succinct and in an easily read format that will likely use sub-headings. It is important that referenced research is used wherever possible as well as detail of the methodology used in any collection of primary data in order to add further credibility. The aim of this page/section is to provide a profile of the target audience(s) and to demonstrate how this matches those of the sponsor. Without telling the sponsor what the profile of its own target audiences(s) is (they already know), there should be a demonstration of implied matches. This is implicitly and explicitly indicating 'sponsorship fit'.

Rights owner attributes and opportunities

This page/section carries sufficient but succinct details of all the rights owner's attributes and the sponsorship opportunities that rights owner has as a whole. The aim is to present a full picture of the sponsorship programme. The sponsorship schedule page/section which follows later is more specific to the sponsor and provides precise details of the attributes and opportunities that are being proposed as sponsorship rights. The benefit of providing some details of the more generic attributes and opportunities here is so that the sponsor can see what is not included as part of their proposed rights. This is critical information for them as they can make judgements on the value of what is on offer to them, identify what is potentially on offer to other sponsors and decide on whether to ask to include some of these other elements in their proposed rights. This is why it is important not to price a sponsorship too soon. There may be more that can be included in the deal.

This page/section can also be used to generally relate to how the sponsor fits in to the programme as a whole.

Marketing schedule

Details of the rights owner's marketing schedule could be included in the previous page/section. They are in effect attributes and opportunities. However, if the marketing programme and associated media schedules are extensive then it is important to create a separate page/section here so that appropriate levels of detail can be included.

This is where specific television, radio and other mass media activity should be included. Indicating only that a 'one hour highlights programme' will be broadcast after the event is clearly insufficient detail as the channels, dates and times that are involved are essential information if a sponsor is going to be able to put a value on the benefits that are on offer. If this is an initial proposal and all that is known at this stage is that negotiations with media suppliers are in progress, then it should be understood that a price cannot be proposed as the value can still not be determined.

Mass media exposure details can be important, but it is also important to include details of all the rights owner's marketing activity. In particular schedules for any managed publicity, direct mailing and promotions are all needed in order for a value to be placed on the offer.

Partners

It may be that the proposal is relatively straightforward in that no other parties are involved in the opportunity. In which case there is no need for this page/section. However, even local events may have an association with the local authority or accrediting bodies. More complex and higher profile sponsorship opportunities can involve various partners that are required in order to deliver the benefits that are on offer. For example, Sports or Arts Governing Bodies, third-party agencies involved in the selling process, associated public sector agencies (for tourism or enterprise) and even national government. If this is the case then the details of these arrangements are required here as the sponsor needs to understand the credibility of the offer.

Sponsors

Similarly, the sponsor needs to know which other sponsors are involved. They will need to determine if they can firstly sit alongside other sponsors and also identify if it can work with them in order to exploit their sponsorship. Brief details of the other sponsors' arrangements can be useful here, but permission to release them in this way will be required from the sponsors concerned.

Sponsorship schedule

This page/section contains a schedule of the proposed rights. It is not a repetition of the previous attributes and opportunities page/section as it provides precise specifications and is a bundle of benefits that is designed, as a whole, in order to demonstrate a specific 'sponsorship fit'. Each area of rights is provided in full detail, including all appropriate specifications (quantities, qualities, sizes, colours, locations, timings, constructions, delivery/collection). Which party provides what, where and when should be made plainly clear.

Finance/deal

This is one of those pages that may not always be in every proposal. A final stage sponsorship solution will contain a page with the details of the exchange. This might be a cash price, the extent and details of sponsorship-in-kind, or both. In addition there may be a requirement for fees and/or sponsorship-in-kind to be supplied in instalments and so details of the dates/deadlines and for what identified amounts may also be important detail at this stage. The alternative is to supply this sort of information in the resulting contract but inclusion here may be cheaper. It may also be necessary for the rights owner to identify in what currency the payments have to be made, how these amounts are to be received (bank draft, direct deposit) and where they are to be made (banking details). Depending on the nature of the deal, and the parties involved, it may also be relevant to identify any amounts that are to be received by any agencies for transparency purposes.

This, or another separate page, may be the appropriate place to identify any further options that are available to the sponsor. For example, this may be a proposal for a 1-year deal but with options for renewal for two further years. The deadlines for opting in and the details for the further exchanges therefore need to be identified.

Evaluation

This is an opportunity to map out the methods by which the rights owner will evaluate the sponsorship and how and when this information will be given to the sponsor. If this involves a cost then it is another consideration for the rights owner's pricing process. The production of evaluation for the sponsor is an indication of the extent to which the rights owner is committed, how far it will go to develop the relationship and demonstrate a return on investment. For sponsorship generally, this practice will also demonstrate the critical importance of evaluation.

Back cover

The back cover can carry the contact details of the author of the proposal (address, telephone and website) but otherwise only serves as an end piece.

Contracting

The sponsorship proposal forms an important part of the contracting process. In essence it provides important 'heads of agreement' and therefore the extent of the rights that need to be included in any contract between rights owners and sponsor.

As it is the rights owner that is doing the selling, it is they that need to prepare the sponsorship agreement. It is clearly in their best interests to form a contract for this purpose in order to protect their interests and whilst legal costs can be an additional expenditure, they may be budgeted for and therefore costed in at the determination of the sponsorship price by the rights owner.

If a sponsorship is multi-national in its nature, a number of legal representations may be required to consider aspects of law and finance, country by country.

Summary

The selling of a sponsorship starts at the very first stage of the sponsorship programme development process and continues throughout. Whilst, the preparatory stages of creating an inventory and researching for targeting are critical elements to a recruitment of the right sponsor, even in the latter stages after an initial sponsorship has been sold, there is work to do to get that sponsor to develop the relationship and opt for a renewal. The actual sale of a sponsorship though is ostensibly implemented at stages two and three where there is an approach to a sponsor and then the provision of a sponsorship solution that meets that sponsors needs. At these stages there are a number of factors that require understanding and consideration.

What expertise is required? Whilst there is an increasing employment of sponsorship expertise in-house, by both rights owners and sponsors, there is also a continued use of intermediaries to not just aid in the selling process but also maintain and manage the sponsorship once sold. The key consideration for rights owner or sponsor, is how much focus and attention an intermediary gives when it also represents other clients.

What role do individuals play? Trust and commitment are key elements to the selling and then the development of successful sponsorships, and as personal communications are required in order to gain trust and then commitment, it is clear that individual executives, whether they are in or out-of house, play an integral part.

What role does a sponsorship proposal play? A sponsorship cannot be sold without a proposal, although in an increasingly innovative technological world, there are a number of different forms that a proposal might take. Whilst one proposal might suffice, any number may be required and it is important to hold back pricing for a proposal that contains a final solution.

At what price should a sponsorship be set and at what price one bought? Both principal parties need to know. Without any current unquestionable and objective methods available, a rights owner needs to adopt a multi-faceted approach that combines a number of methods. By firstly identifying full costs, including those for any sponsorship-in-kind, a profit margin can be determined via a combination of a continuous use of market knowledge, an understanding of what any one sponsor will value a sponsorship at and the determination of media equivalency. It is important though that the limitations of media equivalency methods are fully understood.

How important is presentation? If proposals are an essential element of the sales process, then presentation of the right information at the right time is also important. Proposals can be presented at various stages of the sales process, not just to seal the deal but also to create initial interest and to offer draft solutions. A demonstrable understanding of what the sponsor may require in their final sponsorship solution is eventually required but ensuring that that is fully represented in the proposal, that the details are comprehensively considered and presented, is also essential. The exact nature of the sponsorship, how it will be implemented and paid for is required so that a final proposal can contain the necessary heads of agreement and a contract can follow.

Tasks and discussion points

■ Research and produce three separate and at least nationally significant proposals for initial approaches to each of the following brands:
  – Sprite (Beverage)
  – T-Mobile (Communications)
  – Bang & Olufsen (Audio Visual)
■ Team up with a colleague and consider each others' proposals. Determine which of the three opportunities each brand should take further, if any. Analyse the extent to which each proposal might potentially go on to meet the sponsors requirements and whether a sponsorship fit has been both ably and appropriately demonstrated.

References

Bowdin, G., Allen, J., O'Toole, W., McDonnell, I. and Harris, R. (2006). *Events management*, 2nd Edition. Oxford: Elsevier.

Duff, M. (2004). Give your sponsors more than they expect. *Street and Smith Sports Business Journal*, May 31–June 6, 2004.

Farelly, F., Quester, P. and Mavondo, F. (2003). Collaborative communication in sponsor relations. *Corporate Communications: An International Journal*, Vol. 8, No. 2, pp. 128–138.

Grey, A. and Skildum-Reid, K. (1999). *Sponsorship seekers toolkit*. Sydney: McGraw-Hill.

Masterman, G. (2004). *Strategic sports event management: An international approach*. Oxford: Butterworth-Heinemann.

Masterman, G. and Wood, E. H. (2006). *Innovative marketing communications: Strategies for the events industry*. Oxford: Elsevier/Butterworth Heinemann.

O'Connell, D. and Goodman, M. (2002). The game's up. *The Sunday Times*, 24 February.

Section Three: Successful Sponsorship

The chapters in this section consider three key factors for successful sponsorship return on investment, sponsorship fit, exploitation and evaluation.

Chapter 9 considers how sponsorship can be strategically managed by sponsors in order to achieve objectives and specifically the importance of integrating sponsorship communications.

The case for exploitation is that a return on a sponsorship investment is much more likely if rights are leveraged by sponsors. Chapter 10 assesses the importance of sponsors exploiting their rights including how rights owners can play a part in encouraging this to be undertaken.

If sponsorship is not evaluated, not only will a return on investment be indeterminable, sponsors may turn to other forms of communication for their needs. The responsibility lies with both sponsors and rights owners if sponsorship is to demonstrate that it can provide return on investment. Chapter 11 considers the case for more evaluation and new evaluation methods for sponsorship.

Finally, Chapter 12 raises several issues and provides an overall summary for this text. The increasing use of ambush marketing, the strength of the sponsorship relationship and the ethical management of sponsorship are all discussed here. The increasing trend towards multi-faceted sponsorship is also considered. These issues are used to highlight the need for awareness amongst rights owners and sponsors of the importance of strong sponsorship fit, exploitation and evaluation for sponsorship to continue to develop.

9

Strategic management and integration

The objectives for this chapter are to:

- Further understand the importance of the sponsorship decision-making process
- Further examine the importance of the use of sponsorship as an integrated marketing communications option
- Consider how integrated sponsorship is successfully managed
- Examine corporate, marketing and brand level planning for sponsorship
- Identify and evaluate the role integrated sponsorship plays in marketing strategies

Cosmote and the 2004 Olympics
Cosmote, a sponsor at the 2004 Olympics in Athens, uses the side of a building for
advertising purposes
Photograph: Brian Masterman

Introduction

The focus in Chapter 3 was on the process by which sponsors select sponsorship in order to achieve their marketing communications objectives. By following this sponsorship decision-making process, a sponsor can successfully determine whether sponsorship is the most effective and efficient way of achieving communications objectives, make the decision to sponsor, what to sponsor and then implement that sponsorship.

The process is initiated by the sponsor's organizational mission and objectives and then by the planning of a marketing function (alongside all other organizational functions) in order to achieve those desired outcomes. The exercise of eliminating other possible communication solutions and progressing with a sponsorship is therefore not only a strategic organizational decision, it is also a decision that has been derived out of an integrated process, a process by which the sponsorship is selected on its capacity to work within the overall marketing function.

After the decision has been taken there is the task of managing the sponsorship. It is critical that the sponsorship remains integrated. A sponsorship should not be an incongruent use of communications that does not compliment other communications that are undertaken for the organization or brand concerned. That is not to say that there is a requirement for all the communications activity to be directly linked, but at the very least they should be able to sit alongside each other in harmony. An advertising or public relations campaign, even if not directly associated with a sponsorship, should aim to achieve the same objectives and demonstrate the same attributes. If they don't then the message becomes confused and lacks credibility. This chapter considers the management of integrated sponsorship strategies and tactics.

Sponsorship management

The sponsorship planning process, Figure 3.1 in Chapter 3, acknowledges the important role that sponsorship should play in an integrated communications mix by ensuring that sponsorship options are fully developed and then considered alongside other forms of contact in order to determine the most effective and efficient set of message channels. Whilst sponsorship is always an option worth assessing it is not necessarily always going to provide a solution. However, if and when it does, it is important that it plays a congruent role in any wider communications effort.

The common failure in developing a communications mix is to distinguish between the different communications areas and see sponsorship, advertising, public relations and direct marketing as separate components (Fill, 2002). A more successful multi-disciplinary approach towards the achievement of communications objectives is one that uses all forms of brand or corporate contact as message channels, with each element being managed separately (Shimp, 1997). For example, undertaking advertising activity without relating, associating and linking it with any public relations actions can lead to incongruence. The growth of sponsorship has seen the emergence and development of separate sponsorship agencies and there are cases where their activity has become divorced from the rest of an organization's communications work, particularly if there are other types of communications agency involved. The problem can also occur in-house where a large organization with individual advertising, public relations and sponsorship departments do not integrate. When there is an agency involved, it is essential that the monitoring of their agenda, operation and implementation of sponsorships is done if sponsorship is to be an integrated component of the wider communications effort. The more external agencies there are at play in the activation of communications the more the potential for dysfunction (Fill, 2002; Kitchen, 1999; Shimp, 1997).

Research has shown that integration can be a key success factor for sponsorship with a study by Amis et al. (1999) of Canadian firms demonstrating that those sponsors that made sponsorship an intrinsic part of their overall marketing strategy were more successful at achieving their objectives than those that did not. Communications management with an integrated approach is therefore critical and a key issue if sponsorship is to continue to grow and develop as a significant provider of return on investment (Mintel, 2002).

The focus for integrated marketing communications is on affecting the behaviour of its target audience. This not only requires activity that influences brand awareness but also strategies that can instigate action in order to focus on measurable return (Kitchen, 1999; Shimp, 1997). This could be in the form of sales or less tangible image development and awareness. As the case for an increased use of an integrated approach develops, so will the demands on sponsorship for a return on investment (Tripodi, 2001). This highlights the need for exploitation of sponsorship rights and therefore the integration of sponsorship with other marketing communications in order to achieve and ultimately maximize that return.

Toiletries manufacturer PZ Cussons recognized that its sponsorship rights for the 2002 Commonwealth Games alone were not enough to achieve their marketing communications objectives. In a brand strategy for its soap product Imperial Leather, it avoided the more commonly used 'official' sports sponsorship acknowledgements and developed activities that focused on exactly what its soap does, getting customers clean. This included national television and regional outdoor and print campaigns, event signage, the use of celebrity and former athlete Sally Gunnell in public relations activity, sampling and hospitality for key trade clients. Ten million packs of Imperial Leather carried promotions and the brand was functionally used in the event via ambient forms of contact such as event venue washrooms and the use of giant baths on event concourses (Hawtin, 2004). The common focus for all these communications was getting high-performance athletes clean with an equally high-performing product.

If integration is to be fully realized, then the responsibility of its management lies with the whole organization and not just individuals, single marketing or sponsorship departments or agencies. It is a corporate effort and as such sponsorship management should permeate the whole organization (Roy, 2005). Using the same Manchester 2002 example, PZ Cussons managed their integration by firstly ensuring that all its agencies (BDH/TBWA, Biss Lancaster and Mediaedge:cia) worked together to identify all the opportunities that were available before planning how each one would be implemented in a focused effort to exploit its sponsorship rights.

Sponsorship planning

Despite the critical role that an integrated approach may make to sponsorship success, many marketers do not fully understand sponsorship as a communications tool and as a consequence plan poorly for it. Only a third (37 per cent) of the sponsor respondents in the 2004 European Sponsor's Survey indicated that they thought sponsorship to be a very important part of their organization's overall marketing communications plan (Redmandarin, 2004). This perhaps portrays the relatively small expenditure on sponsorship as opposed to the higher spend on advertising. However, 75 per cent of sponsors said that they thought integrating sponsorship across the organization was very important. This is an encouraging sign that sponsors are at least beginning to recognize the importance of ensuring that the whole of an organization should contribute to sponsorship planning. The recognition of this important factor is not necessarily being followed through in actual planning however.

All sponsorships require planning and whatever the objectives or complexity involved they also require integration, whether it is a sponsorship with objectives that are focused on the local community or one with much wider and global intentions. However, the greater the scope and range of the sponsorship the more the nature and structure of the sponsor organization has an influence on how planning is managed. For example, a centralized organization can achieve a standardized sponsorship strategy across all its markets and if there is one brand involved this can also achieve economies of scale (Roy, 2005). In contrast, a decentralized organization can implement strategies that can target customers locally and if required, address differing customer needs and preferences (Silk and Andrews, 2005). There are also pitfalls to avoid in both cases. For centralized planning, on a national scale for example, it is essential that local customer needs that differ from region to region are identified in the targeting process and addressed with appropriate strategies. Whereas a decentralized organization clearly has to ensure that all parties involved, including numbers of regional teams and possibly out-sourced agencies, are managed so that the sponsorship, whilst offering local differential, continues to be integrated and consistent.

Global sponsorship opportunities present similar issues for sponsorship planning. However, whilst global communications generally present difficulties in crossing multi-cultural and language boundaries, sponsorship has a distinct advantage. Carefully selected sponsorships can cut across those boundaries by having common meaning across the targeted regions. For example, sponsorship of an existing globally renowned rights owner/property such as Michael Jordan, the FIFA World Cup, the Russian State Ballet or the Rolling Stones in concert might have the widest of international markets to target. Similarly, the broad selection of a type or genre of sponsorship can also be successful. For example, field athletics in Scandinavia, where there is strong history of discuss, javelin and shot or R&B music throughout Europe, where club culture has grown rapidly in recent years. The principal still applies for more disparate groups of markets such as those countries that belong to the Commonwealth when, for example, cricket is selected as a focus for sponsorship or for organizations that might want to target North America, Japan and other parts of Asia via baseball.

With poor selections and planning the results can be weak. Heineken, the beer brand, as sponsors of The European Rugby Cup, generally received pan-European awareness but in one territory there was an un-harmonious element. In France, because of bans on alcohol-related sponsorship and advertising, the competition was referred to as 'le H'. Better planning by Coca-Cola, as a sponsor of Team China at the 1998 FIFA World Cup, saw implementation of their sponsorship vehicle for a local marketing programme in China so that it coincided with the event. The universal World Cup brand itself was used here to help break down cultural barriers. Similarly, Samsung continues to use sport sponsorship to create brand awareness via the Olympics. According to research, unaided awareness of the Samsung brand as a mobile communications provider increased from 16.2 per cent after the 2000 Games in Sydney to 70 per cent after the 2004 Games in Athens (Miang, 2006). Its sponsorships are recognized as important contributors to that success.

Critically, sponsorship planning is, or should be, governed by the objectives that are set for it. The sponsorship planning process begins with an organization's mission and objectives so that marketing and then sponsorship-specific objectives can be derived in order to achieve the organization's desired outcomes as a whole. The result of following this process is a sponsorship that is fully integrated into an organization-wide strategy. Rather than taking a narrow view that sponsorship is only a bolt-on communications tactic that is added on to a marketing communications plan, it is assessed at the earliest opportunity for its strengths in playing an integrated role in organizational goals for growth or holding position.

Having determined that a sponsorship is a communications solution in order to achieve organizational and marketing goals, the role of sponsorship planning is to then ensure that alignment with these objectives is maintained throughout its implementation. This is where sponsorship can be specifically used to achieve any of the broad objectives of direct sales, corporate image awareness and development, brand image awareness and development, the development of internal relations and/or competitive advantage (see Chapter 3). Sponsorship planning can therefore be seen as an organization-wide task and one that features at all three levels of organizational planning; corporate, marketing and brand (Roy, 2005).

Corporate level planning

Organizations are dependent on the resources they employ to differentiate them from and compete against the competition (Piercy, 1997). There are schools of thought that suggest that strategies should be developed around those resources that can be developed into distinct areas of competence in order to influence performance (Amis et al., 1999). Furthermore, those resources that are difficult to imitate can also provide competitive advantage.

An organization can have both tangible and intangible resources but it is generally the intangible resources that cannot be imitated (Amis et al., 1999; McGrath et al., 1995). A tangible resource such as a product, whether it is a good or a service, can be copied. However, the equity that is gained by being renowned for superior technology, design, service and quality is an intangible perception that is on the one hand difficult to gain in customers, but on the other of great value once achieved. This is an organization's or a brand's image and reputation, an important combination of intangible resources that forms brand equity; the value a customer places on a product above that which would result for an otherwise identical product without that brand name (Amis et al., 1999; Hall, 1992).

Sponsorship offers opportunities that can help to develop image and reputation and therefore brand equity, and as such is a potentially superior resource (Meenaghan, 1991; Pickton and Broderick, 2001). However, for any competitive advantage to be gained and maintained, a sponsorship must be developed into an area of distinctive competence (Amis et al., 1999). The key is for a sponsor to select a sponsorship well so that it can tie it in with its other facets and then implement it well by ensuring that it achieves the objectives set for it. This is achieved by ensuring that the sponsorship appears synonymous with the image of the sponsor and that there is a strong sponsorship fit throughout the life of the sponsorship.

Any resource has to be continually developed and if it is to be a superior resource that can achieve competitive advantage, it must also be developed into something that is difficult to imitate. If a competitor can easily imitate the opportunity, either via ambush tactics or other sponsorship opportunities and then does so, there is no competitive advantage. However, the association and affiliation that can be achieved between a sponsor and a rights owner is very much a resource that can be made into being difficult to imitate. Firstly, most sponsorships are offered on an exclusive basis and competitors from the same market sector do not sit together in the same sponsorship programmes. This is why sponsorship is generally recognized as a provider of competitive advantage. Secondly, the stronger the fit the more difficult it is to copy.

However, simply taking the sponsorship, even with sector exclusivity assured, is only the first stage. To be superior, a resource also has to be exploited. Competitive advantage can only be fully achieved when the sponsorship rights and the fit are leveraged and a position in the marketplace has been developed to a point where it cannot be copied, especially to ensure that any would be ambush tactics from competitors can be either thwarted or diminished. The costs for an imitator are high and are therefore a barrier to their attempts to copy. The combination of these barriers, exclusive sponsor status, sponsorship fit and leveraged rights, make it difficult for others to copy and therefore a sponsor that can create such a superior resource can achieve competitive advantage.

An important distinction needs to be made at this point. A superior resource is one where an organization achieves a higher level of value in the customer's eyes. Successful sponsorship fit is perceived in the eyes of the target audience, not in the eyes of the managers who construct it. Producing an unmatched level of value for the customer does though require superior operating models that are dedicated to achieving that value (Piercy, 1997) and for sponsorship this will require operational excellence.

If the creation of superior resources were easy then there would be little advantage to be gained through sponsorship. The identification of good fit and then its development into a sustainable superior resource is a considerable task but has, for some sponsors, resulted in significant contribution to the achievement of competitive advantage. The IOC's TOP sponsors can all claim superior resources and the achievement of competitive advantage though not necessarily superiority. Similarly, Scottish Power the UK utilities provider, has been a sponsor of the Royal Scottish National Orchestra for 10 years and use their association to enhance brand awareness by utilizing their fit with the Orchestra in its provision of excellence, a commitment to social responsibility and more specifically, the development of musical education in Scotland.

The task can be even more difficult when, as for many sponsorships, the opportunity arises as a result of another sponsor not renewing and vacating the position. A very successful sponsorship that comes to an end may in fact be a very difficult vacancy to fill. SAGA's insurance brand was used for a sponsorship of the Royal

Horticultural Society Chelsea Flower Show in 2006. Merrill Lynch had been title sponsor of the Show for some years and SAGA found it difficult to make the most of its opportunity and came out of the sponsorship after only 1 year having been unable to demonstrate a convincing fit.

By ensuring that there is a strong fit, and by exploiting the rights, a new and unique resource can result in competitive advantage, as GlaxoSmithKline's stop smoking brand NiQuitin CQ experienced in its sponsorship of the BMW-Williams Formula 1 race team. By following tobacco brands into F1 sponsorship, the anti-smoking brand was ideally positioning itself. The key here is to have clear criteria for sponsorship selection that are focused on previous and competitive sponsors. Ernst and Young for example, consider the extent to which the efforts of previous sponsors are a good fit whenever they consider sponsorship opportunities for themselves (Ingrassia, 2000).

Nextel, the USA-based cellphone telecommunications provider, clearly considered the transition from a previous sponsor to itself as new title sponsor of the Nascar race series very carefully. The previous sponsor was Winston tobacco and by the time they vacated the position they had been associated with Nascar for 33 years. The task of taking over in 2004 was therefore initiated early in mid-2003 whilst Winston was still in contract. In an unusual occurrence of co-operation, Winston worked with Nextel to allow them to announce their $70 million per year 10-year sponsorship agreement in August 2003. The name of Winston was synonymous with Nascar for a long time and for many remains so, and so only more time and exploitation of the Nextel fit will see the new sponsor achieving its goals.

Demonstration of a position of strength can also be a requirement by organizations when they are under threat. At a corporate level, the goal in such cases might be to show that the organization is an attractive proposition for both buyer and shareholder. In other words a position of strength would be one that demonstrates that the organization, or any of its constituent parts, is worth buying or keeping. Nabisco International sought to demonstrate its market strength and used a sponsorship resource to achieve it. In the late 1980s, Nabisco utilized its sponsorship of the Association Tennis Professionals (ATP) Tour, in men's tennis, to demonstrate, that as a conglomerate, it was in a stronger financial position by staying intact, as a whole, and by not selling off its various brands to predators.

The fact that the image and reputation that a sponsorship can bring is an intangible resource raises a point of discussion. How is it to be measured in order to evaluate the return on a sponsor's investment? There have been many instances where sponsors have not renewed their involvements because they have been unable to assess the extent of their competitive advantage and the value of intangible equity. For example, SAGA demonstrated that it was unable to accurately evaluate any competitive advantage and compare that with the costs that were involved in order to determine if there was a positive return for its insurance brand. Successful evaluation, however, can lead to more positive strategic decisions. Vodafone for example, was able to assess in 2006 that it had achieved much in its sponsorship of Manchester United and could come out of that relationship with 2 years still to run on the contract. Having evaluated that the value of its exposure and return of media investment via the fit with its target market segments had been of benefit, the time was right for a change in strategy. Via its Manchester United sponsorship it had addressed its needs in a largely UK-based business with only a growing set of international interests. By assessing that its interests had grown more global however, it decided to come out of that and enter into a relationship with Union of European Football Association (UEFA) as a partner for the Champions League. Having established a fit with football in general it decided to stay with the sport but implement a vehicle that had deeper reaching pan-European and worldwide exposure opportunities (Guardian Unlimited, 2006).

Marketing level planning

With strong resources, an organization can implement strategies for growth. Used in an integrated marketing communications plan, sponsorship can therefore assist strategies for existing products and growth in existing markets (market penetration and expansion), the introduction of new products for identifiable or established markets (product development), existing products for new markets (market development) and entirely new products for new markets (new market development or diversification) (Boone and Kurtz, 2002; Jobber, 2004).

In addition, a strong resource can assist in holding a position in a mature or declining market. Some organizations abandon weaker products and focus on more profitable ones in the mature stage of the product life cycle. They may though be ignoring the high potential of mature markets and their older products (Kotler and Keller, 2006). Maintaining the same market position is also important and a sponsorship can assist in sustaining and possibly rejuvenating mature products. In 1986, John Hancock, the Boston-based insurance provider, entered into its sponsorship of the Boston Marathon in order to rejuvenate its mature offerings and in so doing also helped to rejuvenate the event too (see Case Study 7.1 in Chapter 7). The firm worked to reposition itself from being perceived as a rather old-fashioned company to that of a provider of insurances and investments via a position inspired by its sponsorship of the Marathon. At the time the sponsorship accounted for a large proportion of its total marketing spend with activity that saw the firm work closely with the Boston community at large (Teopaco and Greyser, 1998).

Brand level planning

Once marketing objectives have been determined, the next level of planning involves the production of a marketing mix, for an individual brand, that is designed in order to achieve those objectives. As part of that mix (product, price, place and promotion) there is the formulation of the promotions or communications mix and any sponsorships that will be implemented. In increasingly competitive markets the need at this stage of planning is to differentiate a brand from those of its competitors. 'Positioning' the brand is an approach that attempts to create this differentiation.

The marketing mix is a tool that is used to achieve a desired market position in an attempt to create for the brand a unique place in consumers' minds. The consumers' perception of a product's attributes, uses, quality, and advantages and disadvantages in relation to competing brands is therefore a position in the market from which the organization wants to compete. As such, a desired position provides the direction for an organization's marketing strategies and the marketing mix is used in order to reinforce that position (Boone and Kurtz, 2002; Roy, 2005).

There are several dimensions in which an organization can differentiate its offering: product, service, personnel, channel, image and cost (Kotler and Keller, 2006). For example, it can be a product that has more features, can be ordered more easily, delivered by friendlier more competent staff, available through more outlets or has a greater media profile than the competition's offering. In each of these dimensions there is a part that sponsorship can play. Sponsorship of an event, for example, may be able to allow all of these competencies to be on show via the product providing an event function, the organization's staff being on-site and interacting with spectators/participants, there being product information and sales opportunities on-site and the media have been encouraged to give coverage to the product and these competencies. An official event technology sponsor for example might exploit such rights. LG is a global electronics manufacturer based in Korea and in 2006 was looking to expand its North American brand presence as well as name recognition and sales. The firm makes a number of electronic products and sought a way of including them all in communications that provided interactions with target consumers. As part of a wider encompassing marketing communications strategy, it selected a sponsorship arrangement with the 'Freemont Street Experience', a technologically focused entertainment venue in the heart of the technologically advanced city of Las Vegas. The venue consists of audio/visual displays in a performance-focused environment and LG was able to provide its technology and therefore provide a function within the relationship that included giant screens and projections. The overall marketing position for LG was 'Life is Good' and via branding and advertising that was incorporated within the show, spectators were able to engage with a vibrant and colourful entertainment experience. The aim was to achieve the perception amongst target consumers that this experience was courtesy of LG and thereby demonstrate a good fit.

Events have also provided any number of car manufacturers opportunities to reach their target markets. Taking official transportation rights are an old and trusted way of achieving this if those rights are subsequently exploited. Honda researched that one of its key target market segments in the USA was the Y Generation (those born between 1977 and 1994). Consisting of approximately 75 million people and representing 26 per cent of the population in the USA, this was a market worth pursuing. Honda further identified that whilst in 2003 only 16 per cent of that market were eligible to drive, by 2010 that would increase to 35 per cent. Nearly four million vehicles a year would be sold to Generation Y by 2010 and so Honda launched the model 'Element' in order to exploit this market. They identified that the Element, competing in the truck-based market, could provide function within outdoor sports events and so designed a strategy that included a number of key events in surfing, snowboarding, BMX and mountain biking. The strategy was designed to create a position of being 'the original, the one that the others copy' (Ucmakli and Joostema, 2003). The emphasis across the manufacturer's communications was on the vehicles ability to support the active lifestyle of the target market and the sponsorships were used to promote that via customer interaction.

Once points of differential have been identified there is then the question as to how many differences should be promoted via a sponsorship. On the one hand there are those marketers that maintain that a singular 'unique selling point' (USP) should be utilized. An integrated marketing communications approach would then see the sponsorship as one of several communications tools that would be used to reinforce that position. The sponsorship itself would then also focus on that position throughout all its related communications. An example is how the leading Scottish Malt Whisky brand Glenfiddich has been positioned as 'the spirit of Scotland' in a competitive international market via a sponsorship of the 'Glenfiddich Spirit of Scotland Awards' for piping (bagpipes).

There are risks in utilizing more than one point of differential, for example under-positioning where target audiences will only gain a vague idea of a brand, over-positioning where audiences have too narrow an understanding of a brand, confused positioning where there are too many messages and doubtful positioning where there is little credibility to the position. Those sponsorships that are ill-fitting will certainly lack credibility. On the other hand, single-benefit positioning might be a lost opportunity. If these risks can be eliminated, a set of sponsorship rights that are comprehensively exploited can deliver more. adidas launched a new football boot in early 2006 and whilst it was claiming that it was a brand that was focused on performance, in essence there was more than one position as the 'F50 Tunit' boots were a customized offering with three component parts that could be purchased separately and in a variety of colours. The starter kit was priced at £123 in the UK and with 8 different components, up to 18 variations and a top price of £240, this was also an expensive and fashion positioned brand. Launch-related promotions likened the new product with other target market purchases that were component and custom-built based and bearing similar attributes to those of the iPod music player brand (Goodman, 2006). As for the adidas 'Predator' boot before it, sponsorships via professional footballer endorsement-based contracts were also enacted in order to emphasize the performance position.

When there is little basis for differentiation the strategic approach can be via the use of competition-based positioning. Sponsorship can be used here to demonstrate products in action in an attempt to show superiority. In particular it is the 'function' of a brand within a sponsorship that can be used to demonstrate the attributes, uses and qualities of the brand. If this is done successfully then target audiences can be led nearer to being able to make comparisons with other brands. The perception that 'if Nike golf products are good enough for Tiger Woods, the number one golfer in the world, then they are good enough for me' is clearly a fundamental approach in the use of rights owners to champion the brand via endorsement-focused sponsorships.

Brands often have little time to sustain their differential when competitors can so easily imitate or duplicate the product. Even the potential advantage of being first to market can become a risky option if duplication is so easily possible. Sponsorship though is one way of reinforcing superiority over even very similar competing brands. By associating with a high-profile rights owner, a sponsor can show that their brand carries a credible endorsement and with exposure to large audiences. The development of high awareness can be a critical factor here. If there is little difference between a sponsors brand and those of its competitors and provided the target audience perception is positive, the higher the awareness is, the greater the opportunity for competitive advantage. Shell, for example, demonstrated the economy attributes of its new petrol product via its sponsorship of the Fuel Economy World Record Challenge (see Case Study 7.4 in Chapter 7) in an attempt to show superiority over competitors' brands.

Another critical factor for sustaining differential might also be in the longevity of the relationship between a sponsor and a rights owner. An awareness that is maintained over a long period can also enhance the desired perception of superiority.

In a world where technology is developed so quickly, sustained competitive advantage is extremely difficult to achieve. However, there are successful brands that have achieved target audience perceptions of superiority by providing functions within sponsorships and by developing those relationships over long periods. Kodak, in its relationship with the IOC since 1896, has used its association with the Olympic Games to try and gain superiority in the photographic industry (see Case Study 4.1 in Chapter 4), as has Hewlett Packard in IT markets, via its relationship with the Boston Marathon since 1994, and most recently via its 'HP Athlete Search System' (see Case Study 7.1 in Chapter 7). Other manufacturers have these types of technology but in these cases have been denied the opportunity to access these particular opportunities to create market position.

Positioning can also be planned by focusing on particular goals. The basis of this approach is to articulate the brand's identity and communicate that to the target audience (Roy, 2005). A sponsorship can therefore be a valuable resource on this basis as it can deliver associations with rights owners and their properties that can already have significance with their own target audiences. If there is a strong fit between sponsor and rights owner, then the association can be exploited so that there is a successful articulation, possibly emotionally and physically, that also carries the powerful endorsement of the sponsor/brand by the rights owner and property. This can then be used to achieve marketing objectives. For example, sponsors of Nascar have been reported as seeing increased numbers of customers switching to their brands just because they are associated with Nascar. Nascar's particular target customers have shown that they will switch to a brand when it successfully articulates its affinity with Nascar, the race series, or a Nascar race team. In other words, when it demonstrates that it has a strong fit. Research in 2000, identified that 72 per cent of Nascar fans would 'almost always or frequently' choose a Nascar sponsoring brand over one that was not associated with Nascar and that 46 per cent would still choose that brand when it was up to 10 per cent more in cost. It also identified that 43 per cent of fans would switch from their normal brand of grocery item to try a sponsor brand (Performance Research Europe, 2000). As an example, the Tide brand of soap powder reported that 20 per cent of its consumers switched to try the brand after its Nascar sponsorship began.

Articulating one position on a global scale is not always as possible or necessary as it is with one or few target markets and so an organization needs to be aware of the differences that exist from market to market. Therefore a bespoke approach may be necessary in order to accommodate different cultures, languages and customer expectations. A brand that is targeted at numbers of different geographic markets can use sponsorship to overcome these issues whilst a multi-layered sponsorship portfolio can be used to articulate to target markets at various levels. For example, Coca-Cola's sponsorship programmes operate at local, regional, national and then international regional levels. By matching its brands with world standard events, such as the Olympics and the FIFA World Cup, it is attempting to utilize sponsorships that represent excellence and that have universal meaning whatever the market but by then addressing local needs with tailored activities it is attempting to be seen as a local brand and in touch with individual customers. Coca-Cola does this via internationally negotiated sponsorships and the activation of local offices around the world to communicate with local markets (Business 2000, 2006). One aspect of Coca-Cola's involvement with the 2002 FIFA World Cup is discussed in Case Study 9.1.

Case Study 9.1 Brand level planning: Coca-Cola – 2002 World Cup

Coca-Cola has purchased World Cup rights from FIFA for 30 years and has a comprehensive understanding of the ability of football sponsorship to deliver competitive advantage. It understands the necessity to exploit these rights and as a result plans at all levels to achieve its marketing objectives in most of its markets around the world. The worldwide rights require planning on a global scale and Coca-Cola achieves this by planning its brand-focused sponsorship activities at local levels and by involving a full range of integrated communications; customer promotions, media, public and internal relations.

One example of this exploitation, on one day in one country, demonstrates the level of planning, on a worldwide scale that was required for their objectives to be achieved.

The UK is an important territory for Coca-Cola but was one of many territories where exploitation was implemented outside of the 2002 World Cup host countries. On one day it implemented joint promotions with one of its key retailers, supermarket chain Sainsbury's taking advantage of its right to have the World Cup trophy for one promotional day only. In four Sainsbury's venues around the UK it enabled football fans to touch the Cup, be photographed with it and meet several ex-football players. 3000 lucky fans were able to do this amongst many more fans who were attracted to each store.

The result for Coca-Cola and Sainsbury's was increased sales by half a million cases.

This one small case demonstrates just how much planning has to be coordinated at all levels in order to take full advantage of global sponsorship rights.

Source: Earl (2002)

Customization of the message in order to articulate to different target markets can involve simply translating into local languages but more complexly might also involve the inclusion of local values, traditions and ways of life in order to be successful. Coca-Cola does this via music and fashion for example. The 'Coca-Cola Form and Fusion Awards' is a schools' competition in Ireland. Students design costumes from recycled materials for entry into fashion shows and in 2001, 2400 students took part in the event. Coca-Cola's strategic approach was to take out sole sponsorship in order to maximize the position (Business 2000, 2006).

Morgan Stanley Dean Witter has used sponsorship to cross multi-cultural boundaries. The global financial services organization sponsored 'Stitches in Time – A Tapestry for the Millennium' in 2000. This was a series of six exhibitions throughout the East End of London and targeted at the multi-cultural local communities in the Tower Hamlets and Newham Boroughs in particular. The aim was to increase interest in the firm as a local Tower Hamlets business and to attract employees. The series transformed public buildings and interacted with local participants in an arts-focused effort that aimed to integrate the communities (Sponsorship Consulting, 2006).

Scottish Power has used sponsorship to cross national boundaries in order to reach target markets in Wales. By sponsoring the Welsh National Opera and the internationally renowned National Eisteddfod of Wales, it has attempted to show its capacity as a utilities provider that can serve many geographic markets beyond Scotland. One aspect of its attempt to create a position with these markets was to take its own Scotland-based employees to these events in order to sample and better understand the local culture (Scottish Power, 2006).

Research has shown that sponsorship if selected poorly can result in ambivalence towards the brand. NTL, the UK telecommunications provider, decided to enter into sponsorships of both Glasgow Celtic and Glasgow Rangers football clubs. The sponsorships contained similar shirt advertising rights and the initial approach was taken as a result of previous sponsorships of the clubs where it was found that Celtic fans would alienate themselves from a sponsor brand of Rangers and Rangers fans would reciprocate for sponsors of Celtic. The research identified that the most committed fans of each club were the least accepting of the sponsorships and the perhaps expected positive relationship between support of the clubs and NTL, as per Nascar fans and related brands, was not found (Davies et al., 2006).

Strategy selection

Organizations are constantly attempting to differentiate their brands. Where the challenge is too great to sustain differential, competitors match or exceed the offering, where markets and the economy change and consumer needs develop, there is a need to create new attributes, uses and qualities in an attempt to add value and benefits that will be of worth to consumers. Assuming that products have a limited life, that their sales and profit levels pass through different stages and that their resource requirements change, an organization has to produce appropriate strategies at the right stage of a product's life cycle. Over the lifetime of any one brand then, there are normally several different stages which require appropriate strategies in order to effectively differentiate and position products and achieve competitive advantage.

Whilst there are various product life cycle patterns, bell-shaped, growth-slump-maturity, cycle–recycle, style/fashion/fad cycles for example, most consist of stages of introduction, growth, maturity and decline (Kotler and Keller, 2006). Albeit some stages might occur more than once in a cycle.

Introduction stage

This is the period of slow sales growth, high expense and therefore, non-profit as the product is introduced to a market.

Growth

This is a period of increased market acceptance and sales leading to greater profits.

Maturity

This is the period of slower sales growth as the product is accepted and bought by the majority of the markets so profits become stable or start to decline because of increased competition.

Decline

This is the period of continued downward sales and thus a decrease in profit.

The first two stages may utilize strategies that include sponsorship activity. The adidas launch of its new 'F50 Tunit' boots and Honda's launch of its 'Element' are both examples of the use of sponsorship to aid the introduction of new products into a market. Financial services orientated organizations can also be identified as introducing products with long introduction stages. Nationwide Building Society for example, has targeted children over long periods with significant promotions investment in its sponsorship of the England Football team and previously the Football League (Michael et al., 2002). Whilst children do have savings accounts and Nationwide does offer such products, it is their future value as purchasers of mortgages and loans that are targeted in these strategies.

The previously discussed John Hancock's sponsorship of the Boston Marathon is an example of a strategic attempt to use sponsorship to rejuvenate a brand when it has already reached maturity.

New product development strategies

An organization's strategy for new product development can vary according to the existing portfolio of products (product mix), its overall marketing objectives and the state of the competition. The choice of strategy also depends on the strength in the market position of its existing products. Typically, it has four alternatives (Boone and Kurtz, 2002; Jobber, 2004).

Market penetration and expansion

Market penetration and expansion strategies are for the development of existing products within existing target markets in order to increase sales. Organizations can also modify products, improve their quality or promote new uses for them. Such strategies can be used, for example, to boost the market share of mature products. The most basic way of increasing sales is to win competitor's customers where the use of promotion or distribution or the cutting of prices can be considered. Pepsi was particularly aggressive in its penetration of the Cola market in 2002. It spent heavily on gaining market share in North America with activities that included significant sponsorships (Teather, 2002). For example, it became sponsor of the National Football League (NFL) in the USA. Naturally a response came from Coca-Cola with the launch of Vanilla Coke and a renewal of its sponsorship of the National Basketball Association (NBA).

Another way to expand is to acquire a competitor. This was ably demonstrated in 2005 when adidas bought Reebok. This was an example of the number two in the sports manufacture market buying the number three in order to specifically expand in the USA with a particular strategy aimed at taking share from the number one, Nike. Both the adidas and Reebok brands have so far strategically remained focused on sponsorship of football teams and footballers and on American team sports respectively in order to achieve this objective.

An organization might also expand an existing market with an existing product by converting non-users or by increasing usage in existing users and use sponsorship in its strategies.

Sponsorship is generally utilized to achieve objectives of image development and increased awareness in existing customers or the competitions' customers in the promotions mix that will be required for any of these strategies.

Product development

Product development strategies are for the development of new products in existing target markets. Such strategies are used to take advantage of the success of existing products, in the form of customer awareness and loyalty, in order to introduce and sell new products to them. Approaches here include extending an existing product line with a product at a higher price, upgrading existing products or replacing older products with new ones.

Prior to the completion of its term as a main sponsor of Manchester United, Vodafone identified that there were the global markets that were opening up for its 3G technology. At the same time it withdrew from its sponsorship of the Ferrari Formula 1 team and did so because sponsorship of the McLaren team offered it rights to 3G coverage that meant it could send related pictures to mobile phones. Via a product development strategy Vodafone was able to introduce new products to existing customers.

Market development

Market development strategies are for the development of existing products in new target markets that can involve the promotion of new uses of existing products in new markets. They can also involve the marketing of existing products and their existing uses to new market segments which could simply be new geographical regions.

Approaches here involve entry into attractive new markets when the organization's core competencies are strong enough to carry over to the new target markets. There are two key tasks: (a) to overcome any barriers for market entry and (b) to ultimately achieve and maintain an acceptable level of sales. The barriers for entry need to be surmountable for more benefit than cost and this task is made easier if the new market conditions show similar traits and customer needs as those that are portrayed in existing markets.

Vodafone recognized that its UEFA Champions League sponsorship afforded the firm exposure within 227 countries and four billion television viewers (Guardian Unlimited, 2006). It therefore came out of its sponsorship of Manchester United early so that it could take up this opportunity to develop new markets. The decision was based on there being a greater point of exposure than that which one single team might deliver even if it did play in and win the competition.

American International Group (AIG) replaced Vodafone and became 'Principal Sponsor of Manchester United'. AIG has little presence in Europe or the domestic UK market but does operate in 130 countries beyond. It decided that club sponsorship was right for entry into these new markets and paid a record price for the privilege, £56.5 million over 4 years (Smith, 2006).

New market development

New market development strategies are for the development of new products in new target markets. These are riskier strategies because they are based on the premise that existing core competencies are strong enough that they can be carried over into new products for new target markets. Often termed a diversification strategy, this is an approach by organizations experiencing market leadership and superior market share possibly with little or insufficient capacity for growth. The approach is one of diversifying the portfolio of brands in order to grow. Some organizations look for markets that compliment existing ones. An even riskier approach is to look for completely new directions.

Puma, the sportswear manufacturer has firmly moved into new markets with new products. It has over a number of years adopted strategies that have involved the production of new footwear in particular that, rather than being performance led, have been designed by top fashion designers (Rocha and Starck) in an attempt to gain growth in fashion-focused markets. It has also produced new clothing for a healthier lifestyle via an association with and endorsement from fashion model Christy Turlington and a focus on yoga.

Summary

Sponsorship can be a unique component in an integrated marketing communications approach. For example, whilst global strategies may need to address both cultural and language barriers, sponsorships can cut across those boundaries by having common meaning across targeted regions.

The general aim for integrated marketing communications is to affect the behaviour of its target audience and in order to do this, strategies that can instigate action and provide a measurable return are required. The task of managing this, so that sponsorship is both a congruent and influential element of an integrated marketing approach, is a corporate effort. The task can be difficult as there are some considerable barriers, for example where the nature of the organization can be seen to shape a prohibitive management approach. However, if the management of sponsorship is seen as an organization-wide task and not one that rests with individuals, single marketing or sponsorship departments or agencies, then it can be successfully managed.

Sponsorship planning, as an organization-wide task, can be seen to be managed at all three levels of organizational planning: corporate, marketing and brand. At the corporate level an organization can gain competitive advantage from the development of superior resources. Whilst tangible products and services can be replicated by competitors, it is more difficult to imitate an intangible resource and therefore the same equity that can come from superior technology, design, service or quality. As a strong sponsorship fit is difficult to copy, it can and should be developed as a superior competence in order for it to deliver its objectives and help develop competitive advantage.

Planning at marketing level is focused on the implementation of strategies for the achievement of marketing objectives. Over the lifetime of any one brand there are changing economies, markets and consumer requirements that present any number of strategic challenges, and therefore different types of strategy are required at different stages of a product's life cycle. Strategies are required for the introduction of new products, their growth, when they are in maturity and also when they are in decline. For the development of new products the strategy choices include market penetration and expansion, product development, market development and new market development.

At brand level, sponsorships are planned as part of an integrated marketing communications plan where the need is to differentiate a brand from those of its competitors. An organization can differentiate its offering by focusing on the product, service, personnel, channel, image and/or cost and as sponsorship can be successfully utilized in any of these dimensions it can be developed as a superior competency and play an integral role in the development of brand position.

Tasks and discussion points

- Research examples from the industry and analyse how sponsors have implemented the following types of strategy:
  - Market penetration
  - Product development
  - Market development
  - New market development
  - Market defence
- Identify the criteria that the following brands might adopt for their sponsorships for each of the above type of strategy:
  - Woodpecker Cider
  - O'Neil Surfwear
  - HSBC Bank
- Select one of the above brands and one strategy. Identify or create a sponsorship that would meet all the appropriate criteria and produce a concept that includes the sponsorship rights and the forms of exploitation that would be required.
- Now discuss how this sponsorship will assist the development of that brand's market position.

References

Amis, J., Slack, T. and Berrett, T. (1999). Sport sponsorship as distinctive competence. *European Journal of Marketing*, Vol. 33, No. 3, pp. 250–272.

Boone, L. and Kurtz, D. (2002). *Contemporary marketing 2002*. London: Thomson Learning.

Business 2000 (2006). The Coca-Cola brand and sponsorship. www.business2000.ie/cases/case6 (accessed 25 January 2006).

Davies, F., Veloutsou, C. and Costa, A. (2006). Investigating the influence of a joint sponsorship of rival teams on supporter attitudes and brand preferences. *Journal of Marketing Communications*, Vol. 12, No. 1, pp. 31–48.

Earl, K. (2002). How sports sponsorship can always win. *Admap*. www.warc.com. Article Center (accessed 5 October 2006).

Fill, C. (2002). *Integrated marketing communications*. Oxford: Butterworth-Heinemann.

Goodman, M. (2006). Fashion scores as adidas launches its custom boot. *The Sunday Times*, 29 January.

Guardian Unlimited (2006). Vodafone rings the changes without sentiment in quest for global power, 9 February. www.sport.guardian.co.uk (accessed 9 February 2006).

Hall, R. (1992). The strategic analysis of intangible resources. *Strategic Management Journal*, Vol. 13, pp.135–144.

Hawtin, L. (2004). Imperial Leather: A winning performance. *Admap*, April, 2004. Oxon: World Advertising Research Centre.

Ingrassia, P. (2000). Building a high value event and sponsorship program: Focusing on events as customer relationship builders. *The Advertiser*. www.warc.com/ArticleCenter (accessed 5 April 2006).

Jobber, D. (2004). *Principles and practice of marketing*, 4th Edition. Maidenhead: McGraw-Hill.

Kitchen, P. (1999). *Marketing communications: Principles and practice*. London: International Thomson Business Press.

Kottler, P. and Keller, K. (2006). *Marketing management*, 12th Edition. Upper saddle River, New Jersey: Prentice Hall.

McGrath, R., MacMillan, I. and Venkataraman, S. (1995). Defining and developing competence: A strategic process paradigm. *Strategic Management Journal*, Vol. 16, pp. 251–275.

Meenaghan, T. (1991). The role of sponsorship in the marketing communications mix. *International Journal of Advertising*, Vol. 10, pp.35–47.

Miang, Ng Ser (2006). Speech at Singapore Sports Council Session, 20 January. Shangri-La Hotel, Singapore. www.sscgov.sg/SportsWeb/media_speeches (accessed 23 March 2006).

Michael, J., Clarke, B. and Malhotra, R. (2002). *Catch them young and keep them long: Sponsoring the brand*. ESOMAR. The World Association of Research Professionals, September. www.warc.com (accessed 5 April 2006).

Mintel (2002). *Sponsorship Report*. UK: Mintel.

Performance Research Europe (2000). Viagra and Lycos outperform first year sponsors to Nascar. www.performanceresearch.com (accessed 9 October 2003).

Pickton, D. and Broderick, A. (2001). *Integrated marketing communications*. Harlow: Pearson Education.

Piercy, N. (1997). *Market-led strategic change: Transforming the process of going to market*. 2nd Edition. Oxford: Butterworth-Heinemann.

Redmandarin (2004). *The 2004 Redmandarin European Sponsors' Survey*. Full Report. In Association with The Sponsorship Research Company. London: Redmandarin Sponsorship Consulting.

Roy, D. (2005). Global sport sponsorship: Towards a strategic understanding. *Global sport sponsorship*, Amis, J. and Cornwell, B. (Eds.). Oxford: Berg.

Scottish Power (2006). Our community sponsorship. www.scottishpower.com/pages/aboutus_community (accessed 22 February 2006).

Shimp, T. (1997). *Advertising, promotion and supplemental aspects of integrated marketing communications*, 4th Edition. Fort Worth: The Dryden Press.

Silk, M. and Andrews, D. (2005). The spatial logics of global sponsorship: Corporate capital, cola wars and cricket. *Global sport sponsorship*, Amis, J. and Cornwell, B. (Eds.). Oxford: Berg.

Smith, D. (2006). United in record shirt deal. www.sportbusiness.com/news (accessed 11 April 2006).

Sponsorship Consulting (2006). Morgan Stanley Dean Witter – A case study. www.sponsorshipconsulting.co.uk (accessed 25 January 2006).

Teather, D. (2002). Coke gets a vanilla flavour. *The Guardian*, 16 April, 2002.

Teopaco, J. and Greyser, S. (1998). *John Hancock sports sponsorship 1993–2000 and beyond*. Boston: Harvard Business School.

Tripodi, J. (2001). Sponsorship – a confirmed weapon in the promotional armoury. *International Journal of Sports Marketing and Sponsorship*. March/April, 2001.

Ucmakli, A. and Joostema, K. (2003). *Calibrating new products for Generation Y automotive consumers with emerging market realities*. ESOMAR. The World Association of Research Professionals. www.warc.com (accessed 5 April 2006).

10

Rights exploitation

The objectives for this chapter are to:

- Understand the importance of sponsorship exploitation
- Identify the sponsorship exploitation process
- Evaluate and understand the importance of function for sponsorship exploitation
- Identify the role of rights owners in sponsorship exploitation
- Evaluate how sponsors exploit

O₂ and the Wireless Festival
O₂ utilizes its rights at the 2006 Wireless Festival, Harewood House, near Leeds

Introduction

Throughout this text, the focus has been on demonstrating the key success factors for successful sponsorship. Exploitation is one of those. Sometimes referred to as leveraging or activation, this is where the sponsorship rights are supported by marketing communications by the sponsor in order to achieve sponsorship and ultimately communications objectives. The purchasing of a set of sponsorship rights by a sponsor is invariably not going to be enough for the sponsorship to be successful or to maximize the potential return on investment. The rights need to be exploited via the use of further communications. Traditionally these may be seen as 'extra' because they are not supplied by the rights owner along with a set of rights. However, a significant issue for sponsorship is the prevailing misconception that sponsorship rights alone will achieve their objectives. Another issue is that there is also insufficient understanding and use of these as integrated communications. This chapter will therefore consider the important role that integrated exploitation must play.

Importance of sponsorship exploitation

Sponsorship rights are clearly a critical aspect of the sponsorship relationship. However, it is not in the interest of either the rights owner or the sponsor for the latter to rely solely on its negotiated rights if it is to fully achieve all that is possible from the relationship. In order that the sponsorship is utilized to its fullest potential it is necessary for the sponsor to exploit those rights. By supporting a sponsorship with resources that are over and above the costs of the rights, a sponsor is more likely to reach its target markets to a greater extent. This is achieved by integrating the sponsorship into a wider programme of communications activities.

The research that has been undertaken in this area does indicate that without exploitation, sponsorships are less likely to be as successful (Otker, 1998) and the effectiveness of a sponsorship is reliant on support advertising and promotions that leverage the rights (Meenaghan and Shipley,1999; Mintel, 2002). Indeed research also indicates that the effectiveness of sponsorship is directly related to the degree to which sponsors are willing to exploit their rights (Thompson and Quester, 2000). However, if sponsors, and rights owners, are to be convinced of the importance of exploitation, they need to know to what extent they should support their rights with other communications. Currently there is little empirical evidence to show to what extent exploitation is necessary.

Despite this, there are a number of commentators that propose guidelines for exploitation. In some texts for example, there are rules of thumb for how much a sponsor should spend on exploitation. These are generally based on spending so many more times the amount spent on the rights themselves. Graham et al. (2001) for example suggest 3:1 (three times the amount of the sponsorship rights fees involved). Others are 1:1 (New Zealand Sponsorship Agency, 2004; Redmandarin, 2004) and anything from 50 to 400 per cent (Grey and Skildum-Reid, 1999). In contrast, there are cases of sponsorships where a much greater need has been identified. In 1996 for example, Coca-Cola spent over 10 times the amount their sponsorship rights cost them for the 1996 Olympics in Atlanta (Kolah, 1999; Shank, 2002).

The analysis of data from a 2004 survey of corporate sponsorship decision-makers revealed that collectively they spent an average of 1.3 to 1 (IEG/ Sponsorship Research, 2004). This ratio was higher in 2003 at 1.7 to 1. These are average ratios that have been identified in retrospect in order to evaluate the extent to which some sponsors have exploited their rights and are clearly not intended as the basis for any specific guidelines. In fact it is unreasonable to assume that there can be generic guidelines that suggest how much exploitation is sufficient when the required amount of exploitation can only be determined according to the unique circumstances of each individual sponsor. There is no one optimal level as the identification of what is required is entirely individual to the sponsor concerned, as Coca-Cola demonstrated. Their requirement and judge-ment was to spend at that level in order to maximize their unique opportunity, in their hometown, at that time. Whilst there is little empirical evidence to show how much exploitation is enough, or an optimal level of exploitation, rules of thumb would appear to be redundant.

There is a more effective approach that can be taken for this task however. The evidence that shows that the effectiveness of sponsorship is directly related to the degree to which sponsors are willing to exploit their rights (Thompson and Quester, 2000) does support the case that sponsors should at least be encouraged to exploit more. Even those sponsors that have little other communications activity will need to support their rights with further resources to reach their target audiences effec-tively. The focus for this approach is to consider the nature and extent of the com-munications that the sponsorship is to be integrated into. In particular, how strong the strategy needs to be to reach target markets, with what messages and under what kind of market conditions. The key then is to determine what exploitation is required to meet objectives. There will however, always be limitations to the amount of resources that can be utilized. An unlimited amount of exploitation is never going to be an option. The approach therefore, should be to determine what exploitation is necessary to achieve objectives but then to identify how much of this can be both effectively and efficiently undertaken with the resources that are available.

The importance of exploitation is clearly not wholly understood by sponsors. In many cases sponsors underestimate the investment of money and time required to exploit a sponsorship and turn it into a key competence. Whilst investment in 'collateral marketing communications' is a necessity (Crimmins and Horn, 1996; Roy, 2005) there is evidence to suggest that this is not understood. The IEG/ Sponsorship Research (2004) survey of sponsorship decision-makers revealed that 77 per cent of sponsors spent additional monies to exploit their sponsorship rights. Alarmingly though this figure was higher at 87 per cent in 2003. The respondents listed corporate hospitality, internal communications, advertising, public relations, Internet tie-ins and sales promotion as the top six forms of spon-sorship exploitation. When asked about how much they spent on activation/ exploitation, 60 per cent of the respondents in the 2004 European Sponsors Survey indicated that they spent no more than the same amount as they did in securing the rights fees. Of these, 41 per cent said that no further spending was required. Forty four per cent of all respondents said that they spent less than they did on their rights fees and only 16 per cent indicated that they spent twice the amount of their fees (Redmandarin, 2004).

Beyond specific surveys and other such research, it is generally difficult to identify how much is spent on exploitation. Most figures relating to spend on sponsorship relate only to the totals spent on fees (IEG/Sponsorship Research, 2004; Mintel, 2002). Detail on how much is spent on sponsorship fees is more readily available in the public domain whereas the investment by a sponsor on exploitation is not specifically revealed and is only one element of general marketing spend when reported in corporate accounts. However, in a report by the Chartered Institute of Marketing (CIM, 2004) it was estimated that for the $6 billion spent on European sports sponsorship, up to $5 billion is wasted because sponsors do not exploit.

Planning sponsorship exploitation

There are a number of factors that need to be considered when it comes to planning exploitation.

Process

The identification of what is required in order to make the most of sponsorship rights is clearly an important task. As explained in Chapter 3 this should be undertaken before a decision to sponsor is made. If the success of the sponsorship is dependent on the amount of exploitation undertaken (Thompson and Quester, 2000) then not only are the rights fees a consideration, the resources required to exploit the sponsorship rights also need to be determined so that the total costs that will be involved in making the sponsorship successful are known prior to the decision to spend. Planning exploitation therefore begins at the earliest stages of determining the mix of marketing communications that will successfully achieve a company's communications objectives (see Figure 3.1 in Chapter 3).

Rights

If sponsorship is identified as part of that mix then the exploitation activities need to be implemented. The question of when they should be implemented is, in part, down to getting the most appropriate rights in the first place. Rights come in agreements that have a timeline, a start and a finish, and these are what determine when exploitation can start and finish. For some sponsorships, such as those for events, these start/finish dates may well involve pre- and post-event periods as well the duration of the event itself.

Function

It is also important to ensure that the sponsor and/or its brand/product provides a function within the sponsorship. This was introduced in Chapter 4 as a critical inclusion for all sponsors within the sets of rights they acquire.

The function a sponsor or its brand plays can provide synergy across all communications and ensure that exploitation is integrated. For example, Accenture a sponsor at the 2004 World Economic Forum in New York, provided wireless technology that enabled delegates to download event information whilst they were attending the event. By inviting its target media contacts to the event Accenture was not only able to demonstrate the value of its product, it was also able to do that whilst the product was providing a valuable service and therefore playing a functional role in improving the event. As a result, Accenture was able to get features in key trade-related publications for an audience that extended well beyond the spectators at the event.

Accenture has also functioned with events as a media partner and then grown into a sponsor. In 2003 for example, they worked with the Metropolitan Museum of Art in New York, USA to produce a virtual Manet/Veazquez Spanish painting exhibition via the sponsor's provision of the Museum's website. A similar approach was used in its sponsorship of The Louvre in Paris where Accenture provided a valuable function for all the museum's events, via the creation of a website, as well as providing target market research data that helped to recruit two further sponsors, Credit Lyonnais and Blue Martini Software. In a 3-year arrangement, from 2000 to 2003, the company also provided sponsorship-in-kind in the form of expertise to the value of one million euros and helped to ensure that The Louvre's new Internet strategy was entirely commercially funded (Masterman and Wood, 2006).

Integration

A sponsor's communications that are implemented to exploit its sponsorship rights need to be integrated with all those other communications that it undertakes for the brand/product. As discussed in Chapters 3 and 9, if this is not undertaken, success can be limited as messages can become dysfunctional and then diluted when they act in different ways and at cross-purposes (Boone and Kurtz, 2002; Pickton and Broderick, 2001).

It is also important for sponsors and rights owners to identify common opportunities for integrated communications. In this way the sponsorship relationship will be enhanced. Motorola, a high spending and major sponsorship partner of the National Football League (NFL) in the USA, claims that this sponsorship enables it to reach customers and attain a position that its competitors cannot. At the outset, the sponsorship began with Motorola as official supplier of communications equipment for all NFL coaches and their support teams, where the brand exposure came mainly from the logos on the headsets worn on match days. The relationship was developed to then take advantage of many more exploitation points including exclusive player locker room visits, access to the sidelines on match days, golf events using NFL players and dinners with Hall of Fame members. All of which might be used in consumer or client activities. By considering the challenges of each of its diverse business units, Motorola worked with the NFL to ensure that the rights owner was aware of the objectives it wanted to achieve. As a result benefits have been continually added to the relationship. For example, Motorola now fully participates in several national events so that it can build up customer relationships locally. These events, where players explain the value of Motorola technology to audiences, are specifically created between the sponsor and the NFL in an integrated communications effort. In addition the market position has also been developed to demonstrate that both sponsor and rights owner are caring organizations via a scheme that initiated the collection of used cellular phones at matches. Motorola refurbished the phones and donated them to charitable organizations to help abused spouses. Accordingly the teams promoted this to their fans and in one season 22,500 phones were donated (Weisz, 2003).

A number of other sports sponsorship exploitation examples are featured in Figure 10.1.

Rights owners

There is an added benefit for a rights owner if their sponsor exploits their rights effectively. The extra exposure that is achieved by the sponsor is over and above the communications activities the rights owner undertakes for their own promotion. The exploitation of a sponsorship by a sponsor can therefore have positive results for the rights owner and, because the sponsor is paying, at no direct cost to itself. For example, at its expense, American Express, as the founding and lead sponsor of New York's Tribeca Film Festival, exploited their official credit card status with print news media, billboards, fly posters, television and radio advertising tactics and website, wireless alert and photograph promotions (American Express, 2004) (see Case Study 2.1 in Chapter 2).

There are also benefits to be gained for the sponsorship as a whole. If both rights owner and sponsor are engaging with communications activities, each party gains from an improved exposure of the relationship and target audiences are more effectively reached. As a result further more valuable sponsorships may result from existing or interested potential sponsors that covet the opportunities they have either observed, or been shown. Existing sponsors can then gain an enhanced relationship and an increased number of opportunities to link with other sponsors in exploitation activity.

In addition, appropriate sponsors can bring an amount of credibility to a rights owner that can be an important factor in the development of its brand and appeal to customers. The adding of a specific sponsor may add to a rights owner's appeal and therefore the effectiveness of its communications simply because that sponsor adds value and wider communications reach. For example, a sponsor with associations with charities can not only add to the appeal of an event because of the goodwill it might impart, but also through the links with news media and associated celebrities that then extend the capacity of communications. The 'Coca-Cola Form and Fusion Awards', an event created in 2000 in Ireland, was targeted at schools to educate and promote art and fashion. The event was able to double its number of participants to 2400 students and hold its final in Cork in front of an audience of 2500 with the help of Coca-Cola Ireland's exploitation activities (Business 2000, 2004). By enhancing the event's nationwide media coverage in order to achieve its own communications objectives, the sponsor helped the event achieve greater reach as well.

If a rights owner can benefit from associations with sponsors that actively exploit, it is good management practice for rights owners to put more effort into seeking out those sponsors that will undertake such exploitation. To enable this, sponsorship recruitment should include an assessment of how sponsors can potentially combine their communications efforts directly with those of the event. The mutual benefit of exploitation is that both rights owners and sponsors are likely to be more successful with their communications. A much closer relationship can therefore be achieved and as a result sponsorship renewal becomes more likely. For the rights owner this is also less expensive than the alternative of finding a replacement.

Sponsor relations are enhanced still further when several sponsors can be encouraged to partake in co-promotions. At the 2004 World Economic Forum for example, Accenture needed to combine with Compaq in order to provide the wireless technology that enabled delegates to get improved information. In order to exploit its rights as the official credit card for the 2002 London Film Festival, Morgan Stanley linked with the website 'This is London' and the regional newspaper the Evening Standard, two associated new media products. In so doing, Morgan Stanley was able to provide a one-stop shop for all festival news and coverage and develop brand awareness through new and traditional media (Associated New Media, 2004).

Control

A final consideration for both rights owner and sponsor is control of the other party and their communications so that there can only be positive benefit. On the one hand there is the post-contract task for the rights owner in policing its own sponsors' contractual compliance. Whilst a contract may contain clauses that indicate that a sponsor must seek approval of all its exploitation communications activities prior to implementation, the reality is this may still require processes that ensure that this is indeed what happens. On the other hand a sponsor will want its marks and brand utilized properly by both the rights owner and any other sponsors it has agreed to jointly promote with, so that there are no negative messages that would otherwise disturb an integrated exploitation effort.

How sponsors exploit

Sponsorship rights can provide a strong platform from which to target a clearly defined position. Exploitation of the rights is what achieves this. As with any other promotions or communications mix, all of the traditional tools are available: advertising, public relations, sales promotions, direct marketing and these can translate in to any number of tactical activities such as competitions, links with websites, in-store promotions and sampling. Those sponsors that have developed a key competence from their sponsorships and have been effective at achieving competitive advantage are those that have been creative in their exploitation.

There are examples of sponsorship exploitation that have adopted a successful and bespoke approach to the task and those that have not. A number of these are now discussed.

A critical analysis of how sports sponsors approach the task of demonstrating sponsorship fit:

Gillette
As part of its plans to spend a significant $20 million in exploiting its Nascar sponsorship in the USA, Gillette ran nationwide giveaways of Hot Wheels miniature team cars on-pack for its brand Duracell batteries. This did not demonstrate any function Duracell played within the sponsorship but the company did commit to an allocation of exploitation budget and to working with promotional partners.

Toshiba
Toshiba, official IT partner for the 2006 FIFA World Cup in Germany, ran UK print media promotions that had computer graphics depicting goal scoring celebrations and a competition that entitled purchasers of Toshiba Notebooks to get 66 per cent of the price refunded if England won its games. It used a 'fingers crossed' connotation and a link to '66 (England's 1966 World Cup win) to create affinity with the target audience.

Hyundai
In contrast, Hyundai, also an official 2006 FIFA World Cup partner, advertised its Tucson car in print media during the event with no references to their sponsorship or their function other than the placement/flash of the event logo in the corner of the bought space.

INEOS
INEOS, the third largest chemical company in the world sponsored Rhys Jones in his attempt at climbing the highest peak on each of seven continents. On the successful Everest ascent the sponsor took a full page in The Sunday Times in the UK. The advertisement was a message of congratulations to the youngest person to complete the seven peaks. There were no references to how INEOS provided a function in this sponsorship or of the fit between themselves and Rhys Jones.

McDonald's
As part of its exploitation of its sponsorship of the 2004 Athens Olympics, McDonald's created 'Go Active Happy Meals'. To promote a healthy diet, it printed all its take-out bags with 'Proud' Olympic partner logos and a statement for healthy eating. Various websites were promoted for further information and the message stated that a new Go Active meal came with a salad and water (or soft drink) and a booklet and a stepometer to encourage walking. The fast food retailer was responding to poor publicity over its food range and used its sponsorship to help it reposition itself.

Ariel
The Ariel brand of washing powder was used to sponsor tennis professional Tim Henman. To exploit this around the 2003 Wimbledon fortnight, billboard posters, tube train and station advertising on London Underground's District Line were implemented. There was a risk associated with the sponsorship of an individual, but in this case the choice of Tim Henman was probably well taken as he had appeal to Ariel target consumers whether he won or lost.

Figure 10.1 Sports Sponsorship Exploitation

Microsoft

At the 2002 Commonwealth Games, Microsoft unfortunately struggled to fully exploit its rights as the official IT sponsor. Microsoft UK had never undertaken a sponsorship previously and had the opportunity of exploiting a position of being the first supplier of the single technology platform for an event of this magnitude. Many major international multi-site events for example, utilize a number of suppliers to meet their needs. One of Microsoft's objectives was to showcase itself as a single supplier and demonstrate the quality of that supply. The company started early by supporting UK athletics events in the build-up to the Games and by utilizing Para-Olympian Tanni Grey Thompson in internal promotions. During the Games an Internet Café was set up in the Athletes Village with email and MS Xboxes available. Whilst they did enter into some exploitation activity, the issues for Microsoft UK were that, as a first-time sponsor, it had agreed to its sponsorship quite late in the day and without full consideration of the amount of exploitation potential or resources requirements prior to that decision. Commonwealth Games executives had recognized that Microsoft's lack of sponsorship experience might be an issue and pro-actively staged regular workshops for them, and other sponsors, to make them aware of the deadlines for implementing and exploiting their rights. This included the timing required for the provision of signage and ticket applications for example. However, whilst Microsoft was supplied with case studies to review, these workshops devoted little time to the implementation of exploitation and in retrospect, Microsoft executives have acknowledged their missed opportunities (Church et al., 2003).

Imperial Leather

The challenge for the PZ Cussons soap brand Imperial Leather, and its official sponsor status for the 2002 Commonwealth Games, was to utilize its rights to reinforce its recent repositioning as a 'feel-good, modern, relevant brand that was for every-one' (Hawtin, 2004). This was an integrated strategic decision that was made ahead of sponsorship implementation. The solution was to become less 'official' and focus on the friendly and fun values of the Games and link those with the brand. It wanted to become an 'Official Sponsor of the Commonwealth Fun and Games'. The campaign was launched with low-weight television advertising in the UK that featured archive Games footage mixed with new live action of events and showing a gymnast slipping on a bar of soap after landing from the parallel bars, a diver taking off his trunks to then bathe in the pool and a runner taking a bath in the steeplechase water jump. This campaign was supported by integrated regional outdoor and press advertising across the UK with similar themes, for example, a picture of a high-diver about to dive into a foamy bath. Their rights included event signage across the host city of Manchester and giant bouncy baths on the stadium concourse, but they also supported these with more unusual ambient media in the stadium washrooms.

UEFA EURO 2004 sponsors

The sponsors at UEFA EURO 2004 were very active with mainstream mass communications in support of their status with the event. T-Mobile, Motorola,

Coca-Cola, adidas, Canon and Mastercard all implemented high-cost television and print advertising on a pan-European basis. In so doing, all these companies focused their communications on football and the event in particular. Mastercard for example, used its advertisements to drive consumers to its website for event ticket competitions via a competition that could only be accessed on-line.

Flybe

Exploitation is certainly not limited to high profile or resource rich sponsors. Flybe, a small discount airline headquartered in Devon in the UK, aimed high in its exploitation of its local sponsorship of minor league football club Exeter City FC. In 2004 it used the Brazilian national football team's 90th anniversary of its first competitive football fixture. Incredibly, as this first fixture was against Exeter, Flybe was able to duly create a 'Brazil Festival'. Legends of former Brazil teams played at Exeter's St James Park and in order to attract pre-event media coverage, ticket promotions were distributed to the printed news media whereby readers could win a trip courtesy of Flybe airlines to the event. With some good research, the forging of new and effective contacts at the Brazilian F.A. and the use of its own products as prizes, the airline was able to maximize its sponsorship rights via media exposure tactics for relatively little input of resources.

Toyota

Toyota supplied the official transport for the 2006 Valencia Summit, a conference focused on the use of major sports events as opportunities for urban development. Officials and delegates were met at the airport and taken to their hotels and to the Valencia Congress Hall as part of the arrangement. Toyota used the opportunity to showcase its new Prius car with each one of the courtesy fleet fully loaded with equipment including satellite navigation and branded with manufacturer and event logos. Toyota also provided a team of drivers in smart uniforms. Unfortunately there were delegate complaints that the drivers were not trained in the operation of the navigation systems and also did not know their way from the airport to the destinations required causing a negative perception of the sponsorship.

Warner Brothers

Jaguar cars recruited an unusual sponsorship from film producers Warner Brothers where the former provided products for the film 'Oceans 12', starring George Clooney, Brad Pitt, Matt Damon and Julia Roberts. In return, Warner Brothers, took the unprecedented step of sponsoring the two Jaguar Formula 1 cars and race team for the 2004 Monaco Grand Prix. It was unusual in many ways, not least because it was a one-off sponsorship for the one race. Exploitation of the rights included using the stars of the film in televised walkabouts on the race qualifying day and extensive print and photo media activity across Europe. The televised elements were boosted with the use of race team clothing, pit garage signage and the cars themselves all featuring the name and logo for the film (Masterman and Wood, 2006; *Sunday Times*, 2004).

Samsung

Samsung has also linked up with the film industry. Using its 'Anycall' brand it worked with the producers of 'The Matrix Reloaded' to promote a new camcorder cellular phone product in Korea. In a three-phase campaign, it began with the utilization of guerrilla teams at petrol stations that gave away oil (an expensive commodity in Korea) alongside competitions for film tickets. It then utilized cinema advertising spots and staged 'Anycall' preview parties and followed that with a final phase of street promotions with free film tickets. Throughout the month-long campaign, 14,000 consumers received tickets for the film and unit sales increased by 11 per cent (Event Marketer, 2004).

Budweiser

Anheuser-Busch utilizes its brand Budweiser (Bud) in a number of nationally and internationally significant sponsorships and adopts a strategic and fully integrated approach to their implementation (Greenspahn, 2000). This begins with local marketing personnel and wholesalers conducting evaluations of each opportunity. For larger events the brewer also deploys a team of eight people that converge on a designated market and implement merchandizing, sampling and promotions tactics in order to develop the image of Budweiser.

The 'Budweiser Mobile Beer School' was first used at the 1996 Olympics in Atlanta but continues to visit events throughout the USA. It has appeared in 45 states and 380 designated markets, and 300,000 'students' have graduated as 'Certified Beer Masters'. The School is a mobile classroom where guests engage in presentations about the art of brewing Bud. Similarly, 'Bud World', launched at the Atlanta Super Bowl XXXIV, is another mobile experience where invited guests learn about the history of Bud as well as sampling the product.

To exploit Budweiser's sponsorship of Dale Earnhardt Jnr's Nascar Winston Cup team, and to reinforce its position as the official beer of Nascar, the 'Bud Brew Crew Challenge' was used at Nascar events as a simulated pit stop for consumer promotions. Anheuser-Busch also links up with Nascar through its sponsorship of the Nascar Busch Series. As a result of all these related sponsorships, Anheuser-Busch has been able to integrate its exploitation communications at various levels.

SoBe

SoBe's Adrenaline Rush drink, in its link with Ozzfest (music concerts), was able to engage with 31 local markets. It implemented radio advertising spots, promotional overlays, retailer and bottler ticket incentive promotions and created a dedicated website to create a 'tour' feel. It also took a mobile 'Adrenaline Theatre' to each concert where 90 consumers at a time could experience a movie that showcased SoBe sponsored athletes. In all, 33,000 consumers visited the theatre and 235,000 samples of Adrenaline Rush were served. SoBe were providing entertainment and therefore a function for Ozzfest whilst reinforcing an integrated joint position of excitement and energy (Event Marketer, 2004).

Examples of exploitation of rights for the 2004 Olympics in Athens are featured in Case Studies 10.1 and 10.2.

Case Study 10.1 Sponsorship exploitation: 2004 Olympics, Athens

'Olympic ideals'

The following sponsors of the 2004 Olympics had the opportunity of exploitation that was focused on the promotion of Olympic ideals. The IOC expects and encourages this from its sponsors so that it can promote the Olympic Movement. By tying in, sponsors had the opportunity of using the Olympic ideals as a base for the development of their own objectives for image and awareness through their communications programmes.

Fage

Fage, a Greek yoghurt producer and Grand National Sponsor, developed educational and environmental programmes to bring youths in touch with Olympic ideals, history and the principles of environmentalism. These programmes ran from 2002 through to the Games in 2004 and included the schemes 'Junior wins the Gold medal for the protection of the Environment', Junior educates his friends about Olympic Sports' and 'Junior narrates to his friends stories from the Ancient Olympics'.

Heineken

Another Grand National Sponsor, Heineken, developed activities focused on art in order to promote Olympic ideals. It staged touring public exhibitions of original artworks by Greek painter Dimitris Koukos throughout Greece.

Swatch

Swatch launched its 'Kaleidoscope' project in Athens where Olympians, artists and celebrities from around the world were invited to create works of art by arranging Olympic sport equipment and spare parts from Swatch watches on to canvas. A silent auction of the works was then organized to raise funds for UNICEF and the IOC to provide sport opportunities for youths in Rwanda. The exhibit was toured around the world and on a final day in Athens, $200,000 was handed over to UNICEF.

Alpha Bank

Alpha Bank's 'Panorama of Olympic Sports' was launched in 2001 and toured 64 Greek cities and Cyprus until the Games. The exhibit included 11 Olympic sports demonstrations with well-known athletes.

Source: Athens Marketing Report (2004)

Case Study 10.2 Sponsorship exploitation: 2004 Olympics, Athens

Working with partners

Visa used its sponsorship of the 2004 Olympic Games to create business opportunities for its member banks.

- Visa and Olympic related marketing was implemented in 56 countries around the world.
- In Europe there were 17 national promotions that resulted in 43 million pieces of Visa Olympic marketing materials being distributed to cardholders.
- 58,000 merchants in Athens and the five other Olympic venue cities displayed 300,000 pieces of Visa Olympic point-of-sale material.
- Alpha Bank's 'Olympic Gold Card', issued in partnership with Visa, attracted 110,000 subscriptions by the start of the Games against a target of 30,000.

Source: Athens Marketing Report (2004)

Summary

Exploitation is one of the key success factors for successful sponsorship. The purchasing of a set of sponsorship rights by a sponsor is not enough for a sponsorship to work or to maximize the potential return on investment and research indicates that the effectiveness of sponsorship is directly related to the degree to which sponsors are willing to exploit their rights. Sponsors therefore need to support their rights with communications in order to achieve sponsorship objectives. Whilst exploitation communications have previously been seen as 'extra', because they are not supplied by the rights owner along with a set of rights, they are now an essential component of successful sponsorship.

An issue for even those sponsors that recognize the need to exploit their rights, is how much exploitation is necessary. Whilst there are commentators with rules of thumb for this, there is little empirical evidence that identifies a uniform optimal amount. The solution is an approach that views a sponsorship individually, and then evaluates the extent of activity that is required to meet the objectives that are set for it.

How and when to exploit is another issue for many sponsors that have to date, predominantly shown a lack of understanding of the need to integrate, not only in their implementation of their own supporting communications but also in missing the opportunity to integrate with their rights owners and other sponsors in order to maximize that association. Therefore the process of exploitation is clearly a key consideration. It is necessary to ensure that exploitation is determined prior to the agreeing of a sponsorship for example, so that the whole of the cost of a sponsorship can be identified. Getting the most appropriate rights is also a factor, not only in order to know what can be exploited, but also to know when exploitation can start and end. A final factor for both sponsor and rights owner is that exploitation, because it is at the sponsors expense, is of additional value to the rights owner and is therefore also a key part of the recruitment process.

Tasks and discussion points

- Select an example of exploitation that demonstrates the importance of rights that afford a sponsor a function in the sponsorship. Analyse the extent to which exploitation has been achieved.
- Select an example of a sponsorship programme where there has been active encouragement of sponsor joint promotions and explain how these communications have been used to achieve marketing objectives for each sponsor.
- Identify a local sponsorship in your neighbourhood that has done little to exploit its rights. Identify the rights and devise how this sponsor might make more of its opportunity.

References

American Express (2004). www.americanexpress.com (accessed 9 May 2004).

Associated New Media (2004). www.anm.co.uk/caseStudiesD (accessed 26 April 2004).

Athens Marketing Report (2004). IOC.

Boone, L. and Kurtz, D. (2002). *Contemporary marketing 2002*. London: Thomson Learning.

Business 2000 (2004). Case study: Bank of Ireland. Sponsorship of the Special Olympics: A partnership approach. www.business2000.ie/cases (accessed 26 April 2004).

Church, R., Hunt, S. and Maitland, B. (2003). Microsoft UK's sponsorship of the 2002 Commonwealth Games. *Sport and Technology Newsletter*. Arksports, June.

CIM (2004). The measure of success: Is sponsorship worth the whistle? *The Chartered Institute of Marketing*, April.

Crimmins, J. and Horn, M. (1996). Sponsorship: From management ego trip to marketing success. *Journal of Advertising Research*, Vol. 36, July/August, pp. 11–20.

Event Marketer (2004). Best activation of an entertainment sponsorship awards. www.eventmarketer.com (accessed 6 April 2006).

Graham, S., Neirotti, L. and Goldblatt, J. (2001). *The ultimate guide to sports marketing*, 2nd Edition. New York: McGraw-Hill.

Greenspahn, M. (2000). Maximizing brand presence at special events: Budweiser's approach to special event marketing reinforces its reputation as 'King'. *The Advertiser*, September. www.warc.com/ArticleCenter (accessed 5 April 2006).

Grey, A. and Skildum-Reid, K. (1999). *The sponsorship seekers toolkit*. London: McGraw-Hill.

Hawtin, L. (2004). *Imperial Leather sponsorship wins the 2002 Commonwealth Games*. IPA Effectiveness Awards. Institute of Practitioners in Advertising. www.warc.com (accessed 5 April 2006).

IEG/Sponsorship Research (2004). 4th Annual Sponsorship Decision-Makers Survey. *IEG Sponsorship Report*, Sample Issue. Chicago: IEG.

Kolah, A. (1999). *Maximizing the value of sports sponsorship*. London: Financial Times Media.

Masterman, G. and Wood, E. (2006). *Innovative marketing communications: Strategies for the events industry*. Oxford: Elsevier.

Meenaghan, T. and Shipley, D. (1999). Media effect in commercial sponsorship. *European Journal of Marketing*, Vol. 33, No. 3, pp. 328–348.

Mintel (2002). *Sponsorship Report*. London: Mintel.

New Zealand Sponsorship Agency (2004). *Newsletter*, April. www.nzsponsorship.co.uk (accessed 1 April 2004).

Otker, T. (1998). Exploitation: The key to sponsorship success. *European Research*, Vol. 16, No. 22, pp. 77–86.

Pickton, D. and Broderick, A. (2001). *Integrated marketing communications.* Harlow: Pearson Education.

Redmandarin (2004). *The 2004 Redmandarin European Sponsors' Survey. Full Report. In association with The Sponsorship Research Company*. London: Redmandarin Sponsorship Consulting.

Roy, D. (2005). Global sport sponsorship: Towards a strategic understanding. *Global sport sponsorship*, Amis, J. and Cornwell, B. (Eds.). Oxford: Berg.

Shank, M. (2002). *Sports marketing: A strategic perspective*, 2nd Edition. London: Prentice Hall International.

Sunday Times (2004). Fast alert, 16 May.

Thompson, B. and Quester, P. (2000). Conference paper. Evaluating sponsorship effectiveness: The Adelaide Festival of the Arts. *Australian and New Zealand marketing academy conference*, November–December 2000. Visionary marketing for the 21st century: Facing the challenge.

Weisz, D. (2003). Leveraging sponsorship through events: How to use event marketing to leverage your brand awareness. *The Advertiser*, August. www.warc.com/ArticleCenter (accessed 4 October 2006).

11

Evaluation

The objectives for this chapter are to:

- Understand the importance of evaluation
- Understand the role of continuous as well as post-sponsorship evaluation
- Analyse current evaluation methods
- Critically examine the need for new methods as well as increased levels of evaluation in sponsorship

Sponsorship at the Theatre Antique, De Sanxay
Sponsors including la Nouvelle Republique, France Bleu, Finac.com, Affichage Clodejac, Soregies, Chateau Perigny and Centre Presse are promoted on a poster for an open-air production of La Boheme at the Theatre Antique, a Roman amphitheatre in De Sanxay, France

Introduction

In previous chapters several key factors for success have been introduced and examined. Encouraging the establishment of good practice for successful sponsorship has been an important objective throughout this text and it is now important to address one more critical factor, evaluation, the analysis of information that can show whether there is a return on sponsorship investment. Having established communications objectives and strategically selected sponsorship as a solution, having established a good sponsorship fit and having supported the sponsorship with an integrated programme of communications, the task is to determine to what extent the sponsorship is successful. Knowing the extent of the success or failure is a factor for success as feedback, both during and after a sponsorship has been implemented, is important for any necessary realignment with object-ives and ultimately the determination of whether there has been a return on investment.

All sponsorships should therefore be evaluated. Amis et al. (1999) maintain that a successful sponsorship is achieved when a sponsor has developed a distinctive competence in implementing sponsorship. Therefore the sponsorship decision process should be indicative of all the elements of timing and knowledge that will be required to achieve that competency and experience and analysis should be used to feed back into the decision-making process in order to improve it. Thus continuous and post-event evaluation of sponsorship, against the objectives set for it, enables feedback for improved future performance. It is important to note that both sponsors and rights owners should become active assessors of sponsorship.

Despite the importance of evaluation, it is not common practice and unfortunately current techniques are inadequate (Meenaghan, 2005). This chapter will therefore consider the need for more widespread evaluation as well as new evaluation methods for sponsorship.

The importance of evaluation

When questioned further to ascertain how effective they were at measuring return on investment, less than 25 per cent of the respondents in the 2004 European sponsor's survey reported that they thought that they were 'very effective'. It appears from this that the majority of sponsors do not know by how much or even if they are being successful (Redmandarin, 2004). Further, with only 37 per cent of respondents in the same survey indicating that they thought that sponsorship was 'very important' in their organization's overall marketing and communications plans, there is also a need to educate a wider audience in the virtues of sponsorship. It is therefore critical to examine and demonstrate why evaluation needs to become common practice (Hoek, 1998).

In order to do this here it is important to firstly look at why some practitioners consider it unimportant. Why, for example, do only 37 per cent of organizations consider sponsorship very important (Redmandarin, 2004)? Is there too little evaluation of sponsorship? Are there too few accurate methods of evaluation to show whether there has been a return on investment? Dolphin (2003) also asks if there is so little evaluation because the true cost of sponsorship is too difficult to determine and as a result evaluation cannot ever be that accurate.

Another reason given by sponsors for not conducting evaluation, particularly post-event evaluation, is that it requires resources that sponsors, and rights owners, are keen to devote to their next venture. The traditional view of evaluation is for it to be implemented, if at all, after it has ended. Many events for example, are reluctant to evaluate at all let alone assess the impacts of sponsorship after the event has ended. This is due to their need to move on to the next revenue driven project rather than devote any resources to an exercise that does not directly generate revenue. There may also be a reluctance to evaluate due to believing that it is incumbent upon the sponsor, rather than the rights owner, to engage in such research.

Despite the reluctance to evaluate, evaluation is critical and a continued lack of evaluation will hinder success. If evaluation is both iterative and end-on for example, the results can be fed back to help improve current and future performance respectively. In the longer term, evaluation can also be critical for identifying and then recruiting and renewing sponsors (Thompson and Quester, 2000). Research in this area found that there was a link between those sponsors that experienced shorter sponsorships, of 3 years or less, and those who failed to set objectives and/or evaluate against them (Pope and Voges, 1994). Sponsorship evaluation can therefore lead to indirect revenue generation and a longer term and more enlightened perspective is that researched and analysed data, via evaluation, can be used to demonstrate how an event can help sponsors achieve their marketing objectives. Thus post-event research is also a critical factor in the recruitment of sponsors. In one case the American Junior Golf Association, overhauled its approach by identifying that its sponsors required fulfilment reports. It duly employed a full-time member of staff to produce documented post-event reports for each of its sponsors. It now reports that it has benefited from substantially increased sponsor retention rates.

Continuous and iterative evaluation of sponsorship is necessary as opposed to a reliance on only post-event assessment. As identified earlier in this text, in order to build sponsor relations there is a need for both parties to accommodate change when and where necessary, and the longer the relationship the greater the chance there is that this kind of flexibility will be required. Unfortunately, this is not a widespread undertaking either. The IEG/Performance Research (2004) survey of corporate sponsorship decision-makers for example, showed that 86 per cent of their respondents typically spent less than the equivalent of 1 per cent of the amount of their total sponsorship spend on evaluation. Worse still, nearly half of the 86 per cent spent a zero amount and the most common form of evaluation used by the sponsors surveyed was via the less expensive evaluation method of internal feedback after the sponsorship was concluded. Only 27 per cent of respondents used customer-focused research.

Another reluctance to evaluate stems from the fact that evaluation is not always that easy to undertake. The difficulty with sponsorships that are more global for example is that evaluation becomes more complex (Meenaghan, 2005). Sponsorships that are targeted at a number of different markets for example, are required to meet different objectives and because brands are not always at the same point in their life cycle in every market, the extended scope of the evaluation task is a lot more complex as a greater range of tools and methods are required. When the exposure and popularity of the sponsorship vehicle differs widely from market to market a separate evaluation approach is required in order to fully assess each set of objectives.

Requirements for evaluation

There are three basic questions for sponsorship evaluation to address. How clear was the sponsorship, who took notice and did it achieve the objectives set for it (Masterman, 2004). There is a need to measure if enough of the target audience saw the sponsorship and if they successfully received the desired message. The purpose is to determine how the sponsorship can be improved to communicate the message or to reach more of the audience (Thompson and Vickers, 2002). Therefore, in order to undertake evaluation, there is a need for pre-set sponsorship objectives that are specific and therefore measurable (Meenaghan, 2005; Tripodi, 2001). Those sponsors that fail to set clear objectives or fail to evaluate against those objectives are more likely to experience shorter and less successful sponsorship relationships (Pope and Voges, 1994).

Objectives that are not specifically measurable result in a sponsorship that is impossible to evaluate accurately. Ambiguity is of little value in this regard (Meenaghan, 2005). Specific targets that stipulate the extent of the increases that are required for sales, market share, image and/or awareness are all critical applications for example. Thus the precise sizes and nature of the target audiences must also be measurable at the outset. Another requirement is the identification of the time scales that these objectives should be met within, as meeting objectives, but over too long a period, is ineffective.

This final factor indicates that a degree of flexibility is also required. For example, sponsorships can extend over a number of years and many are also renewed thus creating the need to renew, alter or replace objectives. Therefore, evaluation also needs to be readdressed and aligned to any new objectives and may be required several times in the life cycle of a sponsorship.

Another key question needs to be addressed. Whose job is evaluation? As evaluation is a cost factor, enlightened sponsors may seek to get their sponsorship evaluation undertaken by the rights owner as part of the agreement. A rights owner can therefore make their sponsorship opportunity more attractive if they offer this service. At any rate, if a sponsor does not do its own evaluation then a rights owner has a responsibility itself to perform the task, as discussed earlier. What is important to remember though is that whilst a rights owner evaluation report may well appear to meet a sponsor's needs, the latter needs to understand that this is not an independent report and therefore needs to be tested for objectivity.

Many rights owners will not offer an evaluation report or may also only provide a common report for all sponsors and in these cases the sponsor will need to undertake a more specific and comprehensive evaluation themselves. This can be efficiently achieved by building in all evaluation costs into the initial budget for the sponsorship.

Despite the various approaches and thoughts on evaluation, the overwhelming argument is for a sponsor to evaluate its own sponsorship. It is the sponsor that is closest to the sponsorship exploitation communications programmes they undertake and therefore it is they, or any externally sourced but managed evaluation agency, that are in the optimum position to measure the sponsorship accurately, as a whole and as an integrated marketing communication. An independent evaluation agency, and not the agency that inspired or implemented the sponsorship, is also a more reliable out-sourced supplier of evaluation.

Evaluation methods

Measuring sponsorship is a 'grey' area (Tripodi et al., 2003) as a result of the lack of an implementation of measurable objectives and there being no consensus on uniform methodology for sponsorship evaluation. However, the variety of methods that have been developed can be categorized in to three main areas (Meenaghan, 1991; Tripodi et al., 2003).

Sales effectiveness

If the objective of a sponsorship was to have helped drive sales and sales were made possible via the sponsorship, then sales figures will be a reliable evaluation against the targets that were set. The question is, were the sales directly attributable to the sponsorship?

Traditionally, marketing has been dominated by 'sales'. More recently there has been a swing towards customer-relationship management (Boone and Kurtz, 2002; Kotler and Keller, 2006; Meenaghan, 2005). In sponsorship too there has been a tendency not to look to sales as a measure. For example, there was a low priority afforded to sales objectives by the respondents in the 2004 European sponsor's survey. This was mainly to do with their issues over how the impact on sales should be evaluated (Redmandarin, 2004). The difficulty arises in trying to isolate the contribution of sponsorship to an organization's sales results. For example, an increase in sales at or around the time of the sponsorship cannot be directly attributed to the sponsorship if there were other communications in effect or there were possible carry-over effects from past advertising that may have had an impact on the results. Other external factors such as changing economic conditions and market entry/exit by competing organizations may also impact and therefore distort the results (Bennett, 1999). A causal relationship will always be difficult to prove.

Despite this lack of confidence in sales as measures, there is sense in using other sales-related results in order to evaluate sponsorship. In particular, whilst sampling is not sales, sponsorship has the capacity to 'showcase' products and can do so as an integral functioning element of the sponsorship. Making the product 'hands-on' to consumers in this way can lead to sales leads and provided they are considered as exactly that they can be used as a measure of sponsorship effectiveness. The numbers of samples given away and the numbers of tests of the product are therefore important data to gather.

If this sampling can also be associated with 'intentions to buy' then this provides a further step towards the measurement of sponsorship effect. Performance Research (2000a), for example, and as referred to in Chapter 5, found that 72 per cent of NASCAR fans would almost always or frequently choose the brand they associate with NASCAR over one that is not. This is data that certainly makes NASCAR sponsorship appear attractive. It was also found that 46 per cent would pay as much as 10 per cent more for a NASCAR-associated brand and 43 per cent are influenced enough to switch from their normal brand to try a NASCAR-associated brand. Again this is useful evaluation for both NASCAR and existing and potential sponsors.

Having played down the use of sales per se, there is a more recent development that is critical for the future. There is in fact an increasingly demonstrable and measurable link to tangible sales in sponsorship. As discussed in Chapter 3, direct sales objectives can be built successfully in to sponsorships. A sponsor that secures rights that afford it opportunities to sell through its association with the sponsorship can directly attribute those sales to the sponsorship. For example, a sponsor that provides a function at an event and secures sales as a result. This could be an 'official supplier of beer' that sells its brew to the attendees at the event. It could also be an 'official credit card' that is used by ticket buyers to purchase their event tickets. The sales in both these cases would not have occurred without the association between the sponsors and the rights owners and as such are directly attributable to the sponsorship.

Media coverage/exposure

Applying subjective impact values, counting frequencies of reports and measuring opportunities to see or hear in the form of determining circulation coverage are popular choices of evaluation, particularly in sport sponsorship. Audits of the quantity of media exposure (print and broadcast) are also a common approach and involve an assessment that puts a price on the amount of exposure gained that is equivalent to the amount it would have cost if it had been bought at rate-card prices (equivalent media methods).

Media equivalency methods were the most popular evaluation tools among the respondents of the 2004 European Sponsor's survey (Redmandarin, 2004) and probably because such methods appear to provide such impressive results. For example, Joyce Julius and Associates in the USA provide sponsorship-related research services and work for both sponsors and events. In 2004 they conducted research for a mid-west University and the task was to determine media value for a proposed sponsorship package that included title rights for a single match plus use of season-long scoreboards and other signage. The results indicated that 66 per cent of the exposure any sponsor would receive would stem from scoreboard signage and 39.3 per cent of that would be attributable to the main scoreboard in the stadium (Joyce Julius and Associates, 2004). This type of information is useful for rights holders in order to decide which rights should be included in a sponsorship and possibly at what price.

In some cases sponsors are content to simply collect and count up exposure and coverage, the total number of pages/column inches in the press and how many broadcast seconds have been achieved can be used here. For example, Sports Marketing Surveys Ltd, an international evaluation agency with offices around the world, provided a comparative study of Formula 1 car sponsorship. The research considered the length of time all F1 race cars appeared on television so that it could produce comparable exposure figures for each sponsor logo position on each car. As a result they were able to advise on improving appearance or placement of sponsor logos. It claimed that for one team, whilst on-screen exposure increased by

40 per cent between 2005 and 2006, its advice to modify logos resulted in increased exposure for the sponsors by as much as 600 per cent (Sports Marketing Surveys, 2006). For websites too, evaluation techniques can also be fairly simple. For what it is worth, sponsors often record how many visits there were to the website and associated statistics such as which pages are viewed how often and for how long in order to produce a 'hit' total. These lists of media coverage are then used to demonstrate how successful, or not, the sponsorship has been.

A slightly more sophisticated approach, also common, is to attempt to put a value on this coverage and too often it is a comparison between advertising and sponsorship that marketers seek to achieve this. In order to justify the selection of sponsorship as a communications tool and then to demonstrate success or otherwise, evaluation is undertaken using 'equivalent advertising and media value' techniques. This is where press coverage data and numbers of seconds of sightings of logos/advertisements that have been heard or seen in broadcasts are totalled up and then priced according to advertising rate-card costs. Joyce Julius and Associates for example, indicated that its mid-west University client's sponsorship package would draw $720,000 of media value over the season (Joyce Julius and Associates, 2004; Masterman and Wood, 2006). Similarly, the results of an evaluation of Imperial Leather's sponsorship of the 2002 Commonwealth Games consisted of a mixture of media coverage/exposure measures (Hawtin, 2004):

- 89 per cent share of television exposure on the first day of the athletics that generated six and a half hours of TV presence (logo sightings).
- 253 branded photographs in national press during the athletics days.
- Exposure of the brand in the UK media equated to £889,882 of additional coverage.

In both these cases, the value of editorial coverage, because it is not paid-for advertising, can also be subjectively factored up. Depending on the sponsor, a purely individual and therefore non-standardized multiplier can be used to boost the value of newspaper or magazine coverage. Some sponsors have been known to factor-up by as much as three times (Meenaghan, 2005).

Despite the attraction and continued use of 'equivalent value' evaluation techniques, there are signs that sponsors have begun to become sceptical. A considerable flaw of the application of rate-card prices is that they are prices that are seldom paid in the advertising industry. False prices are therefore being applied. Secondly, the fact that paid-for advertising coverage does not have the same qualities as editorial coverage means that the basis of the comparison is also flawed. As a result, sponsors are now 'discounting' equivalent media values as they become increasingly aware that television and radio advertising in particular offers a quite different form of communication (Gillis, 2005). Whilst the scepticism is well founded here there is also an issue in knowing what discount to apply. Again purely subjective discounts are being applied by individual sponsors so that, for example, the sighting of a logo might be valued less than a verbal acknowledgement by a presenter. By applying a weighting to types of coverage the technique attempts to arrive at a realistic value to the coverage. However, it remains at best, a subjective and non-standardized measure.

When this type of evaluation was first undertaken it was via the manual use of stopwatches and viewing diaries. Technology has enabled more accuracy to be developed and in a sense more standardization in that computer-read data can be reliable and valid. However, new techniques are continuously being developed and then offered as a paid-for service in many cases. A sponsor therefore has more choice, but as a result there is arguably now even less standardization. One such service was launched by Nielson Media Research, a USA-based media tracking research organization. Its 'Sponsorship Scorecard' was designed to count how many times event television audiences saw sponsors advertisements and for how long. In what it called an 'assessment of the value of a sponsorship' it reported on how often a logo, for example, was seen in one broadcast, by how many people and for how long. This resulted in what it they called 'impressions' (*Sports Business Daily*, 2004).

Whilst these techniques may be of use in assisting with an overall picture, measuring reach and exposure for example, unfortunately they are not a reliable evaluation of the quality of awareness levels or shifts of such over time. The results of this type of evaluation are more numbers of sightings than they are a measurement of the quality of the effect of the exposure. The problem generally, as reported in Chapter 1, is that whilst they are a valid indicator of any exposure a sponsorship delivers, they say nothing about the effect of that exposure on target audiences. Generally the issues are as follows:

- Counting up media exposure results in a total amount of publicity achieved, but it does not measure the effects of that publicity on target audiences.
- Media exposure and coverage is only one aspect of most sponsorships. Thus any measurement of such is only ever able to achieve an evaluation of those elements and not the wider implications of the effect of sponsorship, in particular the communication effect that can be achieved via the rights owner/sponsor relationship.
- As long as sponsors continue to individually vary their use of media coverage evaluation techniques there will remain a lack of standardization.
- This in turn will continue to raise doubts as to the value of sponsorship and its capacity to achieve return on investment as sponsors and rights owners will be prone to exaggerate the achievements of a sponsorship.

Communications effects

Some sponsors look to measure awareness and image. The quest here is a measure of the quality of the effect of the communication, the extent of the awareness. Techniques are used to assess the quality and depth of actual audience perceptions as opposed to just the extent to which they have heard or seen a sponsorship via the publicity generated through media coverage/exposure. Research into whether a sponsorship has achieved its intended communications objectives can generally be more reliably assessed using target market and attitudinal surveys, focus groups and interviews. Data showing increased awareness of a particular sponsors brand is not of much use if the level of perception is not measured. For example, numbers of sightings of logos and advertisements does not indicate the perception of brand values, benefits, pricing and availability whereas questioning intended targets can. A more comprehensive approach to evaluation will also utilize research data that is collected at different time intervals in order to track movement and shift.

Evaluation of the effects of communications can also utilize advertising effect-iveness techniques, such as recall and recognition measures with both 'top of the mind awareness' and prompted approaches. The extent of the effect of the sponsor and/or the brand involved is often measured via these techniques. Performance Research Europe (2000b) conducted telephone research in the 2 weeks following UEFA EURO 2000. They reported that despite watching an average of 13 EURO 2000 matches many fans struggled to identify tournament sponsors, and were often confused by the presence of non-EURO 2000 sponsors. During spontaneous spon-sorship awareness questioning in the 2 weeks that followed the tournaments con-clusion, 50 per cent of the fans in the sample (221 fans that reported watching or attending at least 3 EURO 200 matches) were unable to name any sponsors involved. Only 2 out of 10 identified McDonald's and 1 out of 10, Coca-Cola and Pringles in an unprompted/top of the mind awareness approach. A prompted recall approach achieved a higher awareness with 85 per cent of fans identifying Umbro, the England team kit sponsor whilst 75 per cent identified Carlsberg another England, UK television coverage and tournament sponsor. The research also showed that Carling, a non-sponsor, achieved nearly as much recall at 69 per cent and another non-sponsor, Nike, achieved 71 per cent which was ahead of tourna-ment sponsor adidas (70 per cent). Whilst this data does not prove or disprove the effectiveness of sponsorship, no doubt all parties involved, or not involved, in the event would have found this evaluation useful.

Companies do rely heavily on measuring sponsorship awareness (Thompson and Quester, 2000) and the use of unprompted versus prompted recall and recog-nition appears to be a common research method to do it. For example, it can be seen from Performance Research Europe's survey results above that there was an increase in awareness recall after the use of prompts. Whilst this is a well-used approach it is, nevertheless, disputed that prompted or unprompted recall is any-thing more than simply an 'identification' of a sponsor (Johar and Pham, 1999).

Tripodi et al. (2003) have conducted research into the use of prompts and the types of questions that get asked. They also wanted to determine if a particular sequence of questions could be important for sponsorship awareness measure-ment. They devised the following prompts.

Prompted sponsorship recall approaches:

- Event sponsorship prompt – 'When you think of (event A), which sponsors come to mind?'
- Brand sponsorship prompt – 'When you think of (brand B), what sponsor-ships come to mind?'
- Category sponsorship prompt – 'When you think of (category C), what spon-sorships come to mind?'

Prompted sponsorship recognition approaches:

- Brand recognition prompt – 'I am going to tell you some of brand B's current or recent sponsorships. For each one, tell me whether you were aware of brand B sponsoring that event, before today (describe each sponsorship).'

Whilst it is common practice in market research to measure spontaneous (event or brand cued) recall first and then follow that by recognition, Tripodi et al. (2003) found that simply adding prompts did not always result in better recall and indeed might be deemed to be interfering with it. They also concluded that as evaluation is a diagnostic measure that is used to aid future decision-making, it is a problem when different methods and approaches for testing produce different diagnoses. Therefore they do not recommend the use of ad hoc measures as they are likely to produce less validity. However, they do recommend the use of recall measures but only as supplementary methods that are conducted consistently.

Another level of evaluation is audience attitude or image of the brand. Techniques here can survey the extent of image transfer from the rights owner and the sponsored property to the brand/sponsor, in other words, an attempt to measure the effect of the sponsorship relationship (see Case Study 11.1). Survey methods include the use of Likert scales conducted both prior to and after the sponsorship so that the extent of change can be measured.

The perception of sponsorships and the 'signals' that the sponsorship relationship inspire are seldom considered as a measure. However, it would appear to be an

Case Study 11.1 Sponsorship evaluation: S-COMM – The effectiveness of football sponsorship

S-COMM

S-COMM is a leading sponsorship research and evaluation consultancy that works with both sponsors and rights holders.

In 2001 it conducted a study focused on the English Premier League and television viewers. The objectives were to assess the following:

- Recall of names and logos at football matches:
  - perimeter advertising boards,
  - team shirts,
  - on-screen credits.
- Attitudes to advertising at football grounds.
- Attitudes and perceptions to sponsorship within football.
- Demographics and lifestyles of football viewers.

Methodology

The sample consisted of 150 television football fans, 18- to 35-year-old males watching football on television at least once a season, based in the London and Home Counties region. The sample closely reflected the socio-economic breakdown of the UK but with a slight bias towards C1 (middle/junior management).

No football match involving a London-based team was used in an attempt to limit bias in support and knowledge of teams. Over 75 per cent of the sample watched more than 10 matches per season. The sample was recruited via an approach on the street in six areas: Barking, Sutton, Maidstone, Ilford, Luton and Kingston.

Three Premier League matches were selected from the 2000/2001 season featuring one team both home and away, Everton versus Aston Villa, Leicester versus Everton and Leeds versus Liverpool. Clips of 15 minutes were shown to the whole sample in a large hall and included shots of advertising boards at ground and upper levels, player interviews against sponsorship backboards, broadcast commercial break bumpers and on-screen credits. Questions were asked before and after the clips.

Results

Recall of perimeter boards

- 52 per cent can recall the sponsor/brand on at least one board unprompted.
- Highest level of recall for any one board was 23 per cent.
- Four brands achieved a recall of 10 per cent or more.
- Rotating boards on the centre line received minimal awareness in the test – due to poor design and sun glare.
- Sponsors with boards on the second tiers of the grounds gained little awareness.
- A consistent supply of boards at matches increases awareness.
- Carling, Sony PlayStation, McDonald's and Yorkie were the brands that were consistently recalled – these sponsors used extensive exploitation in support of their sponsorships, a factor that was considered to be critical for their consistent recall. Other brands (Siemens, Wash&Go, HSBC, Lunn Poly) which do not exploit to the same degree did not achieve the same level of awareness.
- A minimum of three well-positioned boards at a stadium optimizes awareness.

Recall of shirt sponsors

- 53 to 55 per cent was the average recall of a team's shirt sponsor (home or away).
- The length of the sponsorship association impacts on recall – the longer the sponsorship the higher the recall.

Recall of on-screen activity

- Carling's on-screen presence was recalled by 24 per cent of the viewers.
- Cisco (match facts service provider) did achieve awareness despite only one showing.
- Virtual branding on the pitches was recalled by 70 per cent of viewers – this was of the clubs crests and logos rather than sponsor brands.

Fans attitudes towards brands

- 32 per cent of viewers said that they would be more likely to consider buying from sponsors of their own team – this rises to 42 per cent amongst avid fans.
- 23 per cent said that they definitely would not buy the products from the sponsors of their main rival teams.

Source: S-COMM Research Ltd (2001)

important area of measurement when considering the links between a sponsor and a rights owner/sponsored property are what sets a sponsorship apart from other communications. Little enough evaluation has been undertaken in order to identify if this is indeed proving to be a key aspect of differential, but from what has been done we can begin to speculate that sponsorship has the capacity to change a consumer's perception of a specific sponsor and that in turn it can have an effect on the perception of that sponsor's brand. This becomes even more important when a consumer is then willing to purchase that brand. Consequently evaluation scales of trust, liking and respect should be considered as useful measurements (Harvey, 2001). Hansen and Halling (2001) also considered this aspect of evaluation and concluded that much more significant effects of sponsoring can be established when evaluation of attitudes towards the sponsorship, liking the sponsor/brand, linking between the sponsor and sponsorship and emotional responses are undertaken.

The importance of tracking (measurements taken over time to cover different stages of the life of the sponsorship) is vital for much sponsorship evaluation. Where a sponsorship extends over a number of renewals or if rights change over the initial term, there is a need to track how awareness is changing. Taking measurement at different points over time and comparing fresh results with previous ones also carries more validity than ad hoc measurements that can only represent one snapshot in time. For example, it was important for CGU Insurance to measure the effects on awareness and the performance of its sponsorship of the National Cricket League in the UK. The sponsorship was begun in 1999 and by focusing market surveys on the question 'have you heard of a company called CGU' the brand was able to measure its objectives for building brand awareness prior to and during the sponsorship (see Figure 11.1). Between September 1998

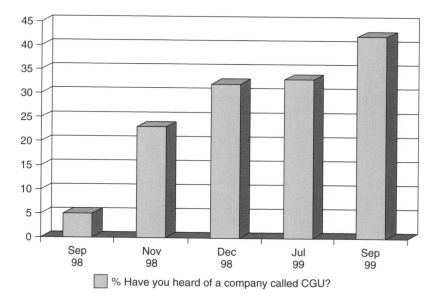

Figure 11.1 CGU: Brand Awareness Tracking Evaluation (% of Respondents That are Aware of CGU) (adapted from Ipsos-RSL (2006) and Connexus (2006a))

and September 1999 the brand was able to measure an increase from 5 to 42 per cent awareness amongst ABC1 males.

Siemens Mobile, took measurements prior to and after their sponsorship of Sky television movies channels. Customer surveys were used to identify opinion on the modernity of the brand, whether it was trustworthy, cutting edge and value for money. Figures 11.2 (pre-sponsorship) and 11.3 (post-sponsorship) show that in each category, the image of the brand developed positively by 78 per cent (modernity), 90 per cent (trust), 114 per cent (edge) and 75 per cent (value), respectively.

Comparisons with other brands can also be made over time and in order to specifically identify where change has occurred in relation to the competitive market positions that the sponsor has taken. Figures 11.2 and 11.3 show how Siemens was able to compare its mobile brand with other leading competitors, Nokia, Ericsson and Motorola. Again this evaluation shows how the Siemens brand was able to compare its brand position in the market pre- and post-sponsorship in order to measure sponsorship effect. Figure 11.4 shows that it was also able to make a further comparison of customer brand recall against a wider list of competitors in order to identify a sponsorship effect that saw it rise from a market position of sixth (pre-sponsorship) to third (post-sponsorship). Finally the brand was able to make comparisons of its own marketing communications strategies by measuring the effects of its English Premier League football sponsorship against the effects of its independent advertising, partnership/co-operative advertising and its sponsorship in Formula 1 motor racing (see Figure 11.5).

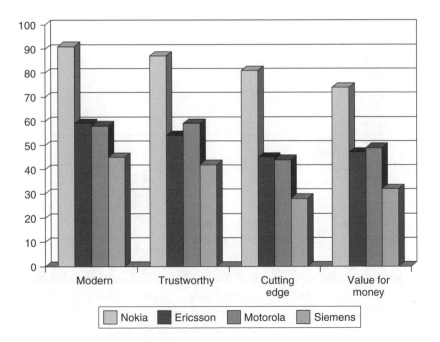

Figure 11.2 Siemens: Effect on Brand Imagery (% of Respondents – Pre-Sponsorship) (adapted from Connexus (2006b))

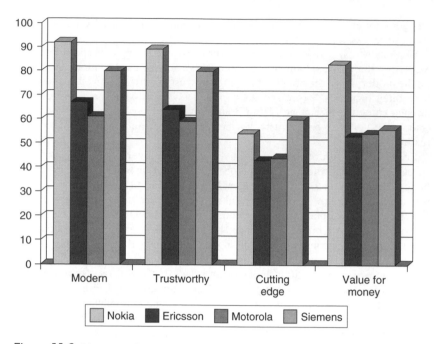

Figure 11.3 Siemens: Effect on Brand Imagery (% or Respondents – Post-Sponsorship) (adapted from Connexus (2006b))

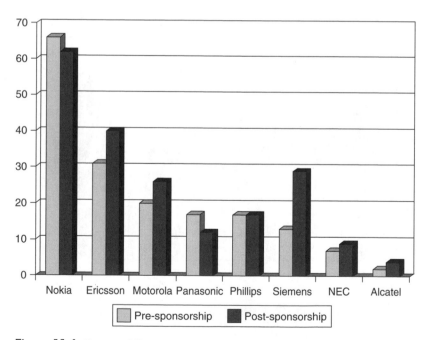

Figure 11.4 Siemens: Effect on Purchase Considerations (% of Total Spontaneous and Prompted Viewer Mentions) (adapted from Connexus (2006b))

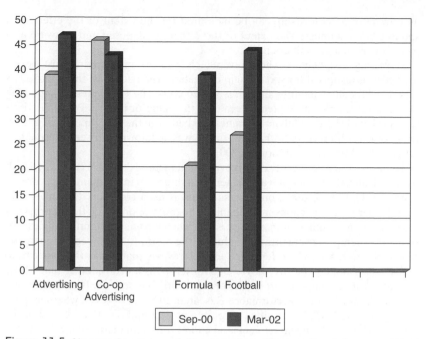

Figure 11.5 Siemens: Comparison of Communications Effect on Brand Awareness (% of Unaided Brand Awareness amongst Those Aware of Siemens) (adapted from Connexus (2006b))

The effect of a sponsorship can also be measured, again commonly via Likert scale methods, by surveying those that were aware (prompted and unprompted) and those that were not aware of the sponsorship, as opposed to just measuring brand awareness. By asking all survey respondents questions about the brand, questions that are specifically image related, a comparison can be made between those that were aware and those that were not aware of the sponsorship. The difference is then used as a measure of the extent of the effect of the sponsorship. For example, a survey (unprompted) of 600 British males, aged 15 to 69 years, with an interest in football, scored Manchester United's shirt sponsors Vodafone with the highest awareness and Premier League sponsors Barclaycard second overall (European Football Monitor, 2003). Coca-Cola, sponsors of The Championship and Worthington, sponsors of the League Cup, scored significantly lower. Nike and adidas, team kit suppliers and Nationwide, a F.A. partner all scored the same. A measurement of sponsorship awareness can indicate the extent to which a brand is associated with a rights owner/property and is also considered to be an indication of the success the sponsor has had in communicating that link to the target audience.

There are commentators that question a focus that compares 'aware' with 'unaware'. The criticism is based on the fact that the unaware may not have been exposed to the sponsorship and therefore an evaluation of sponsorship effect that includes them, will be misleading. Instead, evaluation could focus on a comparison of the exposed and non-exposed (Walshe, 2000). By focusing on degrees of exposure, for example comparisons of audiences with chances and greater chances to see or hear the sponsorship, the argument is, that evaluation can be totally focused on the effect of a sponsorship. Those audiences that are exposed and aware of a sponsorship can be measured for the extent of the effect on a sponsor brand's image. The extent of those that are exposed and unaware also provides important evaluation.

Measuring cost–benefit, where revenue changes are measured against associated costs, is also used for sponsorship evaluation. The issue with this approach is that it is difficult to identify all the associated costs. The US General Accounting Office, for example, attempted to evaluate the value of the US Postal Service's sponsorship of the 1992 Olympic Games and had to, in the end, report that overall profit or loss with respect to the sponsorship was 'unknown' (General Accounting Office, 1993; Miyazaki and Morgan, 2001).

There are other financially driven evaluation methods that are concerned with overall financial gain and the assessment of a return on investment that is organization wide. For example, one measure that is used considers the changes in shareholder wealth in sponsor companies. The premise on which this approach is based, by some commentators at least, is that when it comes to significantly expensive sponsorship investments, the value of the 'bottom-line' needs to increase. Research for NASCAR, referred to earlier, reveals that it has the capacity to deliver sales and competitive advantage for its sponsors considering that 72 per cent of NASCAR fans almost always or frequently buy sponsor brands over that of non-sponsor brands (Performance Research, 2000a). However, whether sponsorship of NASCAR is a positive corporate project and one that nets all of the costs associated with the investment is an entirely different metric of accountability that will no doubt be critically considered in the boardroom (Pruitt et al., 2004).

The argument for using shareholder wealth as a measure is: (a) that a measure of awareness and recognition for a sponsorship that consists of numerous integrated communication activities is going to be extremely difficult to measure and (b) that ultimately an objective of a return on investment starts with a measure of whether all the costs of the sponsorship have been retrieved. Sponsorships may be either more, or less, than the sum total of their traditional assessment metrics and so this is why a measure of changes in stock prices have been used to assess sponsorship accountability (Pruitt et al., 2004). Mathur et al. (1997) and Agrawai and Kamakura (1995), for example, have used stock price changes to determine impact for sponsors in celebrity endorsements and Clark et al. (2002) used stadium sponsorships (naming rights). A study by Cornwell et al. (2001) that addressed the 'value of victory' (race wins) in USA motor sports and specifically the Indianapolis 500 series revealed that only the sponsor companies that were associated with the consumer automotive industry saw positive increases in stock prices. These sponsors increased their net-of-market stock prices by 3 per cent around the time of their Indianapolis victories.

Several commentators have focused on market value. Miyazaki and Morgan (2001) looked at the market value of sponsors of the Olympic Games. Pruitt et al. (2004) focused their research on the question of whether NASCAR sponsorships provide economic value based on stock changes. In other words did NASCAR stockholders view sponsorships as particularly good or poor investment decisions? In 2004, the average breakeven target figure for NASCAR sponsors was $10 million per season with top teams costing up to $18 million in sponsorship investment. Their findings were that for the 24 primary NASCAR sponsors they studied between 1995 and 2001, there were generally positive increases in stocks. The average increase in wealth being over $300 million and $500 million for those sponsors that were directly associated with the automotive industry. Miyazaki and Morgan (2001) also found that the market saw Olympic sponsors as positive investments.

Whilst there has been a certain amount of research in the area of using stock and market value changes as measures for sponsorship evaluation, these approaches suffer from the same issues as most other current measures. A rise in stock is not indisputably a direct consequence of a sponsorship. Other factors such as economic conditions, competitor activity and inactivity may have influenced the outcome. Interestingly, it might have been worthwhile for the above commentators (Cornwell et al., 2001; Pruitt et al., 2004) to have assessed sponsorship relationships and fit in their studies as there was a strong case for assuming that the links between automotive sponsors with motor racing proved to be a critical factor.

Summary: a way forward?

If the 'tough nut' of sponsorship evaluation can be cracked then the way forward for sponsorship could indeed become very positive. After all, sponsorship has not come this far without there being this promise. However, as can be seen from the above discussions, the state of sponsorship evaluation is far from satisfactory. There is too little evaluation and too few reliable and valid techniques available.

The result is that there is no standardization and any evaluation that is performed is open to variable interpretation or even misuse. For UEFA EURO '96 one particular sponsor used one set of evaluation data to confidently claim that their association with the event was recorded at 70 per cent awareness. A different evaluation by IpsosRSL showed a different result at 15 to 20 per cent (Jackson and Lowde, 2000). This is one example of how different techniques can result in different interpretations.

Another issue is that different evaluators can produce evaluation with different interpretations. Depending on who produces the analysis, a final report can be open to misinterpretation and used to accentuate any case required, whether that is for external or internal relations at a sponsoring organization. The important point to understand here is that results that show a negative achievement still form essential information for future decision-making, whether that be to realign a sponsorship or curtail it. Of course, the message that is put out externally as publicity can be one thing, but internally the truth of the evaluation should be candid and comprehensive.

Standardization will only be achieved once there are reliable and valid techniques. Whilst we await their development, there remains a critical need for sponsorship to show when it does, or does not, provide a return on investment. Therefore there is the pressing need to encourage more rights owners and sponsors to evaluate.

The way forward is a sponsorship evaluation framework that consists of a combination of current measures (Tripodi et al., 2003). As sponsorship essentially involves many different types of communication, it is likely that a more extensive range of measures will be required than for other forms of communications (Meenaghan, 2005; Walshe, 2000). Thus sponsorship evaluation, depending on what objectives are set, should consist of techniques that measure sales, awareness and image, and also the effects of all sponsorship-related communications, in a 'total communications' approach. As sponsorships strategically take advantage of the developing range of new media opportunities it has become increasingly difficult to evaluate all communications accurately. Respondents find it difficult to separate and accurately identify what and where they saw and heard. Despite this proviso, it is important to evaluate the wider communications that are used by sponsors to exploit their sponsorship rights.

There are issues for the management of sponsorship evaluation. How, for example is sponsorship evaluation managed in either multi-faceted or multi-regional sponsorship programmes? When there are different target audiences involved, however near or far apart they are, it is critical that evaluation is considered for each audience. Therefore this may require a degree of local autonomy in order to undertake accurate evaluation which in turn may require the assignment of local evaluation budgets in order to measure against different objectives (Meenaghan, 2005).

Sponsorship evaluation should be conducted alongside measurement of the competition, as other brands will be affecting the market and possibly the sponsor's performance. It is therefore necessary to identify whether this was the case, and to what extent, in order to fully consider the sponsorship effect. A substantial programme of sponsorship communication may still lead to an insufficient return on investment if competitors have better results for example. On the other hand a successful return on investment may have been achieved, but a contributory factor may have been little competitor activity or impact in the marketplace.

The development of a different approach to sponsorship evaluation, one that gets closer to demonstrating that sponsors can achieve returns on their investments, will help encourage the use of more evaluation. The solution, for the present at least, is multi-faceted measurement of the effect of sponsorship (sales, awareness, image and total communications), an important area of development for sponsorship evaluation. What is critical to develop though is a focus on the sponsorship relationship itself. If sponsorship is to be judged as an independent communications tool there should be further development of techniques that can accurately evaluate all the aspects of the critical differential that sponsorship has over other forms of communication, namely the value of the sponsorship relationship and the effect that has on audiences. The sponsor brand message for example, is/should be contained in the link between a sponsor and rights owner/sponsorship property (Thompson and Vickers, 2002). By measuring the effect this link has on a sponsor brand, sponsorship evaluation will edge nearer to achieving more accuracy in the extent to which sponsorship can deliver a return on investment. Whilst clearly this is an approach that requires both consideration and development, it can utilize existing metrics for sales, awareness, image and communications but with a focus on the sponsorship and its effects on the brand/sponsor it will further isolate the effect of sponsorship for more accurate evaluation.

Tasks and discussion points

- Select an event and consider how it could develop research and evaluation in order to develop its sponsorship programme.
- Select a sponsor and identify a methodology for the post-evaluation of its sponsorship.
- Consider the evaluation of football sponsorship in Case Study 11.1 and critically analyse how the evaluation approach might be improved.

References

Agrawai, J. and Kamakura, W. (1995). The economic worth of celebrity endorsers: An event study analysis. *Journal of Marketing*, Vol. 59, No. 3, pp. 56–62. www.warc.com/ArticleCenter (accessed 5 April 2006).

Amis, J., Slack, T. and Berrett, T. (1999). Sport sponsorship as distinctive competence. *European Journal of Marketing*, Vol. 33, No. 3, pp. 291–313.

Bennett, R. (1999). Sports sponsorship, spectator recall and false consensus. *European Journal of Marketing*, Vol. 33, No. 3, pp. 291–313. www.emeraldinsight.com (accessed 5 November 2004).

Boone, L. and Kurtz, D. (2002). *Contemporary marketing 2002*. London: Thomson Learning.

Clark, J., Cornwell, T. and Pruitt, S. (2002). Corporate stadium sponsorships, signalling theory, agency conflicts and shareholder wealth. *Journal of Advertising Research*, Vol. 42, No. 6, pp. 16–32.

Connexus (2006a). CGU case study. www.conexus-sponsorship.co.uk/hist-cgu2 (accessed 23 November 2006).

Connexus (2006b). Siemens mobile case study. www.conexus-sponsorship.co.uk/hist-siemens2 (accessed 23 November 2006).

Cornwell, T., Pruitt, S. and Van Ness, R. (2001). The value of winning in motorsports: Sponsorship linked-marketing. *Journal of Advertising Research*, Vol. 41, No. 1, pp. 17–31.

Dolphin, R. (2003). Sponsorship: Perspectives on its strategic role. Corporate communications: *An international journal*, Vol. 8, No. 3, pp. 173–186.

European Football Monitor (2003). Sport + market AG. Wave 1, Cologne, Germany 2002/2003 in Meenaghan, T. (2005). Evaluating sponsorship effects. *Global sport sponsorship*, Amis, J. and Cornwell, B. (Eds.). Oxford: Berg.

General Accounting Office (1993). Postal Service 1992 Olympic sponsorship profit or loss is unknown. Report to the Sub-Committee on Federal Services, Post Office and Civil Service, Committee on Governmental Affairs, US Senate. GAO/GGD9389, July 23. Washington, DC: General Accounting Office.

Gillis, R. (2005). The media value problem. *Sportbusiness*, February 2005.

Hansen, F. and Halling, J. (2001). Estimation of emotional and evaluating effects of sport sponsorships. Forum for Advertising Research, May. www.warc.com/ArticleCenter (accessed 4 October 2006).

Harvey. B. (2001). Measuring the effects of sponsorships. *Journal of Advertising Research*, Vol. 41, No. 1, January/February. www.warc.com/ArticleCenter (accessed 4 October 2006).

Hawtin, L. (2004). Imperial Leather sponsorship wins the 2002 Commonwealth Games. IPA. www.warc.com (accessed 5 April 2006).

Hoek, J. (1998). Sponsorship: An evaluation of management assumptions and practices. *Marketing Bulletin*, Vol. 10, pp. 1–10.

IEG/Performance Research (2004). 4th annual sponsorship decision-makers survey. *IEG Sponsorship Report*. Sample Issue. Chicago, IL: IEG.

Ipsos-RSL (2006). CGU case study. www.conexus-sponsorship.co.uk/hist-cgu2 (accessed 23 November 2006).

Jackson, M. and Lowde, M. (2000). Sponsorship, oh well just add it to the brand tracking study. *Market research society annual conference*, 2000. www.warc.com/ArticleCenter (accessed 5 April 2006).

Johar, G. and Pham, M. (1999). Relatedness, prominence, and constructive sponsor identification. *Journal of Marketing Research*, Vol. 36, August. pp. 299–312.

Joyce Julius and Associates (2004). www.joycejulius.com (accessed 6 February 2004).

Kotler, P. and Keller, K. (2006). *Marketing management*, 12th Edition. Upper Saddle River, NJ: Prentice Hall.

Masterman, G. (2004). *Strategic sports event management: An international approach*. Oxford: Butterworth-Heinemann.

Masterman, G. and Wood, E. H. (2006). *Innovative marketing communications: Strategies for the events industry.* Oxford: Elsevier/Butterworth-Heinemann.

Mathur, L., Mathur, I. and Rangan, N. (1997). The wealth effects associated with a celebrity endorser: The Michael Jordan phenomenon. *Journal of Advertising Research*, Vol. 37, No. 3, pp. 67–73.

Meenaghan, T. (1991). The role of sponsorship in the marketing communications mix. *International Journal of Advertising*, Vol. 10, No. 1, pp. 35–47.

Meenaghan, T. (2005). Evaluating sponsorship effects. *Global sport sponsorship*, Amis, J. and Cornwell, B. (Eds.). Oxford: Berg.

Miyazaki, A. and Morgan, A. (2001). Assessing the market value of sponsoring: Corporate Olympic sponsorships. *Journal of Advertising Research*, Vol. 41, No. 1, January/February. www.warc.com/ArticleCenter (accessed 5 April 2006).

Performance Research Europe (2000a). Viagra and Lycos outperform first year sponsors to Nascar. www.performanceresearch.com (accessed 9 October 2003).

Performance Research Europe (2000b). British football fans can't recall Euro 2000 sponsors. www.performanceresearch.com (accessed 10 September 2003).

Pope, N. and Voges, K. (1994). Sponsorship evaluation: Does it match the motive and the mechanism? *Sport Marketing Quarterly*, Vol. 3, No. 4, pp. 38–45.

Pruitt, S., Cornwell, T. and Clark, J. (2004). The NASCAR phenomenon: Auto racing sponsorships and shareholder wealth. *Journal of Advertising Research*, Vol. 44, No. 3. www.warc.com (accessed 5 April 2006).

Redmandarin (2004). *The 2004 Redmandarin European Sponsors' Survey.* Full Report. In Association with The Sponsorship Research Company. London: Redmandarin Sponsorship Consulting.

S-COMM Research Ltd (2001). The effectiveness of football sponsorship: Summary report. Buckinghamshire: S-Comm UK Ltd.

Sports Business Daily (2004). Nielson unveils service measuring sports sponsorship. www.sportsbusinessdaily.com Vol. X, No. 48, 23 April. (accessed 23 April 2004).

Sports Marketing Surveys (2006). *The Inside track.* Surrey: Sport Marketing Surveys Ltd.

Thompson, B. and Quester, P. (2000). Conference paper. *Evaluating sponsorship effectiveness: The Adelaide festival of the arts.* Australian and New Zealand Marketing Academy Conference. November–December 2000. Visionary marketing for the 21st Century: Facing the challenge.

Thompson, I. and Vickers, S. (2002). Sponsorship: The real deal. *Admap*, October, Issue 432. www.warc.com/ArticleCenter (accessed 4 October 2006).

Tripodi, J. (2001). Sponsorship – a confirmed weapon in the promotional armoury. *International Journal of Sports Marketing and Sponsorship*, March/April.

Tripodi, J., Hirons, M., Bednall, D. and Sutherland, M. (2003). Cognitive evaluation: Prompts used to measure sponsorship awareness. *International Journal of Market Research*, Vol. 45, No. 4. www.warc.com/ArticleCenter (accessed 4 October 2006).

Walshe, P. (2000). What price 'sponsorship awareness'? *Admap*, July. www.warc.com/ArticleCenter (accessed 5 April 2006).

12

Sponsorship aware!

The objectives for this chapter are to:

- Identify and evaluate current and future issues for the development of sponsorship as a communications tool
- Consider the barriers to sponsorship return on investment
- Highlight the importance of sponsorship fit, exploitation and evaluation for sponsorship success

Nike Ambush Marketing, Prague
Nike takes advantage of the 2004 UEFA European Championships held in Portugal by
promoting around Europe using giant footballs
Photograph: Trish Coll

Introduction

Many texts culminate with a final chapter on contemporary issues and elaborate on future issues for their subject focus. The intention for this chapter is more than that. Whilst a number of key issues for the development of sponsorship are identified here, issues that are indeed of future importance, they are used to collectively demonstrate the key message for this text, that sponsorship has got to proactively demonstrate its value. Essentially this comes down to a clear demonstration of return on investment.

Fair or foul, ambush marketing involves direct attack on competitors and their sponsorships and as such spells out the danger for sponsorship. If ambush marketers are selecting ambush versus sponsorship communications and are basing that decision on there being a lack of demonstration of sponsorship value, then that gap has to be filled or sponsorship per se is under considerable threat.

Sponsorship value is also intrinsically linked to the strength of the sponsorship relationship between a rights owners and a sponsor, and so how it is ethically managed as well as controlled are important issues. For example, it is necessary to consider which sponsorships are ethically right to be involved with and should sponsors be in control of how a sponsored property is managed. Further issues are that rights owners are becoming increasingly dependent on sponsorship and a polarization effect is in evidence with already powerful rights owners becoming more powerful at the expense of others. However, whilst sponsorship continues to flourish independently in a number of sectors, the growing trend of using multifaceted sponsorships that incorporate any number of industry sectors is an important trend for communications and an approach that will require an adjustment by many sponsorship managers. The message here is that sponsorship should be aware of already developed trends and consider how it will live up to the enormous promise it has thus far shown as a communications tool.

This chapter considers these issues and their collective impact on sponsorship return on investment by concluding that there are three key components that both rights owners and sponsors need to get right for successful sponsorship, a sponsorship fit, exploitation of the rights and evaluation.

Ambush marketing: fair or foul?

Ambush-marketing tactics have been much utilized since the early 1990s and have become a considerable issue for both sponsors and rights owners. The ongoing concern for rights owners is the threat to sponsorship value and that sponsors will consequently pay less or even prefer other communications options. The further issue is that rights owners have the expense of meeting their sponsors' increasing expectations for their sponsorship rights to be protected from ambush tactics. The greater the threat of ambush, the harder the job of recruiting sponsors therefore becomes. Equally the threat to sponsorship value is a concern for sponsors. If they are exploiting their rights they are, in effect, creating new platforms for their competitors to exploit.

Sponsors have retaliated by making it known that they believe ambush marketing to be unscrupulous. This is supported to some degree by those commentators that see event ambush marketing as the tactics of those companies that seek to associate with an event without paying any sponsorship fees (Kolah, 1999). However, the other and more correct view is that free markets are fair game. Considering that most event ambush marketing is not illegal, it is more appropriate to view it as competitive use of communications, even use of innovative communications (Masterman and Wood, 2006). When a sponsor has strategically created its own market position its competitors have the right to see this as a legitimate opportunity for direct and competitive communications activity. Nike consistently positions itself as anti-establishment and prefers ambush-marketing tactics as opposed to sponsorship (Gratton and Taylor, 2000). The increasing danger for rights owners is if companies decide that ambush tactics are more successful than using sponsorship and do not then become or continue as sponsors. Nike, for example, achieved higher recall in fans attending UEFA's EURO 2000 football championship than many of the sponsors, recording 71 per cent recall whilst sponsors Mastercard (56 per cent), JVC (48 per cent) and Fuji (48 per cent) were someway behind (Performance Research Europe, 2002). Meanwhile adidas, the sportswear manufacturer and a UEFA sponsor, recorded less recall at 70 per cent.

Perhaps of more concern are those brands that sponsor and then prefer other tactics. One such brand, the Proctor and Gamble snack, Pringles, as former sponsors of UEFA and EURO 2000 decided on ambush tactics at UEFA's EURO 2004 Championships. The brand used individual high-profile footballers and their images on-pack in a 2 million deal and of course the beneficiaries did not include the event rights owners. There is nothing illegal here but the concern is that a sponsor has decided that ambush tactics were a more effective route than sponsorship renewal. In another example, Absolut vodka produced branded postcards and distributed them throughout Europe 1 month before the same event. On one side of the card there was the tag line 'Absolut kick-off' and a representation of the actual tournament competition draw, team-by-team, group-by-group, and depicted in the shape of the brands distinctive bottle. There was no reference at all to EURO 2004 as Absolut were not an event sponsor however, their perceived association with the event was all too clear. Again, the concern for the organizers was the devaluing of the value of their sponsorships (Masterman and Wood, 2006).

The use of advertising space to ambush was at one time a lot more common. The acquisition of television broadcast sponsorship was once an independent opportunity in the 1990s but in an attempt to police ambush marketing, many events rights owners started to work with the television media. By negotiating with their broadcast partners prior to their approach to sponsors, events are now able to secure combined rights of broadcast and event sponsorship for their eventual sponsorship programmes.

Individual rights owners have also sought legal protection of their rights with sports celebrities such as Muhammad Ali, Tiger Woods, Eddie Irvine, Franz Beckenbauer and the model Linda Evangelista all having successfully sued for the unauthorized commercial use of their names and images (Harrington, 2002). The intent is to protect the value of those rights when they come to be sold to sponsors.

Despite the increasing need by sponsors for their rights to come ready protected, this often requires a difficult and resource sapping effort by rights owners. One area of rights that has proved very difficult to protect in the sports events industry is where sponsorship of individuals or teams is used tactically against the event's paying sponsors. Even major international events have difficulties here. The sponsorship of one sports team or an individual player by a sportswear manufacturer and then that team competing in an event that has a different sportswear category sponsor is difficult to prevent and as a result is often not 'policed' at all. The effect is that, to all intents and purposes, the event rights owners offer their sponsors a take-it-or-leave-it set of rights (Masterman and Wood, 2006). The FIFA World Cup currently has an official sportswear manufacturer in adidas and readily accepts that it cannot, and would not, prevent Brazil from competing and often achieving a high profile in the competition whilst wearing its Nike sponsored team kit. Nike, via deliberate ambush tactics, widely uses other communications and in particular television at pertinent times to support these opportunities. For example, its television advertisement, featuring Brazil and Portugal in Nike team kit, was broadcast on a pan-European basis in the build-up to the UEFA EURO 2004 Championships in order to compete in that market directly with adidas, the official sportswear sponsor for this event.

There are nevertheless considerable measures of protection that are more easily taken by some rights owners, including FIFA. The standard rights package for the 2006 FIFA World Cup event includes ambush-marketing protection (FIFA, 2004). FIFA maintain that 'profiting from the popularity of their event, without making any financial contribution directly to it or the game of football, undermines the integrity of the event and its marketing programme and also the interests of football worldwide'. Consequently, the international governing body has developed a worldwide 'Rights Protection Programme' that focuses on the prevention of illegal use of trademarks and associations with the event. Aside from seeking the protection of the law there are also measures of protection that involve early pre-event planning and the formulation of media schedules. To prevent potential ambushing companies buying advertising billboards outside event stadia, the simple protection measure is for the rights owners to make early reservations of these spaces themselves and then offer them to their sponsors. In effect this can be done as far ahead as is required and clearly long before any event sponsors are actually even in place. When sponsors are recruited the spaces are then confirmed, still well ahead of the event, and offered to sponsors. Sponsors can then exploit and support their newly acquired rights. At the same time this is a good way for rights owners to proactively encourage sponsors to exploit generally.

Most cities that bid for major international sports events are in fact very conscious of the expectations of their sponsors and some have recognized the need for the long-term planning that is required by securing opportunities for their potential sponsors' exploitation communications in advance. On occasions this requires changes to local by-laws and as cities can effectively do that, in these cases that is exactly what they do to provide protection. For example, enforced and supported by a city instigated 'executive order', a city can reserve local public advertising space. By doing so a rights owner not only offers its sponsors opportunities to support their sponsorships, they offer them a degree of built-in ambush protection. If a sponsor such as adidas has first option on the advertising billboards around a football ground it might feel more secure of the position it can create via a potential sponsorship if it can restrict a competitor such as Nike via the same process. In a move to protect potential sponsors of a New York 2012 Olympics, NYC2012 secured the majority of the outdoor media that would be available in New York City for 2012 and it did this prior to making its bid in 2005 when it did not know if it would host the event or not. This amounted to contacting the owners and securing 95 per cent of the 600,000 advertising signs (billboards, transport, street signage) available. This was quite a remarkable piece of forward planning. To achieve this it had to negotiate a price with commercial suppliers 8 years in advance (NYC2012, 2004). The extent of the planning involved and indeed the level of built-in protection here surprised and impressed many at the time of New York's bid and certainly set a precedent.

Whilst the advanced effort that has been undertaken in order to offer the level of protection New York intended is new, rights owners have been undertaking protection measures for some time. This has been extended to include the 'policing' of spectators at events. For example, at the Sydney 2000 Olympics, officials were confiscating Pepsi drinks from spectators at Olympic venues (Hobson, 2004). At the 2003 Cricket World Cup in South Africa any non-Pepsi drinks were confiscated. At the 2004 Athens Olympics spectators were warned that they could not enter a venue with any food or drink, including water and icetrays. They also found their entry barred if they wore promotional clothing, if that clothing did not bear the brands of official Olympic sponsors. Opportunities for co-ordinated group promotions, where spectators might sit/stand/walk next to others so that graphics on their clothing might be seen to spell out non-sponsor brand messages, were also monitored and banned (Hobson, 2004).

The levels to which events in particular go to protect their rights are themselves open to questioning. Whilst New York City offered its local independent commercial suppliers of advertising sites an above-the-rate and index-linked price for the right to reserve sites 8 years ahead of a potential Olympic Games, the question as to how far the City should have been allowed to insist that sites could be reserved was raised. Additionally, the rights of individuals to buy and eat what they like was clearly something the individual who was ejected (because he had non-Pepsi products) from the 2003 Cricket World Cup took very seriously by taking his case to court.

With ambush tactics becoming more widely used, the question of whether ambush tactics are fair or foul has been raised. The answer of course is that in a free market a competitor is entitled to compete and sponsors are therefore fair and legitimate targets for aggressive and even direct marketing communications tactics. The real issue and question each sponsor should therefore ask is whether it is doing enough to defend the platform and market position it creates when it becomes a sponsor. As some commentators suggest, the problem appears to be that companies think that the public cannot differentiate between official partners and those that ambush (Poole, 2004). If this were true there would be little point in becoming a sponsor. Clearly though, there is a need to do more than simply take and use sponsorship rights.

The solution is exploitation. Whilst taking a sponsorship usually offers exclusive and therefore unique potential for achieving positioning objectives, in order to consolidate any promise of competitive advantage, a sponsor needs to fully exploit its sponsorship rights. Exploitation is therefore a requirement in order to make sponsorship work because it is the way to defend a position and sponsorship communications platform. Following this, the task is then to ensure that evaluation is undertaken so that any return on investment can be demonstrated, thereby confirming effective use of sponsorship as opposed to other forms of communications, including ambush tactics.

Some sponsors have also been known to show their initiative and take advantage of opportunities that they are not sponsoring. In fact they use the communications that they execute in support of their exploitation of their sponsorship rights to do this. One example is Northern Rock, shirt sponsor of Newcastle United. They dressed Newcastle player Michael Owen in his club strip and then draped him in a St George's flag for a programme of advertising prior to the England team departing for Germany and the World Cup in 2006. It clearly becomes a very difficult job to 'police' an event such as the FIFA World Cup when on a worldwide basis even local advertisers see opportunities to 'associate' with powerful media opportunities.

The tactics of some ambushing brands are worth noting. Some can be extremely innovative and for those sponsors that do little exploitation they can provide inspiration. The Bavarian Beer Company, a Dutch brewer, provided orange coloured trousers to a large number of Dutch football supporters at Holland's game with Ivory Coast at the 2006 World Cup. The supporters, fully clad in their national colour but also branded with Bavarian Beer Company logos were asked to leave the stadium by officials or stay but without their trousers on. The response was for the supporters to stay. This was simple yet innovative. The Bavarian Beer Company, not an official FIFA sponsor, achieved some small-scale exposure at the event but much wider awareness via worldwide reporting of the story. The irony, like the case at the 2003 Cricket World Cup above, is that the event might have limited this exposure had they not 'policed' the incident. The Bavarian Beer Company clearly needed a response in order to make this a successful tactic.

Sponsorship ethics

There are some important ethical issues in sponsorship. These are issues that exist as a fine line between what might be considered innovative and welcomed by society and what is not socially acceptable. For example, the use of sponsorship by tobacco manufacturers to reach target markets was once acceptable but then banned. Despite the angst at the prospect of losing sponsorship income, key sports such as motor racing and snooker have managed to survive.

There are other sectors that questionably remain in sponsorship. Hoek et al. (1997) reported some time ago that alcohol had caused ethical concerns because of its potentially negative effects on society. The combination of alcohol and sport in particular, but also the arts and music, remains a potent partnership and exposure to young fans continues unabated. The support of football teams and then the production of replica team jerseys that carry their alcohol brand names is one such example. Children who are legally not allowed to drink are wearing clothing that bears alcohol related branding.

The targeting of younger markets via sponsorship does raise further concerns. For example, another more recent issue relates to the exploitation of the young as endorsers. Across the USA there are young skateboarders and BMX riders that have been given product provided they accept that it remains bedecked in branded logos. Some of these children have been given contracts to ensure this. For example, in 2003, 'Little Tricky' Mitchie Brusco, a 6-year old skateboarder had sponsorship from Jones Soda, Lego and Termite, and had appeared on several national television programmes (Talbot, 2003). Dylan Oliver was only 4-year old when he received sponsorship from Nice Skateboards and at the age of 13, footballer Freddy Adu was paid $1 million by Nike. Also in 2003, Mark Walker, only three and half at the time, had a contract with Reebok that facilitated him with his own website address (markwalker.reebok.com, 2004). On that website there was footage of Mark playing basketball, referring to himself, as being the future of basketball and uttering the words, 'I am Reebok'. The ethics are not clear here, but the communications decisions by Reebok were deliberate. They were exploiting a sponsorship and in many ways innovatively.

Again in the USA, companies have been keen to do in schools what they have been doing in colleges for some time with naming rights and sponsorship in general. The needs of schools to raise additional revenue have led to some innovative sponsorship rights being offered. In Texas for example, Alice Costello School raised $100,000 by selling the naming rights to its gymnasium to Shoprite and three further schools sold their rights to their stadia for over $1 million each. Eastern Financial Florida Credit Union sponsored Everglades High School's stadium for $500,000. Whilst these might appear to be examples of normal commercial enterprise the principle becomes ethically questionable when a doughnut producer buys in to similar opportunities. Krispy Kreme Donuts did just that at Plano High School in Texas with rights that included signage in the end zone of their playing field. The Plano High School board were very commercially minded with the appointment of a school marketing director and the setting of income targets of $1.9 million in 2003 (Pennington, 2004). However, the dilemma for the person in this role is that targets can become all consuming to the point where the ethics of selling sports rights to producers of fast foods become ignored. Sweetwater High School in San Diego, California, has received sponsorship from Pepsi and local pizza producers.

Obesity in children has become an issue for societies around the world including the USA and the UK and clearly the targeting of children by fast food companies has become a debateable ethical concern. Equally, if sponsorship is an acceptable form of communication then there are also ethical issues in societies making rulings on which companies should be allowed to sponsor what. In October 2003, it was reported that the UK Education Secretary, Ruth Kelly, expressed a concern that 'junk food' advertising was aimed at children and therefore should be stopped. She claimed at the time that the Culture Secretary Tessa Jowell, was trying to do that. The irony is that Ms Jowell was also the minister responsible for the 2012 London Olympics, an event that has fast food supplier McDonald's as a sponsor (Campbell, 2004).

The question that is raised here in this text, a text that is concerned with the production of successful sponsorship, is not so much about whether these sponsorships are ethically correct, but whether these sponsorships can even work as relationships if they are socially challenged in these ways. Is there a good sponsorship fit when public perception, even if in a minority, raises ethical issues and is this factor considered by these sponsors when they undertake their marketing decision-making for example? Reebok for example, removed the Mark Walker website in April 2004 having reconsidered the content of its message, reach, perceived value and whether its objectives were being best met.

Sponsorship control

Innovation in sponsorship is being produced in a new area of ambient marketing communications. However, as branding becomes an increasingly imaginative and innovative exercise, it appears to get closer to that ethical line of what is and is not socially acceptable. On the one hand transparent speed-skating suits (revealing the commercial brands and logos that are painted on the skater's body) may continue to be described as innovative until banned by the governing body. The athlete Linford Christie's wearing of contact lenses that depicted the shape of his sponsor Puma's logo was novel when used at media conferences back in 1996. 'Body billboarding' in boxing, the use of commercially related body tattoos, is however under pressure from television broadcasters to get it banned (Christie, 2002; Masterman, 2004a). The ethics involved are complex, but of equal concern is the move by media to attempt to play a part in the governance of sport. As sponsorship revenues increase so do the expectations of sponsors, and with the emphasis clearly on sponsorship for a return on investment, the power of the media grows. Sponsors need to be concerned because the more that the integrity of arts, music, sport and rights holders in general are affected, the less powerful sponsorship communications will become (Masterman and Wood, 2006).

There is a question concerning the extent to which rights owners should sell themselves into the hands of sponsors. Whilst events are keen to receive the financial support that might be the difference between running or not, there are lines that need to be drawn when it comes to how 'close' a sponsor should get or be allowed to get. A close relationship that has the capacity to develop is a fundamental part of the successful delivery of mutual benefits but the control of the sponsorship property remains with the rights owner. Rock musicians consistently resisted for some time the overtures of sponsors whilst expressing their desires to retain control of their artistic license and integrity. As with sport, popular music has now surpassed that but there are still such barriers within other forms of music and the arts generally. Whilst sponsorship of music festivals is commonplace and even rock stalwarts such as Neil Young, Bob Dylan and the Rolling Stones have long succumbed to the sponsorship dollar, there remains a concern for ballet, theatre and opera to develop anything more than simple, even solus, sponsorship programmes in an effort to ensure artistic integrity is maintained (Masterman, 2004b).

This maintenance is important. In an effort to exploit its rights as a sponsor of Major League Baseball (MLB) in the US, Columbia Pictures and Marvel Studios wanted to put logos for its upcoming film 'Spider-Man 2' on the bases and on-deck circles in 15 stadiums in 2004. Playing surfaces had long been considered sacrosanct in USA major league sports and as a result there was an instant reaction and media coverage that labelled baseball as reaching a 'greedy new low' (Rovell, 2004). As a consequence MLB quickly reversed its initial decision to provide these rights realizing that they had given away too much for the sponsorship to be considered acceptable. A different example occurred in 1998 when the media widely reported the claim that Nike had forced the manager of Brazil to play its injured player Ronaldo in the FIFA World Cup final (BBC, 2002). This was vehemently denied but no doubt took its effect on the sponsorship of Brazil by the sportswear manufacturer. Product placement in film and television programming has similar issues. There are regulations that restrict the use of programme sponsor products in to the programmes with which they are associated but with film there are many brands that are 'written-in' to the script. In order to ensure optimum sponsorship fit, it is critical for a sponsorship to be credible and so those sponsorships that are lopsided because they are sponsor controlled, probably with the intent on maximizing a return on their investment, will ultimately achieve something a lot less.

Multi-faceted sponsorship

Sponsorship has become part of a larger movement that has seen a convergence with entertainment in order to reach consumers. In many ways sponsorship is the catalyst that brings sport, media and music together to form entertainment properties (Cornwell and Amis, 2005). As such a driver, sponsorship has the capacity to reach global audiences simultaneously but as this continues to develop, sponsorship managers need to grasp and understand these wider virtues. For example, an understanding that sponsorship can be used across a number of sectors simultaneously negates the need for sponsorships to be labelled, as specifically being sport, music or arts focused. There is an argument for there being no sports, arts or music sponsorship, only sponsorship. What is required is an advanced understanding of the need for the acquisition of appropriate rights, that exploitation of these rights is necessary and that exploitation can cut across all walks of life and even include other sponsorships. In what is now a broad set of opportunities, an Olympic sponsorship for example, can include sport-, arts-, music- and community-linked activities.

Conclusions

Combined forces are threatening the development of sponsorship. Whilst rights owners become increasingly dependent on sponsorship as a source of required, as opposed to extra, revenue, those rights owners with the most attractive sponsorship opportunities are becoming more powerful. Consequently, whilst events are being cancelled due to a lack of sponsorship, the most popular sponsorships, and those in sport in particular, continue to grow. Some significant rights have come under threat. In 2002 for example, Glyndebourne, the opera house, had to turn to the recruitment of consortiums of individual backers after it started to lose the interest of its corporate clients as providers of £300,000 fees. British American Tobacco and Barclays had both halved their numbers of sponsored operas (O'Donnell, 2003). When Deutsche Bank pulled out of its sponsorship of a concert organized by the Nelson Mandela Foundation in 2003, this event too had to be cancelled, despite its headline acts of U2, Elton John, Sting and Bob Dylan. The bank pulled its $1 million sponsorship only a month prior to the intended event date of February 2nd and as a result also had a wider impact as the concert was to raise funds for Aids/HIV charities (Carroll, 2003). At a time when economic forces were significant, due to impending war in Iraq, these examples show that sponsorship can be the first of communications to be culled when cuts are required.

There is a response to these threats. If sponsorship rights that are threatened by cancellation or those sponsorship opportunities that are beyond the most obvious of rights can demonstrate a return on investment, then the threat might be turned into a greater opportunity. New and innovative use of sponsorship is being demonstrated by brands such as Rizla, Durex, Carling, Smirnoff and Nescafe which have all turned to clubs and dance sponsorship to reach their youth audiences and to achieve sales as well as develop brand image and awareness. Ballantyne, the whisky brand, has sponsored 'Urban High', an event that tours urban locations and has been staged in Moscow's Red Square with an audience of 240,000 people. As part of its involvement with club events in Ibiza, brewer

Miller created the 'Miller Yacht Party' where clubbers could win tickets to an exclusive party on board a private yacht where the brand received sole and exclusive exposure (Bagnall, 2002). By pursuing an approach that continually evaluates whether there is a good fit and what opportunities there are to further and better exploit rights, sponsors can also achieve longevity in sponsorship. Such an approach by brewer Stella Artois, in its sponsorship of the Stella Artois Tennis Championships at Queens Club, has remarkably seen this sponsorship last more than a quarter of a century.

The purpose of this text has been to highlight the three key components of successful sponsorship. By creating a sponsorship that demonstrates a good fit, by maximizing the exploitation of the rights and then evaluating against the objectives that were set, there is an opportunity for sponsors to achieve and then identify a return on sponsorship investment.

Tasks and discussion points

- Identify one innovative example of ambush marketing and analyse the impact on the targeted sponsorship.
- Using the same example, determine ways in which the sponsor might have exploited its rights to defend its position.
- In groups, discuss the ethics involved in targeting children via sponsorship communications. As sponsorship managers, how far would you go to achieve your objectives?
- What future issues concern you most and how are you going to address them in your sponsorships?

References

Bagnall, M. (2002). Event sponsorship: Is it the worst yet to come? *Admap*, April, Issue 427. www.warc.com (accessed 5 April 2004).

BBC (2002). The great World Cup final mystery. www.news.bbc.co.uk/sport3/worldcup2002 (accessed 12 December 2006).

Campbell, N. (2004). Will fast food sponsors go the same way as tobacco? *The Guardian*, 13 October.

Carroll, R. (2003). Sponsor pulls plug on Aids concert at Mandella jail island. *The Guardian*, January 2003.

Christie, J. (2002). New meaning to bottom feeders. *The Globe and Mail*, 23 January 2002. www.sportsethicsinstitute.org/sports_marketing_ethics (accessed 28 March 2003).

Cornwell, T. and Amis, J. (2005). Global sport sponsorship: What now? What's next? *Global sport sponsorship*, Amis, J. and Cornwell, T. (Eds.). Oxford: Berg.

FIFA (2004). www.fifa.com/en/marketing/partners (accessed 12 May 2004).

Gratton, C. and Taylor, P. (2000). *Economics of sport and recreation*. London: E & FN Spon.

Harrington, D. (2002). Whose face is it anyway? *The Guardian*, 25 March.

Hobson, A. (2004). The logo games. *The Guardian*, 2 August.

Hoek, J., Gendall, P., Jeffcoat, M. and Orsman, D. (1997). Sponsorship and advertising: A comparison of their effects. *Journal of Marketing Communications*, Vol. 3, No. 1, pp. 21–32.

Kolah, A. (1999). *Maximizing the value of sports sponsorship*. London: Financial Times Media.

Markwalker.reebok.com (2004). www.markwalker.reebok.com (accessed 28 April 2004).

Masterman, G. (2004a). *Strategic sports event management: An international approach*, Oxford: Butterworth-Heinemann.

Masterman, G. (2004b). A strategic approach for the use of sponsorship in the events industry: In search of a return on investment. *Festival and events management: An international arts and cultural perspective*, Yeoman, I., Robertson, M., Ali-Knight, J., Drummond, S. and McMahon-Beattie, U. (Eds.). Oxford: Elsevier.

Masterman, G. and Wood, E. (2006). Innovative marketing communications: Strategies for the events industry. Oxford: Elsevier.

NYC2012 (2004). 2012 Olympic Bid Document: Theme 7, Marketing p. 127. New York, NYC2012.

O'Donnell, J. (2003). City loses its taste for opera. *The Sunday Times*, 5 January.

Pennington, B. (2004). Reading, writing and corporate sponsorship. *New York Times*, 18 October.

Performance Research Europe (2002). British football fans can't recall Euro 2000 sponsors. www.performanceresearch.com (accessed 9 October 2003).

Poole, D. (2004). Sponsorship: An uneven playing field. *The Guardian*, 8 July.

Rovell, D. (2004). The tangled web of sports and advertising. www.sports.espn.go.com (accessed 5 May 2004).

Talbot, M. (2003). Play date with destiny. *The New York Times Magazine*, 21 September 2003.

Index